Chicago®

MAGAZINE'S

GUIDE TO

CHICAGO

Chicago®
MAGAZINE'S

GUIDE TO

CHICAGO

Chicago Magazine
Chicago

EDITOR AND
PROJECT DIRECTOR
Daniel Santow

PRINCIPAL WRITERS
AND RESEARCHERS
Carla Kelson, Allen Kelson
David Novick, Daniel Santow, Anne Spiselman

BOOK DESIGNER
Steven Bialer

COPY EDITOR
William B. Kelley

TYPOGRAPHY
Paul Baker Typography, Inc.
Paul Baker, Kier Strejcek, Jack Weinberg

FACT-CHECKING
Christopher Bayard
Kathlyn Penirian, Jennifer Engle

First Edition
Printed in the United States of America.

Make no little plans;
they have no magic to stir men's blood.

— DANIEL HUDSON BURNHAM, 1846–1912
Author, *The Chicago City Plan*

Contents

Getting Around

WHILE GETTING AROUND Chicago is no breeze, it's not a nightmare, either. The Chicago Transit Authority (CTA) runs scores of bus routes and one of only two 24-hour el/subway systems in the country (the other is New York's). Still, the bottom line — unless you live near a bus or el line — is that it helps to have a car. Some of the lines stop running at a certain time, or don't run on Sundays, or only run part of their routes at off-hours, and yes, the subways can be dangerous after dark. That said, though, it *is* still possible to get around without a car; if you know the schedules and keep your wits about you late at night, there should be no problem in getting where you want to go. In addition, there are many train lines in and out of the city (more on that later).

Fare on CTA buses and trains is a dollar. On buses exact fare is required, though the buses are now outfitted to take dollar bills, which is a great improvement. Transfers, which allow the rider to switch twice in a two-hour period from bus to bus, train to train, or bus to train (and vice versa), cost an extra quarter. For senior citizens and the handicapped, the transit fare is 50 cents and transfers are 20 cents. Monthly bus/train passes are available all over the city, in currency exchanges and in many grocery stores. They are good for one calendar month and cost $50 ($25 for senior citizens and the handicapped).

There are CTA buses on almost every major street, and during rush hour many of them run express to certain parts of the city. While many buses run all night (owl service), some do not. It's best to check the bus-stop sign or call the CTA before planning on a late-night bus excursion. The CTA is pretty good about keeping bus signs and routes posted and up-to-date.

The CTA rapid-transit system (the el and the subways) maintains four lines, each of which has an A route and a B route, which more or less means that the trains stop at every other stop. In the Loop and other busy neighborhoods, many stops are A/B and all trains stop there. Designated stops allow free interline transfers.

The **Howard-Englewood-Jackson Park** line runs under the State Street Mall, then traces the near-lakefront north to Chicago's tip as well as south, the south-segment A train eventually heading west to Ashland Avenue, the B train east to University Avenue.

The **Lake-Dan Ryan** line runs from the Loop, either south to 95th Street or west to suburban Oak Park.

The **O'Hare-Congress-Douglas** line runs from the Loop northwest to O'Hare Airport, and south and west, the A train to Forest Park, the B train to Cicero-Berwyn.

The **Ravenswood** line zigzags southeast through the city, beginning on the Northwest Side, meeting the Howard-Englewood line at Belmont Avenue, and continuing down to the Loop and back again.

At Howard Street, the Howard-Englewood line meets up with both the **Evanston Shuttle** and the **Skokie Swift**. During weekday rush hours, the **Evanston Express**, which costs $1.20, runs nonstop from Evanston directly to the Loop, a great timesaver for those suburbanites.

For CTA travel information, call 836-7000. The hearing-impaired can get information by calling 836-4949.

For trains that take you out to the suburbs, there are four stations: Union Station,

Getting Around

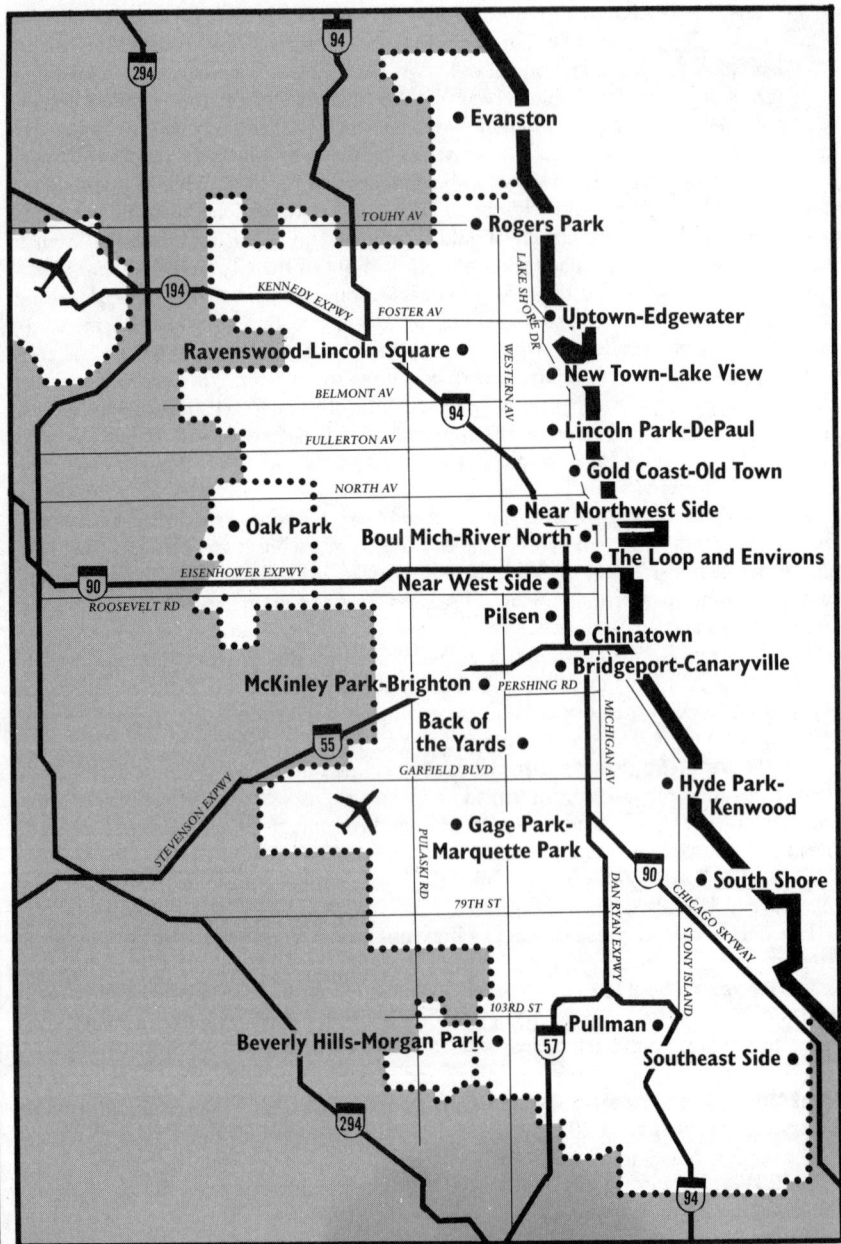

Map showing Chicago neighborhoods and surrounding areas:

- **94** / **294**
- Evanston
- Rogers Park
- TOUHY AV
- LAKE SHORE DR
- KENNEDY EXPWY
- **194**
- FOSTER AV
- Uptown-Edgewater
- Ravenswood-Lincoln Square
- WESTERN AV
- New Town-Lake View
- BELMONT AV
- **94**
- Lincoln Park-DePaul
- FULLERTON AV
- NORTH AV
- Gold Coast-Old Town
- Near Northwest Side
- Oak Park
- Boul Mich-River North
- The Loop and Environs
- EISENHOWER EXPWY
- **90**
- ROOSEVELT RD
- Near West Side
- Pilsen
- Chinatown
- McKinley Park-Brighton
- PERSHING RD
- Bridgeport-Canaryville
- **55**
- Back of the Yards
- GARFIELD BLVD
- Hyde Park-Kenwood
- MICHIGAN AV
- Gage Park-Marquette Park
- PULASKI RD
- **90**
- South Shore
- 79TH ST
- DAN RYAN EXPWY
- STONY ISLAND
- CHICAGO SKYWAY
- STEVENSON EXPWY
- 103RD ST
- Beverly Hills-Morgan Park
- Pullman
- **57**
- Southeast Side
- **294**
- **94**

at Adams and Canal streets; the Chicago & North Western Station, at Madison and Canal streets; the Illinois Central Gulf Station, at Randolph Street and Michigan Avenue; and the La Salle Street Station, at 414 South La Salle Street For routes and passenger information regarding the nine suburban lines, call 322-6777.

Getting out to O'Hare Airport from downtown can cost as little as a dollar if you go by subway (the O'Hare-Congress-Douglas line). If you give yourself an hour, there should be no problem. Another alternative is Continental Air Transport, an airport express bus that leaves from various downtown hotels and suburbs. For fare and time information, call 454-7800.

If you're going to drive, it's a good idea to get a map to see the web of expressways and streets for yourself. Here are some of the major highways:

The **Stevenson Expressway** (Interstate 55), which travels southwest from McCormick Place to Springfield and St. Louis.

The **Eisenhower Expressway** (Interstate 290), which extends west from the Loop.

Interstates 90 and 94, which bear a different name on each side of their intersection with the Eisenhower: To the south the road is the **Dan Ryan Expressway**; to the north, it slants northwest and is the **Kennedy Expressway**.

The **Edens Expressway** (Interstate 94), which veers off the Kennedy about eight miles north of Chicago's center and heads to the northern suburbs.

Northbrook, Northlake, Park Forest, Forest Park, River Forest, River Grove: Even long-time Chicagoans have trouble keeping things straight. The following alphabetical listing of nearby suburbs and outlying communities gives the latest approximate population, the municipal office phone number, and the distance from the Loop.

The suggested auto routes from the Loop leave by expressway and point toward the destination's center.

I-55 South: Stevenson Expressway
I-88: East-West Tollway
I-90 West: Kennedy Expressway (becomes Northwest Tollway)
I-90 East: Dan Ryan Expressway (becomes Chicago Skyway)
I-94 East: Dan Ryan Expressway (becomes Calumet Expressway)
I-94 West: Edens Expressway
I-290 West: Eisenhower Expressway
I-294: Tri-State Tollway

Arlington Heights (71,100)
253-2340
24 miles (I-90 west, Arlington Heights exit)

Barrington (9,285)
381-2141
36 miles (I-90 west, Ill. 53 north, U.S. 14 west)

Barrington Hills (3,800)
551-3000
38 miles (I-90 west, Barrington Rd. exit north, Ill. 62 west)

Brookfield (19,395)
485-7344
13 miles (I-290 west, 17th Ave. exit south)

Buffalo Grove (30,700)
459-2525
29 miles (I-90 west, Ill. 53 exit north, Dundee Rd. east)

Clarendon Hills (6,827)
323-3500
19 miles (I-290 west, Ill. 83 exit south)

Getting Around

Country Club Hills (16,000)
798-2616
24 miles (I-94 east, I-57 south, 167th St. exit east, Crawford Ave. south)

Deerfield (17,432)
945-5000
27 miles (I-94 west, Deerfield Rd. exit west)

Downers Grove (43,843)
964-0300
23 miles (I-290 west, I-88 west, Highland Ave. exit south)

Elgin (67,000)
695-6500
38 miles (I-90 west, Ill. 25 or Ill. 31 exit south)

Elk Grove Village (30,476)
439-3900
26 miles (I-90 west, Elmhurst Rd. or Arlington Heights Rd. exit south)

Elmhurst (44,275)
530-3000
17 miles (I-290 west, St. Charles Rd. exit west)

Evanston (73,706)
328-2100
13 miles (Lake Shore Dr. north, Sheridan Rd. north)

Flossmoor (8,000)
758-2300
25 miles (I-94 east, I-57 south, Vollmer Rd. exit east, Governor's Hwy. northeast)

Forest Park (15,700)
366-2323
10 miles (I-290 west, Harlem Ave. exit south)

Franklin Park (17,500)
671-4800
15 miles (I-290 west, 25th Ave. exit north)

Glen Ellyn (24,738)
469-5000
24 miles (I-290 west, Roosevelt Rd. exit west, Park Blvd. north)

Glencoe (8,880)
835-4111
22 miles (I-94 west, Dundee Rd. exit east)

Glenview (33,131)
724-1700
20 miles (I-94 west, Lake Ave. exit west)

Highland Park (31,012)
432-0800
26 miles (I-94 west, U.S. 41 exit north, Central Ave. east)

Hinsdale (16,726)
789-7000
18 miles (I-290 west, I-294 east, Ogden Ave. exit west)

Hoffman Estates (44,000)
882-9100
30 miles (I-90 west, Ill. 53 exit south, Higgins Rd. west)

Kenilworth (2,708)
251-1666
17 miles (I-94 west, Lake Ave. exit east, Green Bay Rd. north)

Lake Forest (17,000)
234-2600
31 miles (I-94 west, U.S. 41 exit north, Deerpath Rd. east)

Lincolnshire (4,856)
945-8500
31 miles (I-90 west, I-294 west, Ill. 22 exit west)

Lincolnwood (11,900)
673-1540
12 miles (I-94 west, Touhy Ave. exit east)

Morton Grove (24,000)
965-4100
17 miles (I-94 west, Dempster St. exit west)

Mount Prospect (52,634)
392-6000
24 miles (I-90 west, Elmhurst Rd. exit north)

Naperville (67,371)
420-6000
30 miles (I-290 west, I-88 west, Naperville Rd. exit south)

Norridge (16,483)
453-0800
14 miles (I-90 west, Harlem Ave. exit south)

Northbrook (33,206)
272-5050
25 miles (I-94 west, Dundee Rd. exit west)

Northfield (4,900)
441-6113
20 miles (I-94 west, Willow Rd. exit west)

Oak Brook (7,300)
990-3000
19 miles (I-290 west, I-88 west, Spring Rd. exit north, 22nd St. southwest)

Oak Forest (25,018)
687-4050
22 miles (I-94 east, I-57 south, 159th St. exit west)

Oak Lawn (60,000)
636-4400
14 miles (I-94 east, 95th St. exit west)

Oak Park (55,006)
383-6400
9 miles (I-290 west, Austin Blvd. or Harlem Ave. exit north)

Olympia Fields (4,146)
748-8246
28 miles (I-94 east, I-57 south, U.S. 30 exit east)

Park Forest (22,000)
748-1112
30 miles (I-94 east, I-57 south, U.S. 30 exit east)

River Grove (10,500)
453-8000
12 miles (I-290 west, First Ave. exit north)

Riverside (9,100)
447-2700
11 miles (I-290 west, Harlem Ave. exit south)

Roselle (19,683)
980-2000
28 miles (I-290 west, U.S. 20 exit west, Roselle Rd. north)

Schaumburg (64,035)
894-4500
29 miles (I-290 west, Ill. 72
exit west, Roselle Rd. south)

Schiller Park (11,458)
678-2550
15 miles (I-90 west, River Rd.
exit south)

Skokie (60,278)
673-0500
16 miles (I-94 west, Dempster
St. exit east)

Wheaton (46,327)
260-2000
25 miles (I-290 west, I-88
west, Naperville Rd. exit
north)

Wilmette (28,229)
251-2700
16 miles (I-94 west, Lake Ave.
exit east)

Winnetka (14,447)
446-2500
18 miles (I-94 west, Willow
Rd. exit east)

CULTURE AND ENTERTAINMENT

Parks and Zoos

CHICAGO'S OFFICIAL MOTTO, *URBS IN HORTO* — "city in a garden" — was ironic hyperbole when it was adopted in 1837, but the Chicago Park District motto, *HORTUS IN URBE*, tells the story today. Most of the lake shore is devoted to parks, and the city's western edge is lined with forest preserves. A once-grand boulevard system links a chain of inland parks, designed by some of the country's foremost landscape artists around the turn of the century. Hundreds of small neighborhood parks and play lots dot the map. Recreational facilities range from old-fashioned croquet and horseshoe courts to a trendy obstacle-fitness course and roller rink.

GRANT PARK

But for a happy accident 150 years ago, Chicago's lakefront would be much like its industry-laden riverbanks. When land along the proposed Lake Michigan-Mississippi River canal was platted, the canal commissioners designated the east side of Michigan Avenue, from Madison Street to Roosevelt Road, "Public Ground — A Common To Remain Forever Open, Clear and Free of Buildings or Other Obstructions." After the Fort Dearborn reservation was dismantled, the public land was extended north to Randolph Street.

The impoverished, young city never developed "Lake Park" and accepted an Illinois Central Railroad offer in 1851 to build a breakfront-trestle in the lake between Cermak Road and Randolph Street. Although the deal seemed reasonable at the time, Chicago's first big lakefront blunder embroiled the city in a 60-year legal battle with the railroad over ownership of the space between the tracks and the old shoreline as it was gradually land-filled. Montgomery Ward conducted a 20-year war in the courts to keep Lake Park "open, clear, and free," which earned him an "anti-progress" label rather than public gratitude.

The World's Columbian Exposition of 1893 provided a vehicle to finish Jackson Park and led to the Chicago Plan — a comprehensive blueprint for a better city. Conceived by Daniel Burnham, the fair's manager, the determinedly neoclassical and symmetrical scheme envisioned a universe of improvements, building on the existing park and boulevard system. Although many of the projects came to naught, Roosevelt Road was widened; Wacker Drive displaced South Water Market; a bridge was built over the river at Michigan Avenue; and the street was widened to the north, which opened the Near North Side to intense development.

By the 1933 Century of Progress fair, Edward H. Bent's Grant Park design was a reality. The **Field Museum of Natural History** opened in 1920 (see Museums). The **Clarence Buckingham Fountain**, a rococo structure flanked by rose gardens and illuminated by an intricate, computer-operated light show, dates from seven years later. The Holabird and Roche **Soldier Field** was completed in time to accommodate the 250,000 who packed the stands for the 1926 World Eucharistic Congress. A crowd of 145,000 saw the Dempsey-Tunney long count here, but the stadium isn't ideal for most sports, although the Bears make do.

The handsome, octagonal, domed **Shedd Aquarium** (see Museums), across Lake Shore Drive from the Field Museum, was finished in 1929. Farther east stands the 1930 pink-marble **Adler Planetarium** (see Museums); its 12-sided building housed the

Parks and Zoos

United States' first sky-projection system.

The other big institutions in the park are the **Art Institute** (see Museums) and the **Goodman Theater** (see Theater), the former having spread beyond its original boundaries.

The **James C. Petrillo Music Shell** behind the Art Institute is where the summer Grant Park Concert Series takes place. In addition, the Gospel, Blues, and Jazz festivals are all focused there.

The park commissioners added to the landscaped space in 1979. For years, a 2,700-car parking lot marred Grant Park north of Madison Street, but construction of the Richard J. Daley Bicentennial Plaza has roofed the space over. Besides 12 lighted tennis courts, there's a skating rink (ice in winter, roller in summer), cross-country skiing in January and February, and field-house activities all year.

Monuments and sculptures honoring illustrious citizens (some of Chicago, some "of the world") and various maidens and goddesses dot the park. Sculpted by Carlo Brioschi and erected in 1933, the **Christopher Columbus Monument** symbolizes aspects of Columbus's expedition that resulted in you-know-what. (During World War Two, people thought one of the pedestal relief carvings looked like Mussolini and wanted it removed.) The original statue of Polish astronomer **Nicolaus Copernicus** adorns the façade of the Polish Academy of Sciences' Staszic Palace in Warsaw. Our copy, with soil sealed in the base from six locations connected with his life, was erected in 1973. Another great Pole honored, **Thaddeus Kosciusko**, was an American Revolutionary War hero.

Other American heroes commemorated by monuments in the park include **Abraham Lincoln**, with a statue by Augustus Saint-Gaudens, and **General John A. Logan**, who was a commander in chief of the Grand Army of the Republic.

The Greek goddess of youth and cupbearer to the gods, **Hebe**, was sculpted by Franz Machti in the early 1890s and placed in the park. The south wing of the Art Institute is home to Lorado Taft's five classic maidens, *Spirit of the Lakes*, symbolizing the Great Lakes. The highest (Lake Superior) spills the waters of her basin into the one held by Lake Michigan, who in turn empties hers into Huron, Erie, and Ontario.

BURNHAM PARK

The city's Lake Front Ordinance of 1919 called for a connecting link between Grant and Jackson parks. Named Burnham Park, it occupies landfill east of the Illinois Central Gulf tracks from Roosevelt Road to 56th Street, and Northerly Island.

The famous **55th Street Promontory (the Point)** is an example of what the park could have been, but after the Century of Progress, which celebrated the city's 100th anniversary, the Point remained the only developed area. It is a favorite spot among Hyde Parkers for sunning, running, ball playing, and musicmaking.

In 1934, Chicago's 22 park boards were consolidated into one highly politicized body, and the new Chicago Park District endorsed a plan by then-Mayor Edward J. Kelly to erect an amusement park in Burnham Park. Although pastoralists screamed, the Illinois Legislature passed a bill allowing the park district to devote ten percent of its space to expositions and fairs. The city couldn't float the amusement-park plan, and Northerly Island lay fallow until **Meigs Field** was constructed in 1947 and named for an aviation enthusiast and publisher of the *Chicago Herald and Examiner* and the

Parks and Zoos

Chicago American, Merrill C. Meigs.

Another Chicago publisher spearheaded the next Burnham Park land grab. Robert C. McCormick of the *Chicago Tribune* had little trouble promoting a lakefront convention hall. With the *Tribune's* considerable political power behind it and with Mayor Richard J. Daley's blessings, the project easily sailed over myriad objections and lawsuits. The hideous first McCormick Place opened in 1958 and quickly fulfilled its opponents' worst fears. After it burned down nine years later, **McCormick Place** unfortunately rose again, consuming acres of irreplaceable lakefront. Distant from hotels and restaurants, the hall is the site of some of the nation's largest trade shows.

A long stretch of Burnham Park to the south is still unlandscaped.

JACKSON AND WASHINGTON PARKS

Burnham and Grant parks have been continually besieged by commercial and political empire builders, but Jackson Park, along the Hyde Park neighborhood's lakefront, escaped such shenanigans. Paul Cornell, Hyde Park's founder, saw the advantages of a city-supported park at the edge of his property holdings.

Plans for Jackson and Washington parks, with their connecting link, the Midway Plaisance, were drawn up by the firm of Olmsted and Vaux. Land was acquired, but, true to the Chicago spirit, costs overran the $75,000 budget by $3,425,000. Work had started on Washington Park when the Chicago Fire destroyed the blueprints and interrupted the project. Still, the northern half of Washington Park opened in 1874 and Chicagoans were enthralled. Thousands came to roam and enjoy one of the largest expanses of grass in the system.

Washington Park exhausted the South Park Board's funds, so selection of Jackson Park as the site of the 1893 World's Columbian Exposition was a godsend. Olmsted returned to draw up plans for the fairgrounds. More lagoons, gardens, and rare plantings sprouted to frame the wildly successful "White City's" magnificent neoclassical buildings, which turned the lake's marshy shore into an amazing fairyland for millions of visitors.

After the fair closed, Jackson Park was gradually converted to park land along the lines suggested by Olmsted. Although demands for organized recreation brought dozens of facilities to the park, some of its bucolic character remained. The fair's Fine Arts Palace housed the Field Columbian Museum until the Grant Park building opened. It then entered a period of decay until rescued as Julius Rosenwald's **Museum of Science and Industry**. The park system's first golf course — 18 short holes — was built in 1900 along Jackson Park's southern edge, and the lagoons became boat harbors.

Throughout the Depression, the war years, and the complacent 1950s, much of the park's beauty was allowed to decay. The park district's army of patronage workers couldn't maintain the gardens and lawns formerly tended by trained experts. But for the repeated protests of neighborhood groups, Lake Shore Drive would have been widened to eight lanes through Jackson Park. As it is, cars dominate the park's northern edge, particularly around the Museum of Science and Industry, and whiz perilously close to 57th Street Beach. Hyde Parkers in the know swim off the rocks at "the Point" (55th Street). The bathing pavilion at 63rd Street Beach is sadly deteriorated.

Except for modern structures on its periphery and general neglect, Washington Park probably resembles Olmsted's plan for the South Park's twin jewels more closely than

Parks and Zoos

Jackson Park. It has no attraction to equal the Museum of Science and Industry, although the **DuSable Museum of African American History** (see Museums) occupies the old South Parks Administration Building — a dollhouse version of the Jackson Park museum. The sunken plot in front of the DuSable has been turned into a sculpture garden by the museum. Burnham's firm also designed the refectory that stands near a WPA swimming pool and a modern field house.

Although Washington Park is frayed at the edges — the lagoons are overgrown, the formal gardens are shadows of the past — it's not unused. On summer weekends, Washington Park is alive with families barbecuing. Cricket and soccer games draw West Indians (and others) from all over the South Side to the open meadow. Once a stable, the **Washington Park Drama Shop** houses the park district's enormous costume collection and props for the extensive drama program. Nearby buildings contain a riggers' shop, electrical equipment, and more.

Between the two parks, the Midway Plaisance might have been a sculpture garden if Lorado Taft, whose studio overlooked it, had had his own way and the money had materialized. Taft's **Fountain of Time**, one of Chicago's largest and loveliest classical monuments, was unveiled in 1922 on the Midway's west end, just inside Washington Park. The opening lines of Henry Austin Dobson's "The Paradox of Time" — "Time goes, you say? / Ah no! / Alas, Time stays, *we* go" — inspired the sculpture. The shrouded figure of Father Time leans on his staff, surveying a mass of humanity — about 100 figures — across a reflecting pool.

John Dyfverman's statue of **Carl von Linné** (Carolus Linnaeus), a copy of Johannes Kjelberg's sculpture in the royal gardens at Stockholm, was moved from Lincoln Park in 1976. It depicts the Swedish botanist in the costume he reputedly wore to roam his native countryside. **The Republic** is a scaled-down replica of Daniel Chester French's sculpture, which stood in the Court of Honor at the World's Columbian Exposition.

WEST PARKS — DOUGLAS, GARFIELD, AND HUMBOLDT

Perceived as unsafe, the West Parks elicit little casual use. Few strollers or joggers trace the winding paths, and benches by flower gardens attract almost no pigeon feeders or sunbathers. During the week in warm weather, the parks come alive with kids when school lets out. On weekends, Douglas Park is jammed with people and cars. The home of Latin American soccer in Chicago, the park lawns are filled with players, observers, and picnickers. Weekend baseball and softball are big in Douglas and Humboldt parks, while Garfield hosts weekly concerts at the bandstand, as well as sports activities.

The 1869 law that created the South Park Board also set up the West Park Board. Local developers were eager to sell some of their holdings for parks, removing the parcels from their tax bills and increasing the value of their remaining land. The 1870s were spent acquiring land. William Le Baron Jenney was retained to supervise conversion of the arid, treeless prairie into wooded gardens. Although far from fully landscaped, the parks opened in 1880. O. R. DuBois succeeded Jenney as West Park architect and continued his work, but the parks didn't really become beautiful until Jens Jensen's tenure at the beginning of the century.

Under the self-taught genius's guidance, the three parks flowered with formal gardens and rustic walkways. At Humboldt, for example, Jensen installed a rose garden with three pergolas designed by Schmidt, Garden, and Martin; and he redesigned the

Parks and Zoos

lagoon with a half-mile miniature replica of the Rock River. Boating pavilions/refectories were built in all the West Parks (now gone or unused), as was the **Garfield Park Conservatory**. The huge, seldom-visited conservatory dwarfs Lincoln Park's and shares its familiar schedule of shows. More than 5,000 varieties of plants include orchids, ferns, succulents, and economically valuable flora. Don't miss the two Lorado Taft marble figures — *Pastoral* and *Idyl* — at the entrance to the Palm House.

LINCOLN PARK

Chicagoans with a confirmed Second City complex mourn our deprivation — no park like New York's Central Park — but on anything but the most literal level, they're misled. To thousands of savvy North Siders, Lincoln Park *is* the central park, bigger and, in some ways, better than New York's.

Zoo for zoo, tennis court for tennis court, statue for statue, meadow for meadow, garden for garden, Lincoln Park holds its own. In addition, our park boasts something New York's can't hope to offer: the lakefront. From North to Ardmore avenues, Lake Michigan's waters define Lincoln Park. Sandy beaches break the rock-lined shore, two boat harbors pinch the land to impossibly narrow waists, and a third is firmed by a crooked finger of land reaching out from the Montrose Avenue peninsula.

But people, not things, make the comparison between the two parks natural. Lincoln Park is populated from dawn to dusk seven days a week, particularly when the weather's nice. The youthful lifestyle that makes New Town, Lake View, DePaul, and Lincoln Park 24-hour-a-day neighborhoods also makes for lots of daylight leisure. In the early morning and after work, a myriad of joggers tread the cinder paths where horses once trotted.

On summer weekends, Lincoln Park is a circus. The weekday crowd is joined by nine-to-fivers, families from all over the city, and an endless stream of adolescents, particularly at the beaches. Each bathing area has a particular personality. Fullerton Avenue Beach attracts the young professionals from the hip lakefront neighborhoods; the strip south of Belmont Avenue is a gathering place for gay sunbathers. Montrose Avenue Beach is a bit tough and menacing. The drives and parking lots to the west have a well-deserved reputation as a drug supermarket. Foster and Hollywood beaches are primarily working-class family spots. The shiplike **North Avenue Beach House** and nearby **Chess Pavilion** draw a mixed crowd — part Old Town eclectic, part Cabrini-Green, and part Gold Coast glitter — but the most popular body-watching spot in the city is probably Oak Street Beach.

After the beaches, the park's biggest attraction is probably the **Lincoln Park Zoo** (see Zoos in this chapter).

The **Lincoln Park Conservatory** is much smaller and more crowded than Garfield Park's, but some ancient specimens grow in the oldest hall, built in 1891. Lincoln Park's finest formal garden stretches for a block in front of the conservatory, past the *Storks at Play* **Fountain**, sculpted by Augustus Saint-Gaudens and Frederick MacMonnies in 1887.

About 20 other sculptures in individual natural settings are scattered throughout Lincoln Park between Diversey Parkway and North Avenue. The **John Peter Altgeld Monument**, sculpted by Gutzon Borglum, honors the Illinois governor who pardoned the Haymarket Riot participants and was described by Vachel Lindsay as

Parks and Zoos

setting "himself tasks which took a lion's courage and a martyr's heart." Edward McCarten's tribute to Chicago poet **Eugene Field** depicts scenes and characters from Field's children's poems. Three great Americans — **Ulysses S. Grant**, **Alexander Hamilton**, and **Abraham Lincoln** — are all honored with statues, Lincoln's being the work of Saint-Gaudens, with a setting and chair designed by Stanford White (Lorado Taft called it "the greatest portrait statue in the United States"). Also of note is the **Johann Wolfgang von Goethe Monument** by Hermann Hahn. Since it's dedicated to Goethe, "the master mind of the German people," World War Two sentiment was for melting it into a bomb.

OTHER PARKS

Besides the giants, the Chicago Park District runs hundreds of other operations. About ten field houses in the system were designed by D. H. Burnham and Company in 1904-05. The oldest, McKinley Park's, predates any in the country. Here are a few more parks:

Auburn Park (406 West Winneconna Parkway) — A stream runs through the 8½-acre, long, narrow park and is crossed by several rustic stone bridges. Some nice 1920s houses line the northern edge. A hidden treasure.

California Park (3843 North California Avenue) has the only indoor sports arena in the system.

Hamilton Park (513 West 72nd Street) has a nice art deco field house.

Indian Boundary Park (2500 West Lunt Avenue) — The name recalls the pioneer-days treaty, but the lovely space has everything an urban park should: a Tudor field house, benches beneath shade trees, tennis courts, playgrounds, a migratory-waterfowl pool, and a vest-pocket zoo — with sadly cramped bears, deers, goats, and more comfortable, smaller wildlife — all provided on a rotating basis by Lincoln Park Zoo.

Marquette Park (6700 South Kedzie Avenue) was one of the West Park Board's last major projects. The WPA executed a large part of the grounds. Half the park is given over to a nine-hole golf course. There's a lovely rose garden in the southwest corner, and the undistinguished field house, which was once a golf shelter, has all the usual park-district offerings.

Portage Park (4100 North Long Avenue) — The Olympic-size swimming pool is used for tournaments.

Pulaski Park (1419 West Blackhawk Street) — William Zimmerman's magnificent Prairie-school–Tudor field house dwarfs the park and stands in striking contrast to the rest of the neighborhood's rococo churches. A classical mural graces the assembly hall's proscenium, although the rest of the series has been painted over. The park has a very full schedule of activities, two large gyms, and a pool.

Riverview Park (river's east bank, north of Belmont Avenue) is owned by the city, not the park district. There's rare access here to the river, with a path for strolling and an exercise course.

ZOOS
Brookfield Zoo
8400 W. 31st St.
Brookfield
242-2630

Seeing the dozens of major exhibits at Brookfield Zoo — with its more than 2,000 animals on 204 acres — in one day is near impossible.

Lions, tigers, bears, monkeys, mountain sheep, and goats romp in their craggy natural habitats (surrounded by moats). Zebras, antelope, camels, bisons, and rhinos roam outdoor ranges. Birds soar in the Perching House. Reptiles slither about their diorama. Swans glide across a formal pool. King penguins keep cool in refrigerated indoor cases. African birds, primates, and hippos survey intruders in the steamy Tropic World (an indoor re-creation of a rain forest). Small nocturnal, carnivorous cats haunt habitats in the Predator Ecology Exhibit (guided tours only). A Tasmanian devil holds forth in the Australia House. New zoo babies join domestic animals in the ever-popular Children's Zoo, which features many demonstrations.

The Seven Seas Panorama, newly completed in June 1987, houses dolphins, walrus, seals, and sea lions. The skylit dolphin theater has an 800,000-gallon performance pool set amid a tropical beach scene (and 2,000 seats). The outdoor seascape replicates shores of the Pacific Northwest, and the dolphin arena evokes a Caribbean coast.

For an overview of the zoo, take the Motor Safari guided tour. There's also a great bookstore (on the bird plaza) carrying more than 4,000 titles.

Lincoln Park Zoo
2200 N. Cannon Dr.
294-4660

After the beaches, Lincoln Park's biggest attraction is probably the zoo. In fact, the Lincoln Park Zoo is the most-visited zoo in the United States. Founded in 1868 with a gift of two swans from New York's Central Park, it has grown over the years to include more than 2,000 animals representing 393 species.

The Great Ape House, with its underground, climate-controlled habitats, provides spacious areas for the apes behind a winding, glass-walled passageway. In the Polar Bear Habitat, the animals swim around in a 265,000-gallon polar-bear pool, the largest such tank in the country. The bears can be viewed from either underwater or outdoors.

A highlight of the zoo, as well as an urban rarity, is its Farm-in-the-Zoo, an actual five-acre replica of a red-barned Midwestern animal farm. Opened in 1964, the Farm-in-the-Zoo was completely renovated in 1987 with upgraded facilities, modernized graphics, and expanded educational programs. There's a main barn for exhibits and demonstrations, a poultry barn in which the kids can watch chickens lay eggs and hatch, a livestock barn with pigs, sheep, and steers, a dairy barn with cows, calves, and goats, and a horse barn.

In addition to the renovated Farm-in-the-Zoo, the Children's Zoo recently underwent a similar transformation.

Other Lincoln Park Zoo attractions include the Penguin-Seabird House, the Water-

Parks and Zoos

fall Lagoon and Flamingo Dome, and outdoor areas for antelope, zebras, and other large mammals.

Grant Park

► **Buckingham Fountain**
Foot of Congress Dr.

► **Christopher Columbus Monument**
Columbus and Roosevelt drives

► *Hebe* **sculpture**
1100 S. Michigan Ave.

► **Thaddeus Kosciusko Monument**
Solidarity and Lake Shore drives, west of Adler Planetarium

► **Abraham Lincoln Monument**
Congress Dr. between Michigan Ave. and Columbus Dr.

► **General John A. Logan Monument**
900 S. Michigan Ave., in the park

► **James C. Petrillo Music Shell**
Jackson and Columbus drives

► **Soldier Field**
425 E. McFetridge Dr.
294-2200

► *Spirit of the Lakes*
South wing of the Art Institute, near Jackson Dr.

Burnham Park

► **McCormick Place**
2300 S. Lake Shore Dr.
791-6000

► **Merrill C. Meigs Field**
Equivalent to 15th St. at Lake Michigan
744-4787

► **55th Street Promontory (the Point)**
55th St. at Lake Michigan

Jackson Park, Washington Park, Midway Plaisance

► *Fountain of Time*
Washington Park, west of Cottage Grove Ave., facing Midway Plaisance

Jackson Park Driving Range
Hayes and Lake Shore drives

Jackson Park Field House
6401 S. Stony Island Ave.
643-6363

► **Carl von Linné sculpture**
Midway Plaisance, just west of University Ave.

► *The Republic* **sculpture**
Jackson Park, Richards and Hayes drives

► **Washington Park Drama Shop**
5746 S. Cottage Grove Ave.

Washington Park Field House
5531 S. King Dr.
684-6530

West Parks

Douglas Park Field House
1401 S. Sacramento Dr.
521-3244

Douglas Park Garden Pergola
Sacramento Dr. and Ogden Ave.

Garfield Park Bandstand
Just east of Hamlin Blvd. and Wilcox St.

► **Garfield Park Conservatory**
300 N. Central Park Ave.
533-1281

Garfield Park Field House
100 N. Central Park Dr.
826-3175

Humboldt Park Field House
1400 N. Sacramento Ave.
276-0107

Humboldt Park Rose Garden
Humboldt Dr. and Division St.

► *Pastoral* **and** *Idyl*
Garfield Park Conservatory

Lincoln Park

► **John Peter Altgeld Monument**
Southeast of Diversey Pkwy., at Cannon Dr.

► **Chess Pavilion**
North Blvd. and Lake Shore Dr.

Diversey Driving Range
Diversey Dr. and Lake Michigan

► **Eugene Field Memorial**
Between Reptile House and Small Mammal House in the zoo

► **Johann Wolfgang von Goethe Monument**
Stockton Dr., south of Diversey Pkwy.

► **Ulysses S. Grant Monument**
East side of South Pond, about 1900 N. Lake Shore Dr.

▶ **Alexander Hamilton Monument**
Stockton Dr., south of Diversey Pkwy.

▶ **Abraham Lincoln Monument**
North Blvd. and Dearborn Pkwy.

▶ **Lincoln Park Conservatory**
Fullerton and Stockton drives
294-2493

Lincoln Park Field House and Cultural Arts Center
2045 N. Lincoln Park West
294-4750

▶ **Lincoln Park Gun Club**
Lake Shore Dr. and Diversey Dr.
549-6490

William Shakespeare Monument
Stockton and Belden drives

▶ *Storks at Play* **Fountain**
Stockton and Belden drives

Theater on the Lake
Fullerton and Lake Shore drives
294-2320

Waveland Golf Course
North of Irving Park Dr., east of Lake Shore Dr.
294-2274

Museums

'WE HAVE BOASTED long enough of our grain elevators, our railroads, our trade. . . . Let us now have libraries, galleries of art, scientific museums, noble architecture and public parks. . . . Otherwise there is a danger that Chicago will become merely a place where ambitious young men will come to make money. . . and then go elsewhere to enjoy it.' So said the Chicago Historical Society's president in 1877, and no other injunction has ever been more heeded by Chicagoans, save for Daniel Burnham's "Make no little plans."

From limestone palaces to little ethnic collections, full-service establishments with every amenity to tiny efforts with limited appeal, the institutions listed here offer something for everyone.

All museums listed are in Chicago, unless otherwise noted.

Major Assets

Adler Planetarium
1300 S. Lake Shore Dr.
322-0300
Sparked by German examples, Sears, Roebuck and Company executive Max Adler funded this country's first planetarium (in recent years greatly expanded and renovated). The astronomical museum has one of the world's largest collections of antique instruments of early astronomers, a navigation display, huge photographs taken of space, and the Doane Observatory with a 20-inch telescope for firsthand heavenly viewing. The show in the Sky Theater changes periodically but is always fascinating and a great educational experience for both kids and adults.

Art Institute of Chicago
Michigan Ave. at Adams St.
443-3600
Justly renowned for its medieval masterpieces and French Impressionists, Chicago's major art museum boasts treasures in every room. Modern painters such as Picasso, Matisse, and Dubuffet are well represented, and the collection includes an impressive array of works by such artists as Rembrandt, El Greco, Renoir, Cézanne, O'Keeffe, and, of course, Seurat, whose *Sunday Afternoon on the Island of La Grande Jatte* may be the museum's most beloved picture. The photography collection has few peers, and a large display of graphics can be seen in the prints and drawings galleries. The various decorative arts departments are active as well, with a fine collection of American and European furniture, silver, and ceramics on view. The museum is also known for its holdings of Chinese art from the last two dynasties, as well as art of the Classical world, African art, and the art of Oceania.

A recent addition to the museum includes the Chicago Stock Exchange Trading Room, preserved from Louis Sullivan and Dankmar Adler's Chicago Stock Exchange building, which was demolished in 1972 and included in the museum in 1977.

Although the museum's affiliation with the Goodman Theater and School of Drama has been severed, the art school flourishes in a dramatic building on Columbus Drive.

Outstanding libraries, a ter-rific film center, free gallery talks, and a wonderful gift shop are additional features. Alfresco dining in McClintock Court can add a sophisticated touch to a day spent in the museum.

Chicago Historical Society
Clark St. at North Blvd.
642-4600
A $15 million renovation and expansion that opens in October 1988 includes 65,000 square feet of additional space, two Atrium Galleries, a new Museum Store, a restaurant, and a Hands-On-History Gallery. The society's 20 million objects include everything from Abraham Lincoln's hat to Walter Payton's jersey.

A fine permanent collection devoted to American, Illinois, and Chicago history includes items as diverse as the *Santa Maria*'s anchor, John Brown's Bible, the *Pioneer* (Chicago's first locomotive), and a large selection of American folk art. The Midwest's only permanent collection of early American history, We the People: Creating a New Nation 1765-1820, features first newspaper printings of the Declaration of Independence, the Constitution, and the Bill of Rights. Special exhibits, featuring photography, architecture, and costumes, reflect the diversity of the museum's collections. A display of old-fashioned toys (at Christmastime) is always a big hit. The library is one of Chicago's finest.

Chicago Public Library Cultural Center
78 E. Washington St.
269-2820
744-6630 (events)
This Greco-Italian Renaissance masterpiece lavished with marble, mosaics, and Tiffany glass was almost demolished when the library's central collection began to burst at its seams, but, fortunately, wiser heads prevailed. Besides the library's fine-arts, language and literature, audio-visual, popular, children's, and special collections, the building houses several exhibit areas, including the Grand Army of the Republic Memorial Hall. There are free tours given, and innumerable free concerts, films, lectures, and art shows.

Field Museum of Natural History
Roosevelt Rd. and Lake Shore Dr.
922-9410
Harry Weese's 1970s renovation of the magnificent building heralded the formerly staid institution's revitalization plan. A new emphasis on the anthropology department (the museum's other traditional divisions are botany, geology, and zoology) has rationalized shows previously considered to be the province of the Art Institute, such as the beautifully mounted Great Bronze Age of China, which focused on another culture through its artwork.

Of course, the grand, marble-clad Stanley Field Hall still has the famous fighting Afri-

can bull elephants and the first freestanding *Gorgosaurus* dinosaur. There are also halls of animal dioramas, plant models, and ethnographic displays, as well as the Hall of Gems, the Egyptian Hall with its walk-through tombs, the Hall of Chinese Jades, and the Maritime Peoples of the Arctic and Northwest Coast exhibit. Even with 20 acres of floor space, the museum can display fewer than one percent of its holdings; scholars use the balance for research.

The museum also offers many excellent films, lectures, concerts, and programs for kids.

Museum of Contemporary Art
237 E. Ontario St.
280-2660
Founded in 1967 and dedicated to the "untried and controversial," MCA functions much like a huge gallery, mounting one major show after another, introducing Chicagoans to new works of neon, paper, video, geometric, monochromatic, op, pop, and other types of art. It also exhibits well-known Chicago and other artists and presents lectures, demonstrations, performances, films, and seminars. The museum houses a renowned collection of artists' books, including selections by such highly regarded artists as Ed Ruscha, Sol Lewitt, and John Cage.

Museum of Science and Industry
57th St. and Lake Shore Dr.
684-1414
More than four million people a year flock to Chicago's most popular tourist attraction to push buttons, pull cranks, and flip levers that animate displays of everything from basic physics to state-of-the-art technology. Bus fleets disgorge hordes of kids who noisily

pack the informative exhibits, which are often financed by trade associations, government agencies, and big corporations. A coal mine, the only German submarine captured on the high seas, and a 16-foot-tall heart you can walk through are also crowd pleasers. Some of the newer exhibits include The Money Center, Food for Life, and Calculating to Computing.

The Henry Crown Space Center and Omnimax Theater, where exhibits are dedicated to space exploration, opened in 1986 and includes the 1968 *Apollo 8* spacecraft that was the first to orbit the moon, among many other holdings. The Omnimax Theater contains a 76-foot-diameter, five-story-high domed screen. The audience sits below, usually held in rapt attention by a stupendous show above.

Quiet corners of the museum include the historic airplanes, bicycles, and autos. Yesterday's Main Street is complete with a silent-movie theater, an ice-cream parlor, and an old-time photographer's studio for souvenirs. The museum mounts lots of special shows; some are quite hip, while others, such as Christmas Around the World, are more traditional. Programs include lectures, demonstrations, workshops, films, festivals, and field trips.

Oriental Institute Museum
University of Chicago
1155 E. 58th St.
702-9521
In addition to the mummies and the famous 40-ton winged bull that once guarded the entrance to the palace of King Sargon II of Khorsabad, this research institution, which was founded in 1911, has

Museums

Sumerian sculpture unrivaled outside Iraq, as well as grand holdings from Turkey, Iran, Egypt, and Israel. Much of the institute's collection derives from excavations sponsored by the university itself.

Sisters of St. Casimir Lithuanian Cultural Museum
2601 W. Marquette Rd.
776-1324
Lithuanian folk arts, textiles, costumes, maps, modern paintings, and several cases of amber are housed in four rooms. By appointment.

David and Alfred Smart Gallery
University of Chicago
5550 S. Greenwood Ave.
702-0200
The permanent collection is strong on 19th- and 20th-century sculpture, Oriental and European art of every period, and 20th-century painting. A growing decorative arts department boasts the dining room suite from Frank Lloyd Wright's Robie House. Intelligent special shows usually explore a period, problem, or premise in depth and are accompanied by films, symposia, free noon-hour gallery talks (by appointment), and expensive catalogues.

The handsome building, part of the University of Chicago's Cochrane-Woods Art Center, was designed by Edward Larrabee Barnes with flexible, well-lit viewing spaces.

Spertus Museum of Judaica
618 S. Michigan Ave.
922-9012
Part of Spertus College, the Midwest's largest Jewish museum mounts extraordinary special exhibitions and maintains a permanent collection rich in decorative arts,

both religious and temporal, Ashkenazic and Sephardic. Many objects, such as intricately wrought silver plates, cups, Menorahs, and torah covers, are grouped by holiday; others, for example, embroidered prayer shawls and calligraphic wedding contracts, are arranged thematically.

The moving Bernard and Rochelle Zell Holocaust Memorial is permanently displayed on the first floor; small rotating exhibits are in the second-floor gallery. The Asher Library is outstanding.

Swedish American Museum of Chicago
5211 N. Clark St.
728-8111
Started as a bicentennial project to document Swedish contributions to American life, the three-story museum houses tributes to Swedish Colonial and Revolutionary War heroes, paintings and photos, costumes, handicrafts, Carl Sandburg memorabilia, and a photo of Gloria Swanson, who grew up in Andersonville, Chicago's Swedish enclave.

Terra Museum of American Art
666 N. Michigan Ave.
328-3400
Founded in Evanston in 1980 by Daniel J. Terra, President Reagan's U.S. ambassador-at-large for cultural affairs and a businessman, the museum expanded in 1987 to new quarters on Michigan Avenue. The collection is composed of more than 400 works of 19th- and 20th-century American art, though it will continue to expand as both Terra and the museum itself make more and more acquisitions. Guided tours, gallery talks, and lectures are all available.

Ukrainian Institute of Modern Art
2320 W. Chicago Ave.
227-5522
Several storefronts remodeled by Stanley Tigerman in the late 1970s house a permanent collection of paintings and sculptures by Ukrainian American and Ukrainian Canadian artists. The museum hosts various rotating shows that are sufficiently important to get reviewed in the art press. Concert series, literary evenings, and children's art workshops serve the community.

Ukrainian National Museum
2453 W. Chicago Ave.
276-6565
Costumes, fine examples of embroidery, woodcarvings, decorated Easter eggs, folk implements, oil portraits, and other distinctive displays fill the upper two floors of an old brownstone and illustrate the Ukraine's diversity. Many of the folk costumes and crafts exhibited probably haven't changed much since the Ukrainian Empire's heyday in the 10th century. The caretakers conduct visitors about with much obvious pride and little English. The museum is open only on Sundays, or by appointment.

Morton B. Weiss Museum of Judaica
K.A.M. Isaiah Israel Congregation
1100 E. Hyde Park Blvd.
924-1234
A fine collection strikingly displayed in a small room includes ceramics unearthed by Moshe Dayan, illuminated parchment wedding contracts dating to 1492, potsherds from Masada, mezuzahs, Megillahs, exquisite spice boxes, and other items tracing the European and Asian roots of many American Jews, as

well as memorabilia of Chicago's oldest congregation (founded in 1847). The 1924 Byzantine temple — a city landmark — is a must-see.

Nature and Science

Argonne National Laboratory
9700 S. Cass Ave.
Argonne
972-2000
Two-weeks-in-advance reservations are required for the 3½-hour Saturday group tours, but individuals can join one by prior arrangement if there's room. It includes an orientation talk and then a tour through some of the labs.

Cernan Earth and Space Theater
Triton College
2000 Fifth Ave.
River Grove
456-5815
This 60-seat wrap-around-screen theater, named for a local astronaut, offers several programs, including laser light shows, sky shows, and various space exhibits. Call ahead for schedule.

Chicago Academy of Sciences
2001 N. Clark St.
549-0606
Situated in Lincoln Park, this small institution nevertheless offers three floors of exhibits, including various lifelike ecology-in-Chicago dioramas. The academy offers lectures on Sundays, as well as daily or weekly classes, and field trips.

Robert Crown Center for Health Education
21 Salt Creek Lane
Hinsdale
325-1900
Formerly the Hinsdale Health Museum, this educational facility offers programs for children in four areas: general health, sex education, drug abuse, and environmental education. Adults may observe classes daily or see the exhibits after school hours. Complex concepts are explained with sophisticated, animated displays, the most popular of which is the talking transparent woman.

Dearborn Observatory
2131 Sheridan Rd.
Evanston
492-3173
On clear Friday evenings from April to October, with prior reservations, you can look through a Civil War-era 18½-inch refracting telescope. If clouds move in, the antique instrument and the film program are still worth a trip to this building tucked into a corner of Northwestern University's campus.

John G. Shedd Aquarium
1200 S. Lake Shore Dr.
939-2426
More than 500 species of fish (8,000 specimens) from all over the world, as well as invertebrates, sea horses, seals, a few penguins, and a freshwater dolphin, inhabit the aquarium, the world's largest. Six galleries are devoted to tropical, cold-, salt-, and freshwater fish. The 90,000-gallon Coral Reef is a popular attraction, especially when divers, equipped with microphones to talk to the crowds, hand-feed the 1,000 colorful Caribbean denizens. Free educational programs for kids are held in the Aquatic Science Center.

In September 1987 the Shedd broke ground on the new, $43-million Oceanarium, a cold-water-mammal pavilion. When completed in 1990, it will be the largest indoor, inland marine mammal facility of its kind and will include seals, sea otters, and penguins, all highlighted by a two-million-gallon pool, housing dolphins and whales.

Smaller and Ethnic Museums

Balzekas Museum of Lithuanian Culture
6500 S. Pulaski Rd.
582-6500
The museum glorifies a country that knew only a few years of modern-day political independence and hasn't had a good decade since the 16th century. Exhibits include Lithuania Through the Ages, which contains arms and armor, prints, books, maps, and works of art, as well as exhibits of beads, jewelry, and decorative objects, and one sponsored by the Women's Guild. The museum also conducts many community activities.

Mary and Leigh Block Gallery
Northwestern University
1967 Sheridan Rd.
Evanston
508-2679
Opened in 1980, this large gallery exhibits everything from paintings and drawings to photography and decorative arts. Lively shows are often thematic and educational. The permanent collection (not on display) is particularly notable for Walter Burley Griffin's drawings.

Museums

Martin D'Arcy Gallery of Art
Loyola University
6525 N. Sheridan Rd.
274-3000
This exquisite collection of medieval, Renaissance, and baroque pieces from A.D. 1100 to 1700 includes a carved, linden-wood, silver-covered head of John the Baptist on a platter; a precious-stone-encrusted ebony jewel case; a rosary bead with tiny, carved Biblical scenes inside; a late-16th-century chest decorated with bizarre winged creatures, angels, and imps; a 14th-century gold chalice; and a sculpture of the scourging of Christ, made of silver, ebony, lapis lazuli, agate, and tiger-eye.

DuSable Museum of African American History
740 E. 56th Pl.
947-0600
Highlights at the country's first black-history museum include Robert With Ames's massive carved-mahogany mural, *Freedom Now*, the Robert B. Mayer Memorial Collection of African Art, and a good selection of black American pop-culture memorabilia.

The museum sponsors activities for community youths, and a multimedia center houses a library and extensive collection of tapes, films, slides, and jazz recordings.

The old Washington Park Administration Building has been renovated; much of the main-floor space has been given over to the museum's offices.

Fermilab
Kirk Rd. and Pine St.
Batavia
840-3000
A free, self-guided tour of the facility, which includes an orientation film, is available. Swans, ducks, and buffalo roam the 640 acres of restored prairie that Fermilab encloses.

International Museum of Surgical Sciences and Hall of Fame
1524 N. Lake Shore Dr.
642-3555
Dozens of rooms on four floors of a mansion modeled on a Versailles building trace medical history thematically and geographically through authentic surgical instruments, paintings, sculptures, and more. A ground-floor 1873 apothecary shop is outfitted with paraphernalia from America's medical past.

Jurica Natural History Museum
Illinois Benedictine College
5700 College Rd.
Lisle
960-1500
Numerous bird, insect, and mammal specimens are exhibited with minerals, fossils, flora, and fauna collected by the late biologist and educator.

Lizzadro Museum of Lapidary Art
220 Cottage Hill Ave.
Elmhurst
833-1616
One of the country's finest collections of carved jade and gemstones is housed in this pleasant, modern museum with a 1,300-pound hunk of jade as a doorstop. Treasures include a huge Chinese screen, a *Last Supper* carved in ivory, faceted gems, and shimmering semiprecious stones.

Mexican Fine Arts Center Museum
1852 W. 19th St.
738-1503
The only museum of its kind in the Midwest exhibits art forms from Mexico and Mexican artists in the United States.

Mitchell Indian Museum
2408 Orrington Ave.
Evanston
866-1395
Splendid examples of beadwork, exquisite baskets, fine Navajo rugs, and photographs are the highlights of this museum located at Kendall College. Opened in 1977 to house the collection of John and Betty Mitchell, the museum also has tools, weapons, musical instruments, carvings, pottery, and jewelry representing Indians of five geographic regions from 3000 B.C. to the present.

Museum of Holography/ Chicago
1134 W. Washington Blvd.
226-1007
More than 75 holograms (three-dimensional, laser-created images) from around the world are on display. The museum also offers lectures, workshops, and classes.

National Italian American Sports Hall of Fame
2625 S. Clearbrook Dr.
Arlington Heights
437-3077
Exhibits are diverse, as one of Mario Andretti's cars and Rocky Marciano's championship belt fill this small but unique museum.

Peace Museum
430 W. Erie St.
440-1860
This is the only museum in the country dedicated solely to issues of war and peace. Recent shows have included an exhibit of art by South African artists and an exhibit about the life and times of Martin Luther King, Jr.

Polish Museum of America
984 N. Milwaukee Ave.
384-3352
Exhibits from the 1939 New

York World's Fair's Polish Pavilion, trapped in this country by the outbreak of World War Two, formed the nucleus of this country's largest ethnic museum. Diverse displays include military memorabilia, a carved-salt icon and other religious art, drawings, costumes, and, of course, an Easter-egg collection. The central rotunda is painted with WPA-like murals and mounted with plaques detailing Polish scientific accomplishments. A separate Paderewski room and an art gallery are opened on request. The library houses thousands of books, periodicals, maps, photos, manuscripts, recordings, slides, films, and genealogical materials.

History and Nostalgia

Bradford Museum of Collectors Plates
9333 Milwaukee Ave.
Niles
966-2770
More than a thousand of the most actively traded collectors' plates are on display with current market prices. The earliest example is an 1895 Bing & Grondahl. The gallery's staff answers questions about the hobby.

Cantigny
1 S. 151 Winfield Rd.
Wheaton
668-5161
The late *Chicago Tribune* publisher, Colonel Robert R. McCormick, left his 500-acre estate as a park. There's a guided tour of his grandfather Joseph Medill's 1896 Georgian mansion. Attend a Sunday chamber concert in the library from October to April, outdoors the rest of the year,

roam the woods or gardens, or visit the First Division Museum — a push-button diorama, complete with sounds and lights, about the glories of war.

Du Page County Historical Museum
102 E. Wesley St.
Wheaton
682-7343
Designed by Charles S. Frost as the Adams Memorial Library, this 1891 Romanesque limestone building now houses a collection heavy on military memorabilia and local period domesticity. A massive model-railroad layout in the basement includes much of the route of the Chicago & North Western, for which Frost designed many stations. There are numerous adult and children's programs, as well.

Evanston Historical Society
225 Greenwood St.
Evanston
475-3410
The 28-room Romanesque chateau of General Charles Gates Dawes, banker, philanthropist, Nobel Peace Prize winner, and public servant (including a term as Vice President under Coolidge), boasts a Jacobean great hall, a Tudor dining room, and a magnificent Renaissance library. Besides the house itself, there are Dawes and Evanston memorabilia, plus the society's excellent research library devoted to local subjects and authors.

Fox River Trolley Museum
Illinois Route 31
South Elgin
697-4676
Open from mid-May to October, this museum offers a ride on the Chicago, Aurora & Elgin or Chicago, North Shore

& Milwaukee interurban electric cars, an open-bench streetcar from Rio de Janeiro, or an old elevated car along three miles of track that traces the Fox River and was once a part of the interurban line between Aurora and Elgin.

Glessner House
1800 S. Prairie Ave.
326-1393
Owned by the Chicago Architecture Foundation, Chicago's only remaining H. H. Richardson building is kingpin of the Prairie Avenue Historic District.

Graue Mill and Museum
York Rd. and Spring Rd.
Oak Brook
655-2090
This 150-year-old building on Salt Creek served as an Underground Railroad way station and is the state's last working gristmill. Tour the extensive Civil War period rooms upstairs. There are demonstrations of weaving, and cornmeal is sold in the shop.

Great Lakes Naval and Maritime Museum
Navy Pier
600 E. Grand Ave.
819-0055
The *Rachel Carson* (an operational research vessel that is in Chicago in the summertime only) forms the backbone of this museum, which includes other vessels as well as informative exhibits about maritime history. A store on the premises has a fine selection of maritime publications and some instruments.

Illinois Railway Museum
Olsen Rd.
Union
262-2266
More than 150 locomotives and streetcars are displayed at this outdoor museum. Several run on a couple of tracks through farmland. There's a

Museums

separate streetcar track, too.

Museum of Broadcast Communications
800 S. Wells St.
987-1500
The recently opened museum and research facility houses a unique collection chronicling media "history."

Naper Settlement
201 W. Porter Ave.
Naperville
420-6010
This Williamsburg-style re-creation of a northern Illinois town circa 1831 to 1885 has 24 historic buildings, including a reconstruction of Fort Payne. Costumed "residents" add to the ambiance.

Printer's Row Printing Museum
715 S. Dearborn St.
987-1059
Nostalgic collections of printing ephemera and working presses in a 19th-century setting are open on weekends.

Seven Acres Antique Village Museum
8512 S. Union Rd.
Union
815-923-2214
This is an an entire afternoon's worth of nostalgia: military memorabilia, 1890s shops, an "Old West" street, the gallows built for the Haymarket rioters, Edison artifacts, and the world's largest collection of antique phonographs.

Widow Clarke House
1855 S. Indiana Ave.
326-1393
Built in 1836 and moved south around the time of the Chicago Fire, the city's oldest building was returned in 1977 to within a few blocks of its original location. Chicago's only surviving Greek Revival house, and a rare example of post-and-beam construction, it has been beautifully restored

and furnished to reflect the life and times of the Clarke family.

Frank Lloyd Wright Home and Studio Foundation
951 Chicago Ave.
Oak Park
848-1500
Tours of Wright's 1889 home and 1898 studio, now a National Historic Landmark, where the architect lived and worked for the first 20 years of his career, are given daily.

Galleries

MORE THAN EVER, Chicagoans are interested in art — buying it, talking about it, creating it. In the last 15 years, the gallery scene has developed to the point that few close and new ones open every year.

Dealers from New York and Europe fall all over each other to exhibit at the ever-growing Chicago International Art Exposition, held every May, the International New Art Forms Exposition, held in September, and the Chicago International Antiques Show, held each summer. Chicago's reputation as a world art center enhances and is enhanced by these grand events.

Interest in Chicago artists grows as the likes of Richard Hunt, Roger Brown, Jim Nutt, Ed Paschke, and Paul La Mantia move toward international reputations. All this encourages more and more artists to stay here to work, giving Chicago art a new excitement and diversity.

The majority of Chicago's art galleries are clustered in and around the River North area, south of Chicago Avenue, between the Chicago River on the south and west and Wells Street on the east. There are still a few galleries on North Michigan Avenue and a few others around the Museum of Contemporary Art on East Ontario Street.

Unless otherwise indicated, all the following listed galleries are in Chicago. There are separate listings for works of art (a term that includes any combination of paintings, drawings, sculptures, graphics, etchings, fiber art, ceramics, and art furniture) and auction houses.

A.R.C. Gallery
356 W. Huron St.
266-7607
Contemporary works of art, many of them by local artists.

Artemisia Gallery
341 W. Superior St.
751-2016
Contemporary art with a feminist bent.

Artisans 21
5225 S. Harper Ave.
288-7450
Wearable art, watercolors, photography, ceramics, and wooden toys.

Arts Club of Chicago
109 E. Ontario St.
787-3997
Art by old masters as well as contemporary artists.

Jacques Baruch Gallery
40 E. Delaware Pl.
944-3377
Artists represented from Eastern Europe, the United States, and Western Europe.

Mary Bell Gallery
361 W. Superior St.
642-0202
Contemporary paintings and sculpture.

Walter Bischoff Gallery
340 W. Huron St.
266-0244
Contemporary paintings, European art, and works on paper.

Roy Boyd Gallery
739 N. Wells St.
642-1606
Contemporary abstract art, mostly by Chicago artists.

Campanile Galleries, Inc.
200 S. Michigan Ave.
663-3885
Nineteenth- and early 20th-century American and European art.

Merrill Chase Galleries
Water Tower Place
845 N. Michigan Ave.
337-6600
Paintings and sculptures

by both contemporary artists and old masters.

Chiaroscuro
750 N. Orleans St.
988-9253
Contemporary works of art, including fine crafts and art furniture.

**Chicago Center
for Ceramic Art**
430 W. Erie St.
649-1777
Contemporary ceramic art.

**Chicago Center
for the Print**
1509 W. Fullerton Ave.
477-1585
Original prints by Midwest artists.

Jan Cicero Gallery
221 W. Erie St.
440-1906
Contemporary art.

Creative Claythings
3412 N. Southport Ave.
472-5580
Ceramics.

Galleries

Dart Gallery
212 W. Superior St.
787-6366
Contemporary American art.

Douglas Dawson Gallery
341 W. Superior St.
751-1961
Textiles, ceramics, sculpture, and other ethnographic arts from around the world.

De Graaf Fine Art
300 W. Superior St.
951-5180
Contemporary art from the Americas and Europe.

Marianne Deson Gallery
340 W. Huron St.
787-0005
Contemporary art from America — much of it from Chicago — and Europe.

East West Gallery
356 W. Huron St.
664-8003
Contemporary art.

Exhibit A
361 W. Superior St.
944-1748
Contemporary ceramics.

Fairweather Hardin Gallery
101 E. Ontario St.
642-0007
Contemporary art, much of it by Chicago artists.

Richard L. Feigen and Company
325 W. Huron St.
787-0500
Old masters from the 14th through the 20th centuries, as well as some contemporary works of art.

Walter Findlay Galleries
814 N. Michigan Ave.
649-1500
Nineteenth- and 20th-century French art, as well as contemporary works of art.

Fly-by-Nite Gallery
714 N. Wells St.
664-8136
European arts and crafts, including art nouveau, art deco, and art moderne works.

Galleries Maurice Sternberg
111 E. Oak St.
642-1700
Nineteenth- and 20th-century American and European paintings and drawings.

Gilman/Gruen Gallery
226 W. Superior St.
337-6262
Contemporary works of art.

Goldman/Kraft Gallery
300 W. Superior St.
943-9088
Contemporary works of art, some of it by Israeli artists.

Grove Street Gallery-Studio
919 Grove St.
Evanston
866-7340
Contemporary, traditional, and naive works of art.

Richard Gray Gallery
620 N. Michigan Ave.
642-8877
301 W. Superior St.
642-8865
Contemporary and modern works of art, including paintings, drawings, sculpture, and prints.

Grayson Gallery
833 N. Orleans St.
266-1336
Contemporary works of art, as well as ancient and primitive art.

Habatat Galleries
340 W. Huron St.
337-1355
Contemporary art, primarily in glass.

Carl Hammer Gallery
200 W. Superior St.
266-8512
Sculpture, textiles, paintings, and decorative arts from the 18th to the 20th century, including works of self-taught artists.

Rhona Hoffman Gallery
215 W. Superior St.
951-8828
Contemporary art.

Hokin/Kaufman Gallery
210 W. Superior St.
266-1211
Contemporary works of art, including art furniture.

Joy Horwich Gallery
226 E. Ontario St.
787-0171
Contemporary works of art, including textiles.

Catherine Edelman Gallery
300 W. Superior St.
266-2350
Contemporary photography.

Edwynn Houk Gallery
200 W. Superior St.
943-0698
Contemporary and modern photography.

Isobel Neal Gallery Ltd.
200 W. Superior St.
944-1570
Works of art by African American artists.

R. S. Johnson Fine Art
645 N. Michigan Ave.
943-1661
Nineteenth- and 20th-century European and American works of art, as well as some old-master prints and drawings.

Rodi Karkazis Gallery
168 N. Michigan Ave.
346-5050
European paintings and 20th-century Chinese art.

Kass Meridian Gallery
215 W. Superior St.
266-5999
Contemporary art.

Douglas Kenyon, Inc.
1357 N. Wells St.
642-5300
Specializes in the works of
John James Audubon and
other similar artists.

Phyllis Kind Gallery
313 W. Superior St.
642-6302
Contemporary American
works of art, much of it from
Chicago Imagists.

Klein Gallery
356 W. Huron St.
787-0400
Contemporary works of art
by American as well as some
Mexican and European artists.

Les Primitifs
2038 N. Clark St.
528-5200
Traditional and modern art
from Africa and Asia.

Robbin Lockett Gallery
703 N. Wells St.
649-1230
Contemporary art.

R. H. Love Galleries
100 E. Ohio St.
664-9620
Nineteenth-century American
art, including folk art and
Impressionism.

Peter Miller Gallery
340 W. Huron St.
951-0252
Contemporary art.

Missouri Gallery
1932 S. Halsted St.
733-7033
Contemporary art.

Monahan Fine Arts
1038-B N. La Salle Dr.
266-7530
Nineteenth- and 20th-century
works of art.

**Mongerson-Wunderlich
Gallery**
704 N. Wells St.
943-2354
Art from the American West.

More by Far
615 N. Wells St.
664-7066
Contemporary art, mostly
by Chicago artists.

N.A.M.E. Gallery
700 N. Carpenter St.
226-0671
Not-for-profit contemporary
art.

Neville-Sargent Gallery
215 W. Superior St.
664-2787
Contemporary works of art,
much of it by local artists.

Objects Gallery
341 W. Superior St.
664-6622
Multimedia works of art, as
well as art furniture.

On Sight Art
906 Sherman Ave.
Evanston
864-7490
Contemporary works of art by
local artists.

Nina Owen Ltd.
620 N. Michigan Ave.
664-0474
Contemporary sculpture.

Perimeter Gallery
356 W. Huron St.
266-9473
Contemporary art.

Prairie Lee Gallery
301 W. Superior St.
266-7113
Art of the Southwest, including works by Indian artists.

Prince Galleries
357 W. Erie St.
266-9663
Eighteenth- and 19th-century
works of art, including
bronzes.

Printworks, Ltd.
311 W. Superior St.
664-9407
Contemporary prints and
other works of art on paper.

Galleria Renata
507 N. Wells St.
644-1607
Contemporary works of art,
many of them by Chicago
artists.

Roger Ramsay Gallery
212 W. Superior St.
337-4678
Watercolors, pastels, drawings, and collages by 19th-cen-
tury and contemporary artists.

Randolph Street Gallery
756 N. Milwaukee Ave.
666-7737
Avant-garde art, mostly by
Chicagoans.

Betsy Rosenfield Gallery
212 W. Superior St.
787-8020
Contemporary works of art,
with an emphasis on works
in glass.

J. Rosenthal Fine Arts
212 W. Superior St.
642-2966
Contemporary art.

Esther Saks Gallery
311 W. Superior St.
751-0911
Contemporary art, much
of it ceramics, glass, fiber,
and multimedia.

**School of the Art
Institute of Chicago**
Gallery II
1040 W. Huron St.
226-1449
Works of art by students at
the Art Institute School.

**Samuel Stein Fine
Arts, Ltd.**
620 N. Michigan Ave.
337-1782
Nineteenth- and 20th-century
works of art.

Galleries

Struve Gallery
309 W. Superior St.
787-0563
Contemporary works of art, including architectural drawings and objects.

Topeka
110 W. Kinzie St.
472-4628
Contemporary art furniture, lighting, textiles, and architectural objects, much of the stock European.

van Straaten Gallery
361 W. Superior St.
642-2900
Contemporary works of art on paper.

Ruth Volid Gallery
225 W. Illinois St.
644-3180
Contemporary art.

Waller-Boldenweck Gallery
5300 S. Blackstone Ave.
363-7446
Contemporary paintings and graphics, as well as limited-edition posters.

Walton Street Gallery
58 E. Walton St.
943-1793
Traditional and contemporary art.

Wild Goose Chase Quilt Gallery
1248 N. Wells St.
787-9778
1524 Chicago Ave.
Evanston
328-1808
Americana, including many quilts.

Worthington Gallery
620 N. Michigan Ave.
266-2424
Contemporary and modern works of art, many of them by German Expressionists.

Yolanda
300 W. Superior St.
664-3436
Contemporary American,
European, and Asian art, focusing on works by naive and folk artists.

Donald Young Gallery
325 W. Huron St.
664-2151
Contemporary art.

Zaks Gallery
620 N. Michigan Ave.
943-8440
Contemporary works of art, many of them by local artists.

Zolla/Lieberman Gallery
356 W. Huron St.
944-1990
Contemporary works of art.

Auctioneers

Christie's
200 W. Superior St.
787-2765

Leslie Hindman Auctioneers
215 W. Ohio St.
670-0010

Sotheby's
325 W. Huron St.
664-6800

Chicago Art Galleries, Inc.
20 W. Hubbard St.
645-0686

Music

THE CHICAGO SYMPHONY ORCHESTRA and Lyric Opera command international plaudits, while less-famous groups spread classical music throughout the city and suburbs. But Chicago's music preeminence extends to every genre. Our blues musicians created and nurtured a unique art form; the number of jazz performances continues to grow; folk clubs thrive here; and the sounds of everything from the accordion to the zither throb in countless ethnic taverns. Since bars and clubs provide the forum for most non-classical performances, neighborhood imperatives dictate most booking policies, and covers or minimums range from nothing to big bucks for big names. (More detailed discussions of clubs can be found in the neighborhood chapters.)

Our wealth of musical performances has one very real drawback: Keeping track of what's going on isn't easy. The most complete listings appear monthly in *Chicago* magazine. Friday and Sunday entertainment listings in the daily newspapers may reflect last-minute changes, and the *Reader*, a free weekly that comes out on Thursdays, offers a wealth of information about neighborhood clubs and bars.

If your thoughts on classical music in Chicago begin and end with the Chicago Symphony Orchestra or the Lyric Opera, you're overlooking a lot. This is one of the most musically active cities in the world, with an enormous reservoir of talented musicians and countless opportunities to hear them perform. All year long, indoors and out, a dizzying array of concerts provides music to satisfy any taste, whether for Renaissance madrigals or for the most challenging modern scores. With everything from organ recitals in neighborhood churches to touring superstars in recital, finding time to even sample the riches creates a pleasant problem.

Skimming the city's classical *crème de la crème* can be costly, even with the savings offered by subscription series, but affordable options abound. Less-than-top-ranked groups performing in halls and churches around town typically command one-half to two-thirds the price of the downtown front-runners. Most school and conservatory concerts are free or inexpensive. On Sundays, you can hear some mighty organ music and choral works in churches for a prayer.

Choral Groups

Apollo Chorus of Chicago
427-5620
Dr. Thomas Hoekstra, musical director and conductor, leads more than 200 voices in mostly sacred music, continuing a tradition that began in 1872. Major performances are a December *Messiah* and one or more large choral works in the spring at Orchestra Hall, plus a concert of shorter pieces at Holy Name

Cathedral, Chicago Avenue and State Street.

Chicago Baroque Ensemble
383-4742
Victor Hildner brings together 16 professional singers and instrumentalists to re-create original baroque performance practices. The repertoire includes hundreds of pieces. The Ensemble performs four times a year.

Chicago Chamber Choir
St. Pauls United Church of Christ
2335 N. Orchard St.
935-3800
George Estevez leads his 40-voice choir in seldom-heard music of all periods. There are four subscription concerts.

Chicago Children's Choir
324-8300
Now in its 31st year, this marvelous organization involves 650 children in various stages of choral training. The 130-voice senior group tours extensively but is always in town for Christmas con-

Music

certs and a June gala, usually in Hyde Park.

Do-It-Yourself *Messiah*
Margaret Hillis conducts the orchestra and you in this popular event. Orchestra Hall fills with joyful voices at two or three sing-alongs in December. The much-sought-after, free tickets are distributed by Talman Home Federal Savings and Loan Association, 72 E. Randolph St., Chicago 60601. Requests must include a stamped, self-addressed envelope, and those postmarked before November 15 are not honored.

William Ferris Chorale
922-2070
Director William Ferris is a composer who celebrates other living composers in concert. The 50-voice chorus performs four major concerts a year at Our Lady of Mount Carmel Church, 690 W. Belmont Ave., with other performances throughout the city.

Music of the Baroque
461-9541
Thomas Wikman's superb singers and musicians perform works from the 15th to the 18th century, but feel most at home in the 17th and are justifiably famed for their interpretations of the great oratorios and *Passions*. The orchestra also does splendidly with instrumental works. Eight programs a year in each of four series: Hyde Park, Evanston, Near North, and the western suburbs.

Oriana Singers
465-5656
William Chin directs this vocal ensemble in everything from madrigals to recent compositions. A four-program subscription series at Chicago and Evanston locations; other concerts, too.

Rockefeller Chapel Choir
5850 S. Woodlawn Ave.
702-6002
One of the best things about Rodney Wynkoop's 25-voice professional choir is that you can hear it free at 11 a.m. Sunday services throughout the academic year. Wynkoop and his assistant director conduct the smaller chancel choir at 9 a.m. Tickets for the subscription series, which include a Christmastime *Messiah*, can be purchased at the University of Chicago box office or at Ticketron.

Ensembles

Bach Society Musicians
Glencoe Union Church
263 Park Ave.
Glencoe
432-4458
Nancy Humphrey is musical director and harpsichordist of this group specializing in solos, trios, and sonatas by J. S. Bach and his contemporaries. There are five concerts a year.

Chicago Brass Quintet
663-4730
Since 1962, five players from major Chicago orchestras have presented the best in brass, as well as their own transcriptions. Programs touch everything from Renaissance works to commissioned contemporary pieces. Three-concert subscription series are at Grace Place, 637 S. Dearborn St. The group also appears around the city and tours nationally.

Contemporary Chamber Players
of the University of Chicago
962-8068
Since the mid-1960s, composer Ralph Shapey's fine

group has championed 20th-century music, especially works by living composers and those ignored by the establishment. The spring Fromm Music Foundation concert is always an important event. Free concerts at Mandel Hall, 5706 S. University Ave.

Harwood Early Music Ensemble
775-6696
John Nygro's nine musicians present carefully-researched, entertaining medieval and Renaissance selections, using replicas of original instruments and appropriate vocal styles. Explanatory narratives and literary readings augment some performances. Five-concert subscription series are at various city and suburban churches.

Opera Companies

Chamber Opera Chicago
822-0770
Now in its sixth season of presenting standard operas sung in English, Chamber Opera Chicago is now performing at the Ivanhoe Theater on the North Side.

Chicago Opera Theater
Athenaeum Theater
2936 N. Southport Ave.
663-0555
Artistic director Alan Stone founded the company in 1973, and it has been delighting Chicagoans with operas in English ever since. Productions range from classics like Mozart's *Così fan tutte* to Chicago premières of contemporary works such as Robert Kurka's *The Good Soldier Schweik*. There are about four operas a season.

Music

Light Opera Works
Cahn Auditorium
Northwestern University
600 Emerson St.
Evanston
869-6300
This company's repertoire includes comic opera, operetta (lots of Gilbert and Sullivan), and operettalike American musicals, all sung in English. Philip Kraus is artistic director; musical chores are handled by Barney Jones. (Not affiliated with Northwestern University.)

Lithuanian Opera Company
Maria High School
6727 S. California Ave.
471-1424
Since 1956, this company has been doing a grand job of producing grand opera in Lithuanian. It has done everything from the war-horses to American premières of rarities like Ponchielli's *I lituani*. There are usually three performances of one opera a year.

Lyric Opera of Chicago
Civic Opera House
20 N. Wacker Dr.
332-2244
A civic treasure, it's one of the hottest tickets in town. Real opera lovers should invest in a subscription for the September-to-February season.

Orchestras

Chicago Chamber Orchestra
922-5570
Dieter Kober's group has been presenting delightful free concerts of well-known and seldom-heard works since 1952. Frequent appearances from winter through spring are at the Museum of Science and Industry, the Art Institute, and

the Chicago Public Library Cultural Center and are capped in May by the Blair Memorial Concert, featuring major soloists, at the Cathedral of St. James, 65 E. Huron St.

Chicago String Ensemble
St. Pauls United Church of Christ
2335 N. Orchard St.
332-0567
Alan Heatherington's 20 to 22 musicians give splendid performances of string-orchestra literature of all periods. There are five subscription concerts.

Chicago Symphony Orchestra
Orchestra Hall
220 S. Michigan Ave.
435-8111
The CSO is Chicago's world-class team. Single tickets for subscription concerts — especially those conducted by music director Sir Georg Solti, or ones featuring Margaret Hillis's superb chorus — are often difficult to come by.

Civic Orchestra of Chicago
Orchestra Hall
220 S. Michigan Ave.
435-8158
The hundred or so musicians in this "training orchestra" of the CSO present some of the finest performances in the area. Principal conductors Kenneth Jean and Michael Morgan put together distinctive programs, placing more emphasis on 20th-century works and American music than is usual for the Civic's home auditorium.

Evanston Symphony Orchestra
Evanston Township High School Auditorium
1600 Dodge Ave.
Evanston
965-2440
Founded in 1945, this 90-

member orchestra gives four concerts annually.

Lake Forest Symphony
Drake Theater
Barat College
700 E. Westleigh Rd.
Lake Forest
295-2135
Seventy musicians and a community chorus perform throughout the year under the direction of Chicago Symphony concertmaster Paul Anthony McRae.

Orchestra of Illinois
341-1975
Musicians for the Lyric Opera have put together America's only self-governed orchestra. Between 60 and 80 of them do everything from keeping the American Ballet Theater on its toes to playing popular concerts for conventions.

Festivals and Series

Allied Arts Association Concerts
Orchestra Hall
220 S. Michigan Ave.
435-6666
The season includes single attractions and several series, which bring in everything from the Orchestre de Paris and Murray Peraiha to Chet Atkins and Judy Collins, carrying on the traditions established by the late Harry Zelzer, one of the last of the great impresarios.

Chamber Music Chicago
663-1628
Now in its 28th season, Chamber Music Chicago performs at various spots around the city, including the Civic Theater, Orchestra Hall, and the Goodman Theater. Each season, CMC highlights a dif-

Music

ferent aspect of chamber music. It also sponsors the Early Talent Recognition program, which involves 1,500 students from nine inner-city high schools in a series of workshops, concerts, and lecture-demonstrations with the Vermeer Quartet.

City Musick
642-1766
Founded in 1985, City Musick specializes in baroque and classical repertoire and performs exclusively on 18th-century period instruments. Its members are drawn from the Chicago Symphony, Lyric Opera, and other smaller ensembles in Chicago. Performances, which have included a costumed production of Mozart's *Idomeneo*, take place at various locations, such as the Shedd Aquarium and Orchestra Hall.

Grant Park Concerts
James C. Petrillo Music Shell
Grant Park
294-2420
Since 1935, Chicagoans have enjoyed free concerts in the city's front yard. The topnotch Grant Park Symphony and Chorus are led by some of the world's most promising conductors in programs ranging from pops to concert opera and ballet. The season runs from late June through August.

Dame Myra Hess Memorial Concerts
Preston Bradley Hall
Chicago Public Library
Cultural Center
78 E. Washington St.
744-6630
An outstanding free series provides exposure and performance experience for young musicians from around the world. Occasionally, established artists are invited also.

Mostly Music
924-2550
More than 70 concerts feature young as well as established artists. From fall through spring, weekly lunch-time concerts of vocal and instrumental music of all periods bring shoppers and office workers to First Chicago Center, Dearborn and Monroe streets; and performances of chamber music in homes and other surroundings are a great success in Hyde Park-Kenwood and on the North Side and North Shore.

Pick-Staiger Concert Hall Series
1977 Sheridan Rd.
Evanston
492-5441
Northwestern University's music school fills this 1,000-seat theater with glorious music from fall through late spring. The Performing Arts Series holds a traditional line-up of orchestras, chamber groups, and soloists; other series lean toward contemporary music, up-and-coming artists, and specialized programs.

Ravinia Festival
Highland Park
728-4642 (May to Sept.)
782-9696 (winter)
Ravinia is more than just a bucolic setting that features the Chicago Symphony: There are visiting orchestras, chamber music ensembles, soloists, pop artists, dance companies, and young people's programs. Special buses (728-4642) and Park 'n' Ride facilities (432-3325) help you get there and back; several dining facilities as well.

University of Chicago Department of Music
Mandel Hall
5706 S. University Ave.
702-1234
The Early Music and Chamber Music series bring notable artists to a nicely renovated hall.

Colleges and Conservatories

Chicago is blessed with some of the nation's finest music schools, and we all reap the benefits of their low-priced — and often free — offerings.

American Conservatory of Music
17 N. State St.
263-4161

Chicago Musical College of Roosevelt University
430 S. Michigan Ave.
341-3780

DePaul University School of Music
804 W. Belden Ave.
341-8373

Northwestern University School of Music
711 Elgin Rd.
Evanston
491-3741

University of Chicago School of Music
5845 S. Ellis Ave.
702-1234

Theater

A DECADE AGO, THEATER IN CHICAGO meant the Goodman, road shows at a few downtown houses, half a dozen dinner playhouses, community troupes, and a handful of struggling Off-Loop groups. Saying there's been a dramatic explosion since then isn't being theatrical. Fueled by a liberalized fire code, government grants, and a wellspring of creative energy, scores of professional and semiprofessional Off-Loop theaters opened during the 1970s. More than a few resulted from college-days collaborations of directors, designers, actors, and playwrights — fruitful shades of Mickey Rooney's "I've got an idea: Let's put on a show!"

The successes of the best helped beget others, and although some companies fold for lack of space or funds, new ones continue to emerge. Synergy sustains the renaissance. Not only do theaters share resources; the very existence of so many keeps a pool of talent in Chicago, contributes to ever-increasing audiences, and prompts private financial backing.

In the fall, the Joseph Jefferson Awards Committee honors excellence in local professional theater with Chicago's equivalent of the Tony awards. Established in 1968 and named for Joseph Jefferson III, a member of the first professional company to play Chicago in 1837, the 40-member committee also maintains a noncompetitive Citations Wing to recognize achievements by non-Equity groups.

HOT TIX booths, which are owned and operated by the League of Chicago Theaters, sell full-price, advance-sale tickets and half-price, day-of-performance tickets for cash only. A small surcharge, prorated on the basis of the full ticket price, is made for handling in both cases. The booths operate Monday through Saturday, with half-price Sunday tickets on sale Saturday. HOT TIX booths are in Chicago at 24 South State Street, in Evanston at the Sherman Avenue garage between Church and Davis streets, and in Oak Park at the Oak Park Atrium, Lake and Marion streets.

These listings are partial, excluding most college and community groups, city arts activities, the Chicago Park District's extensive drama programs, and the growing number of comedy troupes.

All theaters listed here are in Chicago, unless otherwise noted.

Absolute Theater Company
545-0200
After a bang-up start in 1981, artistic director Warner Crocker's group has continued to present proven and new plays — much of its reputation resting on the latter — as well as children's theater.

American Blues Theater
3212 N. Broadway
728-5844
This theater company is known for both presenting new plays and reviving mod-
ern-day classics that spring from the heartland of the Midwest — its people, its steel towns, its suburbs and farms.

Apollo Theater Company
2540 N. Lincoln Ave.
549-1342
The handsome, 350-seat theater with a striking lobby was the first all-new commercial house spawned by the Off-Loop movement. The policy of presenting premières and musical revues that aim for mass appeal and financial success has been virtually supplanted by the practice of
bringing in proven money-makers from elsewhere.

Apple Tree Theater
593 Elm Pl.
Highland Park
432-4335
This tiny 120-seat theater was founded in 1982 and presents both musicals and dramas. Occasionally, it presents a new work as well.

Arie Crown Theater
McCormick Place
23rd St. and Lake Shore Dr.
791-6516
Big Broadway musicals (usu-

Theater

ally road companies with big stars) are the mainstay of this 4,319-seat house with limited visibility from any but the first 15 or so rows. Static-ridden, tinny-sounding body microphones and often inadequately rehearsed orchestras make bad acoustics worse, but sometimes everything does come together for a satisfying night of musical theater. Visiting ballets, operas, acrobats sometimes play here.

Auditorium Theater
50 E. Congress Pkwy.
922-4046
Adler and Sullivan's magnificent 4,000-seat theater houses all types of entertainment — from dance companies such as Joseph Holmes Dance Theater and the American Ballet Theater to other varied types of performances by groups such as the St. Louis Symphony and the Academy of Ancient Music.

Bailiwick Repertory
3212 N. Broadway
883-1091
Founded in 1982, this group has a repertory ranging from theater classics, such as *The Threepenny Opera*, to contemporary plays, such as *The New AIDS Play*. Occupying the Hull House Association's Jane Addams Center on the North Side, the center is used regularly for neighborhood meetings, auditions, and senior citizens' activities.

Beverly Theater Guild
Beverly Art Center
2153 W. 111th St.
238-0742
Not only is this theater group one of the only such on the Far Southwest Side, but it's one of the oldest community theaters in the city.

Body Politic Theater
2261 N. Lincoln Ave.
348-7901

Body Politic mounts a varied subscription season in a 192-seat theater and sometimes rents the space to other groups. Founded in 1966 as the Community Arts Foundation, it is the granddaddy of the Off-Loop theaters. Its current moniker comes from British actor Harley Granville-Barker, who said, "The theater is a body politic and the art of it a single art, though the contributors to it must be many."

Briar Street Theater
3133 N. Halsted St.
348-4000
This group was founded in 1983 and opened its present 399-seat location in April 1985, with the world première of Chicagoan David Mamet's *The Shawl* and *The Spanish Prisoner*. It has continued to produce plays by big-name playwrights, such as Tom Waits and Tom Stoppard, as well as attempting to provide opportunities to include both film and video in its productions.

Candlelight Dinner Playhouse
5620 Harlem Ave.
Summit
496-3000
William Pullinsi, with his mother and grandfather, began the country's first dinner theater in 1959, and the present building, with the first dinner-theater elevator stage, opened in 1964. Rather small, it makes choreography for the major musical revivals difficult. About four shows a year feature Chicago-area talents. Several of its productions have been highly praised, including *Nine* and *Little Shop of Horrors*, which won the Jefferson awards for BEST MUSICAL PRODUCTION in 1985 and 1986.

Chicago Dramatists Workshop
1105 W. Chicago Ave.
633-0630
A not-for-profit theater group dedicated to producing the work of Chicago playwrights, it also hosts public readings and discussions of works in progress and offers classes on play writing.

Chicago Shakespeare Company
2647 N. Greenview Ave.
871-8961
Founded as the Free Shakespeare Company in 1981, this theater group is dedicated to keeping Shakespeare's words alive in the theater. In addition to traditional productions, it hosts experimental late-night performances. Recent productions have included *Measure for Measure*, *Twelfth Night*, and *A Winter's Tale*.

Chicago Theater
175 N. State St.
236-4300
Built in 1921 as a gem in the Balaban & Katz theater chain, the Chicago fell on hard times until being renovated and reopened in 1986. Host to a variety of performances, from concerts (Pia Zadora, Frank Sinatra) to international dance companies to Broadway musicals, the theater is a rococo-lover's dream come true.

Chicago Theater Company
500 E. 67th St.
493-1305
Founded in 1984, this is one of the few black theater companies affiliated with Actors Equity in Illinois. It provides the Chicago theater community a rare but consistent set of plays done from a black perspective.

City Lit Theater Company
4753 N. Broadway
271-8749
Started as a not-for-profit group by Arnold Aprill, David Dillon, and Lorell Wyatt in 1979, this company presents concert readings and full-stage productions of literary adaptations, original works, and scripts that exhibit a love for the spoken word.

Civic Theater
20 N. Wacker Dr.
346-0270
The art deco minimasterpiece seats 878 people at the north end of Samuel Insull's magnificent Civic Opera House.

Commons Theater Center
1020 W. Bryn Mawr Ave.
769-5009
Actors Judith Easton and Michael Nowak and playwright Kathleen Thompson created CTC in 1980. It has since grown to more than 30 actors and produces new plays and a few musicals, often dealing with their plays' subject matter in a witty and humane manner.

Court Theater
5535 S. Ellis Ave.
753-4472
Completed in late 1981 on the University of Chicago campus, CT's 250-seat theater with state-of-the-art light, sound, and stage facilities makes an ideal home for the topnotch productions of established plays, which in recent years have included *Oresteia*, *Tartuffe*, and *Uncle Vanya*. Court also hosts educational programs, which include numerous matinees for high-school audiences, and after-performance audience discussions.

Drury Lane Oakbrook Terrace
100 Drury Lane
Oakbrook Terrace
530-8300
Large-scale musicals and comedies are presented in this 980-seat theater, which offers dinner-theater packages as well.

ETA Creative Arts Foundation
7558 S. South Chicago Ave.
752-3955
Both a school for children beginning at age six and a company, this group, founded in 1971, produces plays and musicals by African American playwrights that speak to the black experience. It also hosts a Reader's Theater for playwrights.

Goodman Theater
200 S. Columbus Dr.
443-3800
A gift to the Art Institute of Chicago from the parents of Kenneth Sawyer Goodman, a dramatist-poet who died in World War One, Chicago's resident regional theater has been producing a wide range of classical and contemporary plays since 1925. With lots of legroom for its 683 seats, a proscenium-arch stage, and excellent sight lines, the theater is a delight. The 135-seat studio houses experimental or developing productions and special events, such as the Chicago début of Milwaukee's Theater X. The Goodman offers newsletters, extensive program notes, and a wide range of lectures and workshops.

igLoo Group
3829 N. Broadway
975-9192
Founded in 1985 in a large second-story loft above a couple of stores, igLoo performs original and lost works and encourages local experimental and performance artists as well.

Immediate Theater Company
1146 W. Pratt Blvd.
465-3107
Founded by 17 actors in 1982, the Immediate Theater Company moved into its current space, which seats up to 98 in the main-stage hall and 55 in the studio, in 1983. Since its inception it has garnered critical acclaim, as well as numerous Jefferson award nominations.

Kuumba Theater Company
1900 W. Van Buren St.
461-9000
Val Gray Ward started the first black professional theater in Chicago — Kuumba — in 1968 to further the black liberation struggle through art controlled entirely by blacks. Besides pioneering a freeform Ritual Theater, the group has produced several plays by both celebrated and not-yet-celebrated authors to educate blacks and whites about black experiences. Kuumba also offers classes and community programs, as well as monthly jazz, blues, and gospel programs.

Latino Chicago Theater Company
1625 N. Damen Ave.
486-5120
Started by the Victory Gardens Theater in 1979 with a grant from CBS, the city's first professional Latino theater company is now independent, maintains several ensembles, tours throughout the city, and performs at its own space. Traditional and original plays about the Latin American experience are performed in Spanish, in English, and bilingually.

Theater

Lifeline Theater
6912 N. Glenwood Ave.
761-4477
Founded in 1982 by a group of actors, Lifeline moved into its own space in Rogers Park in 1985. Dedicated to the ensemble process, each season there is an infusion of new actors and new energy. Lifeline also produces children's theater with a "pay as you can" admission policy.

National Jewish Theater
5050 Church St.
Skokie
675-5070
Dedicated to exploring the contemporary Jewish experience, this group was founded in 1986 and performs regularly in a 250-seat theater at the Mayer Kaplan Jewish Community Center in Skokie.

Next Theater Company
927 Noyes St.
Evanston
475-1875
Started by Brian Finn and Harriet Spizziri in 1981, Next Theater Company has developed a reputation for fine productions of both modern classics and contemporary plays about contemporary issues (its production of *The Normal Heart*, for instance).

Northlight Theater
2300 Green Bay Rd.
Evanston
869-7278
Founded in 1974, Northlight mounts five productions annually. The theater focuses on new plays, producing "lost" classical plays, and creating its own interpretations of contemporary plays drawn from an international repertoire. Committed to serving the community, Northlight also offers outreach programs for students, senior citizens, veterans, and disabled persons.

Organic Theater Company
3319 N. Clark St.
327-5588
The Organic has been called "the theater that never ceases to amaze." Since 1969, the company has been bombarding audiences with productions filled with special effects, action-packed world premières, revivals of its own works, and original adaptations of nondramatic material, such as *Bleacher Bums* and the three-part, sci-fi epic, *Warp*. Taking its name from Stanislavsky's organic process of theater, the ensemble often works closely with Chicago writers to develop plays — for example, the 1974 first professional production of David Mamet's *Sexual Perversity in Chicago*.

Pegasus Players
1145 W. Wilson Ave.
271-2638
Named for the winged horse of Greek mythology, this not-for-profit theater group, founded in 1978, is located at Truman College in Uptown. Pegasus's commitment to Uptown, which is home to many economically disadvantaged people and many elderly, has encouraged the group to keep ticket prices down and to admit thousands free through its Outreach Program.

Reflections Theater Ensemble
5404 N. Clark St.
784-1234
Founded in 1982, this storefront theater group produces plays that reflect changing times, changing attitudes. Its production of Lanford Wilson's *Talley Trilogy: The Fifth of July, Talley's Folly, and Talley and Son* was the first time the entire trilogy was performed together.

Royal-George Theater
1641 N. Halsted St.
988-9000
The newest and the largest of the Off-Loop theaters, it is part of a complex that includes the Cafe Royal and Ruggles, a cabaret.

Second City
1616 N. Wells St.
337-3992
Chicago's venerable comedic institution got its start in Hyde Park bars and has been holding forth on Wells Street for more than two decades. The litany of famous alumni is mind-boggling. The troupe mounts one or two new satiric revues a year, and occasional improvisation. There's also a popular children's theater, with plenty of improvisation and audience participation.

Shubert Theater
22 W. Monroe St.
977-1700
Show place for Broadway musicals such as *A Chorus Line* and *Evita*, the opulent 2,008-seat theater began as a vaudeville house in 1906.

Stage Left Theater Company
3244 N. Clark St.
883-8830
This small, 71-seat storefront theater presents fully produced plays as well as readings by contemporary playwrights.

Steppenwolf Theater Company
2851 N. Halsted St.
472-4141
Steppenwolf is one of the city's premier theater companies. Founded in 1976, it is also one of the first true ensembles of actors, playwrights, directors, and designers; and it chooses its plays — classics, new ones, neglected ones — according to the talents of the group. Its pro-

ductions in Chicago have included works by such playwrights as Sam Shepard, Tennessee Williams, Lanford Wilson, and Caryl Churchill. Numerous productions, including *True West* and *Burn This*, have gone on to be hits on the New York stage.

Victory Gardens Theater

2257 N. Lincoln Ave.
871-3000
Now in its 18th year, this not-for-profit organization houses two theaters, a 195-seat main stage and a 60-seat studio. Victory Gardens produces numerous plays each season, often by local playwrights, and often with a commitment to black and Hispanic theater.

Wisdom Bridge Theater

1559 W. Howard St.
743-6442
Founded in 1974 by actor-playwright David Beaird and named for a painting, this Far North Side theater is off the beaten track but always worth it. It has achieved success with productions ranging from classics to the contemporary.

Dance

SMALL, MOSTLY MODERN-DANCE TROUPES are flourishing artistically, but money and space problems continue to plague them and the many independent choreographers. Many of the companies discussed here offer classes or run full-fledged schools. Chicago Dance Coalition, an organization that promotes dance in Chicago, tries to improve this sometimes chaotic and discouraging situation.

Call the *Dance Hotline* (663-1313) to find out what's happening in dance in Chicago.

Akasha and Company
327-9797
Akasha, a Sanskrit word, translates as "spirit leaping forth." Works by choreographers ranging from Ginger Farley of the Hubbard Street Dance Company to Austin Hartel of Pilobolus are performed by Akasha, a group known for both emotion-filled and theatrical dancing.

American Dance Center School and Ballet Company
22413 Governors Hwy.
Richton Park
747-4969
Now in its 17th year, this company performs the classics; original ballets; jazz, tap, spirituals, and modern dance; and the Christmastime *Hansel and Gretel* ballet, presented with guest artists at the Rialto Square Theater in Joliet. The core group of 14 is augmented by several dozen dancers for most productions. Classes for children, adults, and aspiring professionals are held at the center and at suburban park districts and are offered for credit through Governors State University and Prairie State College.

Chicago Repertory Dance Ensemble
1016 N. Dearborn St.
440-9494
Founded in 1981, this group presents high-quality contemporary dance under the leadership of artistic director Tara Mitton. Instead of going outside the group for inspiration, dances here are choreographed by members within, many of whom use the exuberance and excitement of Chicago as their muse.

Concert Dance, Inc.
Mundelein College
6363 N. Sheridan Rd.
472-8692
Venetia Chakos Stifler founded this ten-dancer company in 1979 and choreographs most of its works.

Ensemble Español
5500 N. St. Louis Ave.
583-4050
The classical, regional, and flamenco dances of Spain are the domain of Northeastern Illinois University's resident company, started in 1976. Founder and director Dame Libby Komaiko Fleming choreographs for her troupe of half a dozen dancers and several apprentices, and they are sometimes joined by guest artists. Besides touring and mounting series for kids and adults at the university, the company hosts the summer American Dance Festival — two weeks of performances, workshops, and seminars.

Gus Giordano Dance Center
614 Davis St.
Evanston
866-6779
Gus Giordano's brand of jazz dance is big, accessible, and highly theatrical and involves a lot of torso and arm movements. The huge, four-studio Dance Center accommodates more than 1,000 students and hosts some concerts. Giordano's company tours nationally and internationally.

Joel Hall Dancers
New School for the
Performing Arts
3340 N. Clark St.
880-1002
Jazz dance is the mainstay of this troupe, whose repertoire includes modern-dance, ballet pieces by Hall and other choreographers. Some works combine dance and drama; others make statements about urban life.

Joseph Holmes Dance Theater
735 W. Sheridan Rd.
975-3505
The special appeal of the exciting ensemble is its energy, its polished dancing, and its appealing choreography — the latter created by Randy Duncan and the company's late founder, Joseph Holmes. Ballet, modern dance based on the Graham technique, jazz, blues, spirituals, dance drama, and African dance are all parts of the repertoire of the JHDT. The company's "Chance to Dance" outreach program provides an opportunity for interested youths to sign up for two free months of special

instruction after seeing a lecture-demonstration-performance presented at schools, community centers, boys' clubs, and the like.

Hubbard Street Dance Company

218 S. Wabash Ave., Third Floor
663-0853
Celebrating its tenth anniversary this year, the Hubbard Street Dance Company is considered by many to be Chicago's premier dance troupe. Artistic director Lou Conte's company has become very popular, with its easily accessible blend of ballet, show, and jazz dance. Uniquely American dance forms, set to Broadway and popular melodies, are performed with great theatrical flair by talented, highly trained dancers.

MoMing Dance and Arts Center

1034 W. Barry Ave.
472-9894
A Chicago dance mainstay, MoMing provides space for and coproduces performances by local and out-of-town dancers and troupes, mimes, multimedia artists, and more. Something new can be seen almost every weekend year-round, and MoMing has helped gain recognition for many fine choreographers who might otherwise have remained unknown. The school offers a full range of dance classes, with a special dance program for kids from four to 14.

Mordine & Company

Dance Center of Columbia College
4730 N. Sheridan Rd.
271-7804
Increasingly important to Chicago dance since its inception in 1969, the DCCC provides one of the few prime performance spaces scheduling more than 30 events a year from October through May. The small resident company, started at the same time by Shirley Mordine, has been getting stronger every year and, unlike most, develops pieces through experimentation and improvisation. Mordine does most of the choreography but also commissions guest artists to create for the group.

Muntu Dance Theater

704 E. 51st St.
285-1721
Eighteen dancers and musicians stage traditional and contemporary West African and African American dances. Muntu was formed in 1972 and currently is in residence at Kennedy-King College, 6800 S. Wentworth Ave.

Nana Solbrig & The Chicago Moving Company

Chicago Dance Center
2433 N. Lincoln Ave.
929-7416
Nana Solbrig, who started the group in 1972, has changed its name and now focuses on her own choreography. The Chicago Dance Center is a rehearsal space for the six to ten dancers and a school.

Sports

Baseball

Chicago Cubs
Wrigley Field
1060 W. Addison St.
878-CUBS
Ivy-covered outfield walls, a manually operated scoreboard, and seating that puts fans on top of the action make Wrigley Field the country's most charming ballpark, but the National League team has been held together with baling wire and chewing gum for years (even though it made the play-offs in 1984, it's not been able to maintain that level of performance for long). Since the Cubs' first game at Wrigley Field on April 20, 1916, all baseball there has been played in the sunshine. The Tribune Company purchased the Cubs in 1981 and since then has fought vigorously for permission to install lights for night games. Despite continuing controversy, the company has finally won, and night games should begin with the 1988 season.

Chicago White Sox
Comiskey Park
324 W. 35th St.
924-1000
When baseball was the all-American game, Chicagoans asked strangers whether they were Cubs or Sox fans before inquiring about such trivialities as ethnicity, religion, or politics. Such die-hards still exist, but now more fans follow fortune's flip-flops from North to South Side and back. Although ancient, Comiskey Park features a state-of-the-art scoreboard and a picnic area. When the team is doing well — and on occasion, they do — good tickets are hard to come by; buy them in advance for important games.

Basketball

Chicago Bulls
Chicago Stadium
1800 W. Madison St.
943-5800
Previously plagued with front-office problems, the Bulls, approaching respectability for years, have finally reached it, with no little help from Michael Jordan — although the cavernous home stadium is in an unsafe neighborhood, cheap seats are far from the play, beer is overpriced, and the hot dogs defy decorous description. For important contests, buy tickets well in advance from the box office or from Ticketron.

Football

Chicago Bears
Soldier Field
425 E. McFetridge Dr.
663-5408
Although the Bears haven't again reached the pinnacle of success they attained in 1984 when they were victorious in the Super Bowl, their defense remains the most brutal in the NFL. The team plays in Coach Mike Ditka's no-nonsense fashion and, because of it, has had the best record in the NFL over the past three seasons. The days when disputes over season tickets could throw estates into probate battles are gone, but a hefty surcharge to a downtown broker is still often the only way to get a seat in this windswept, classical arena.

Golf

Butler National Golf Club
2616 York Rd.
Oak Brook
990-3333
The Western Open, one of the oldest tournaments on the American tour, is played on this difficult course the first weekend in July.

Hockey

Chicago Black Hawks
Chicago Stadium
1800 W. Madison St.
733-5300
Expansion teams have bypassed the Hawks, once the city's proudest franchise. A new coach and some promising rookies may help turn the clock back to those palmier days. Until then, good seats are easy to come by.

Horse Racing

Balmoral Park
Illinois 1 and Elmscourt Lane
Crete
568-5700

Hawthorne Race Course
3501 Laramie Ave.
Cicero
780-3700

Maywood Park
North and Fifth avenues
Maywood
626-4816

Sportsman's Park
3301 Laramie Ave.
Cicero
242-1121

Polo

Oak Brook Polo Club
Oak Brook Hills Hotel
3500 Midwest Rd.
Oak Brook
325-5566
On Wednesday, Friday, Saturday, and Sunday, from May to October, polo fans gather to watch outdoor tournament play; all the trappings, like tailgate parties, too.

Sports

Soccer

Chicago Sting
Rosemont Horizon
693-KICK
Founded in 1974, this professional soccer team has played in twelve play-offs, six division championships, and two Soccer Bowl titles, and won the Trans Atlantic Challenge Cup in 1982. In 1981 it won the Soccer Bowl Championship and was greeted back to Chicago with a ticker tape parade down La Salle Street.

Car Racing

Santa Fe Speedway
9100 Wolf Rd.
Hinsdale
839-1050
Stock cars burn up the track on warm weekend evenings.

Volleyball

Chicago Breeze Volleyball
559-1212
All home games played by Chicago's all-women's professional volleyball team are at Loyola University's Alumni Hall. The team, which made its début in 1987, plays 22 games, three of which are televised by ESPN.

College and University

DePaul University
Alumni Hall
1011 W. Belden Ave.
341-8545
For the last few seasons, the Blue Demons have given Chicago basketball fans something to cheer about as the team piled up victories until tournament time. Still, it was fun riding the roller coaster with legendary coach Ray Meyer; today his son, Joey Meyer, is in his place. The frenzy, though, has obscured the winning seasons of any other DePaul team. Tickets for the men's basketball games, which are held at Rosemont Horizon, are scarce.

Loyola University
274-1211
Although the Ramblers play consistently exciting basketball (home games are played at the Chicago Amphitheater), they labor in the Blue Demons' shadow. Even less attention is paid to Loyola's nationally ranked water polo squad, the good soccer team, or strong women's basketball and volleyball.

North Park College
Gymnasium
Foster and Kedzie avenues
583-2700
In general, this Albany Park college plays with spirit, free from big-time pressures.

Northwestern University
Dyche Stadium and
McGaw Hall
1501 Central St.
Evanston
491-7070
After years as the doormat of the Big Ten, NU's football team has finally showed signs of respectability recently, winning as many as four games in a year. Now that Columbia has broken the Wildcats' consecutive-game losing streak, maybe the clouds have finally lifted. Bill Foster, the new men's basketball coach, has resurrected similarly destitute teams in the past, but has yet to make much of an impact on NU. The best sports action at Northwestern can often be seen on the women's side, where often-excellent teams are fielded in basketball, softball, and field hockey.

University of Chicago
Henry Crown Field House
5550 S. University Ave.
753-4949
The Monsters of the Midway are muggers now, and old castellated Stagg Field, site of so many Maroon victories, has been replaced with a demure, modern facility west of the field house. Today, football is played for fun, not fame, and the same holds true for cricket, crew, rugby, and all the other league or club activities. The U. of C. Track Club, a private organization open to non-students, is home to some of America's most talented competitors.

University of Illinois at Chicago
UIC Pavilion
1140 W. Harrison St.
413-5740
With its relatively new facility at NCAA Division I status in all major sports, UIC finally entered the big time. It has a tough hockey team that keeps up with the likes of Wisconsin, and the gymnasts do well in the Windy City Gymnastics Meet, a national event they host each November.

Joining In

The lake, parks, and forest preserves offer Chicagoans unrivaled athletic opportunities. Although the **Chicago Park District**, or **CPD** (294-2200), does little to encourage the simple enjoyment of nature, it pulls out all the stops for less pastoral endeavors, providing equipment, instruction, and team/league management. The **Cook County Forest Preserve District**, or **CCFPD** (261-8400), maintains sports grounds, but most of the green belt encircling the city is open space reminiscent of state parks. Many of the larger suburbs also offer a wide range of activities open to locals and nonresidents.

Sports

Publicly owned facilities are the least expensive to use, but are often determinedly non-posh, as are many charitable operations such as the YMCAs and other neighborhood clubs. The sheer number of programs and activities they offer is staggering, however, and they warrant exploration.

ARCHERY
CPD has indoor and outdoor ranges; so do many shops. For a list of area clubs and facilities, write to the **Illinois Archery Association**, 506 E. Locust St., Chatham, Ill. 62629.

BACKGAMMON
Join the **Backgammon Club of Chicago**, 2715 W. Peterson Ave. (951-1055), for information about playing backgammon in the city.

BADMINTON
For information, try the **Midwest Badminton Association** in suburban Palatine (882-1566).

BALLOONING
Find out about 90-minute, daylight hot-air rides for two and local races from the **Northeastern Illinois Balloon Association** (948-0506).

BASEBALL
Reserve a diamond for your own big game by calling the specific park well in advance; CPD also has league information. The **American Women's Baseball Association** (729-4594) is always looking for players.

BASKETBALL
Every playground, school yard, and neighborhood club has a budding basketball star; the CPD has an organized program.

BICYCLING
A marked bike path traces most of Chicago's lakefront, and there are paths in the forest preserves. City-street bike-route markings should probably be ignored. The **Northeastern Illinois Planning Commission** (Room 200, 400 W. Madison St., Chicago 60606) offers a six-county, bike-touring map package for $5; **American Youth Hostels** (327-8114) and the **Sierra Club** (431-0158) sponsor biking trips. For information about area biking clubs, write the **Chicagoland Bicycle Federation**, 421 S. Wabash, Chicago, Ill., 60605 (427-3325).

BILLIARDS AND POOL
Most of the city's old-fashioned pool halls have disappeared. There's still plenty of action in neighborhood taverns, though, and tournaments at the **Illinois Billiards Club**, 2435 W. 71st St. (737-6655).

BIRD WATCHING
The best source for information is the **Chicago Audubon Society** (539-6793).

BOATING
The **U.S. Coast Guard Auxiliary** (564-8262) offers classroom instruction in power boating and sailing, navigation, and water safety. **American Youth Hostels** (327-8114) conducts in-water sailing classes. The CPD's **Rainbow Fleet** (294-2270) gives you hands-on experience with small sailboats. CPD maintains boat-launching ramps at several harbors and dispenses harbor moorings. The yacht clubs in public parks are private, as are the key-card-controlled parking lots next to the harbors.

BOWLING
The CPD maintains greens for outdoor bowling. For indoor bowling, just consult the yellow pages and take your pick. Several, including the **Waveland Bowl**, 3700 N. Western Ave., are open 24 hours a day.

BOXING
The CPD offers instruction in all levels of the sport at 26 field houses. The **Catholic Youth Organization** (421-8046) has several coaches and has been sponsoring contests since 1930. Both groups' championship bouts, along with the **Golden Gloves Tournament** (537-7664), are the best amateur action in town.

BRIDGE
Call the **Chicago Contract Bridge Association** (271-0133) or the **Midwest Bridge Unit** (933-9475) for information on play and lessons.

CANOEING
Rent or buy canoes, kayaks, racing shells, materials for building your own, car carriers, books, and other accessories, and tap Ralph Frese's store of knowledge, at the **Chicagoland Canoe Base**, 4019 N. Narragansett Ave. (777-1489). The **Illinois Travel Information Center** (793-2094) can tell you where to use all your gear; **American Youth Hostels** (327-8114) and the **Sierra Club** (431-0185) organize trips.

CHESS

You'll find casual play during summer daylight hours at the **Lincoln Park Chess Pavilion**, near North Avenue. For more serious players and those interested in tournament play, call the **Midwest Chess Association** (246-6665) or the **Chicago Chess Center**, 2923 N. Southport Ave. (929-7010).

CRICKET

You'll find wickets in several city and suburban parks. Call the **U.S. Cricket Association** in Chicago (821-6613) or the **Evanston and Skokie Cricket Club** (761-6668).

DARTS

Give the **Windy City Darters**, 4749 N. Kenneth Ave. (286-3848), a call for information pertaining to clubs and tournaments.

FENCING

The **United States Fencing Association** (248-6785) organizes meets and tournaments. **Chicago Fencing Club** (475-7344), the **Illinois Fencers Club** (835-1888), and the **Great Lakes Fencing Association** (280-4582) give classes.

FISHING

The **Illinois Department of Conservation** (917-2070) publishes a booklet listing fishing areas, regulations, and tips, and sells the $7.50 annual license required for anglers (state residents) over 16 years old. Licenses are also available at **City Hall** and the **State of Illinois Center**. The **CCFPD** also publishes a guide to fishing in its waters. The **CPD** lagoons and lakefront fishing sites are

open from April to mid-November.

FOOTBALL

The **CPD** sponsors neighborhood league play.

GOLF

Senior citizens and juniors pay reduced greens fees at the five **CPD** courses (only Jackson Park has 18 holes) and at the eight 18-hole and three 9-hole **CCFPD** courses.

HANDBALL

With 14 courts, the **Lattof YMCA**, 300 E. Northwest Hwy., Des Plaines (296-3376), is one of the best public facilities. Many health clubs also have courts.

HANG GLIDING

Chicago Hang Gliding Organization (281-3338) meets the first Monday of every month at the Field Museum.

HIKING

During the summer and fall, experienced naturalists, biologists, and curators from the **Field Museum of Natural History** (922-9410) lead adults only in one-day, weekend field trips to nearby nature preserves. **American Youth Hostels** also organizes hikes. For information on the many trails in state parks, call the **Illinois Travel Information Center** (793-2094).

HORSEBACK RIDING

Rent a mount (and buy the required license) at one of the private stables (see yellow pages) bordering **CCFPD**'s 150 miles of year-round trails. For private and group lessons in the city, try the **Coach House Equestrian Center**, 1410 N. Orleans St. (266-7878).

HUNTING

Get information by calling the **Illinois Department of Conservation** (917-2070).

HURLING

Irish Imports (637-3800) will tell you where to catch this traditional Irish game.

ICE SKATING

Almost every good-sized park district has a year-round rink and programs; there are a few private ones as well. When the weather's right, you can skate at the **Richard J. Daley Bicentennial Plaza** (294-2420) in Grant Park, where you can rent skates.

JUDO AND MARTIAL ARTS

Judo is taught at many YMCAs and clubs. The **Chicago Judo Blackbelt Association** (761-7027) sponsors tournaments and can recommend schools.

LAWN BOWLING

Give the **Lakeside Lawn Bowling Club**, 5800 S. Lake Shore Dr. (684-9799) a call for information.

LACROSSE

The **Chicago Women's Lacrosse Club** (985-5260, 262-9275) offers players at all levels the chance to participate.

ORIENTEERING

This is the pedestrian equivalent of sports-car rallies. The **Chicago Orienteering Club** (739-6230) offers activities for all levels. Basics are taught at the **Indiana Dunes National Lakeshore** (219-926-7561).

RACQUETBALL AND SQUASH

Park districts, YMCAs, and private clubs all have courts. The **Illinois Squash Racquets Association**

Sports

(726-2840, ext. 268) has information on tournaments.

ROLLER SKATING
The **Richard J. Daley Bicentennial Plaza** in Grant Park has outdoor skating all summer.

RUGBY
The **Chicago Griffins Rugby Football Club** (588-0350), the **Lincoln Park Rugby Club** (528-8844), the **Naperville Rugby Club** (369-1422), the **Lions Club** (621-1137), and the **Lakeshore Women's Rugby Club** (583-1892) will give you all the info you need.

RUNNING
Marathoners can get information on events, clinics, races, and clubs from the **Chicago Area Runner's Association** (664-0823).

SHOOTING
The **Lincoln Park Gun Club** (549-6490) welcomes nonmembers for trap and skeet shooting, but requires that everyone have an Illinois firearms owner identification card. The **Illinois State Rifle Association** has more information.

SKIING
Cross-country lessons with equipment are available right in the Loop at the Richard J. Daley Bicentennial Plaza in Grant Park. **American Youth Hostels** (327-8114) organizes outings. Give the **Chicago Metropolitan Ski Council** (346-1268) a call for a list of area ski clubs.

SNOWMOBILING
The **CCFPD** has a list of designated areas that may be used if you have a permit. Dealers have more tips, and the **Illinois Association of Snowmobile Clubs** (815-436-8688) will help you hook up with others who share your interests in snowmobiling.

SOARING
Sailplane instruction, rental, and demonstration are at **Hinckley Soaring** (815-286-7200).

SOCCER
The **Illinois Soccer Association** (463-0653) and the **National Soccer League** (275-2850) have info on teams, leagues, and how you can participate.

SOFTBALL
Sixteen-inch softball is as much a Chicago institution as deep-dish pizza, and it's played nowhere else. The **CPD** organizes summer leagues in the parks. Traditionally, some of the best games are at Kelly Park, 4150 S. California Ave., and at Grant Park, where 16 diamonds are in almost constant use after work and on weekends. The **Amateur Softball Association** in Aurora (429-2008) covers all types, including alien 12- and 14-inch softball games that are played with gloves, for cryin' out loud.

SPORTS-CAR RACING
The **Chicago Region Sports Car Club of America** (728-4466) keeps tabs on races, rallies, and meetings.

SQUARE DANCING
Get the lowdown on the hoedown from the **Metropolitan Chicago Association of Square Dancers** (437-5270).

SWIMMING
The **CPD** supervises the city's beaches and public pools and gives lessons, too. Also check YMCAs, Jewish Community Centers, and private health clubs.

TENNIS
The **CPD**'s poorly maintained courts (there are more than 700 of them) are usually crowded, but many are lighted for evening play. The **Chicago District Tennis Association** (834-3727) sponsors leagues and tournaments at all levels of play.

TOBOGGANING
The **CCFPD** has five areas, including **Bemis Woods**, **Jensen Slides**, **Dan Ryan Woods**, **Deer Grove**, and **Swallow Cliff**. There are two runs in Evanston at the **James Park Winter Sports Complex**, Oakton Street near Dodge Avenue (866-2910).

VOLLEYBALL
Most parks and YMCAs have courts. The regional office of the **U.S. Volleyball Association** keeps tabs on league play and tournaments.

WALKING
The **Lakeshore Walking Club** (869-5745) sponsors walks every Sunday in Evanston.

WIND SURFING
Montrose and **Rainbow** beaches are Chicago's official wind surfing beaches—though, unofficially, many wind-surf near Northwestern's beach just north of campus in Evanston. The **Windward Sports Windsurfing Shop**, 3317 N. Clark St. (472-6868), will provide information on this new Windy City sport.

Annual Events

TO EVERYTHING THERE IS A SEASON." In Chicago that means more than flag-waving on the Fourth of July, special exhibits at museums on holidays, or the change of perennials at conservatories. Indoors or outdoors, from the Loop to the sticks, *someone* is always staging *something*. These listings cover established events and some impulses, all of them vulnerable to the vagaries of time and fortune. Current information is best found monthly in *Chicago* and in the newspapers' weekend editions. A phone call is the best protection against disappointment. Although there is an admission charge for most events, the charge at festivities held on Chicago streets is actually a voluntary donation.

JANUARY

Chicago Boat, Sports, and RV Show: Celebrities and entertainment enliven the Midwest's biggest show of boats and sports and recreational vehicles, at McCormick Place. 836-4740.

Chicago Sport and Boat Show: 791-7000.

Chicagoland Sport Fishing and Outdoor Show: 299-3131.

Cubs Fan Convention: Chicago Cubs baseball fans from all over the United States revel together in Cubness. There are screenings of games and season highlights, photo and autograph booths, baseball clinics, a Wrigley Field flea market and auction, and chalk talks with Cubs coaches. 951-CUBS.

Illinois Winter Special Olympics: Handicapped athletes compete in Alpine and Nordic skiing, speed and figure skating, and tobogganing, in Galena. 800-892-9299.

University of Chicago Folk Festival: 702-9793.

FEBRUARY

Azalea and Camellia Show: Masses of lovely blooms transform the conservatories into springtime scenes of the Deep South, at Lincoln Park and Garfield Park conservatories. 294-2493.

Batavia Orchid Society: More than 1,000 blooming orchids are displayed by hobbyist and professional growers, in Aurora. 232-0597.

Black History Month: Special programs and exhibits throughout the city, particularly at the Chicago Public Library Cultural Center and the DuSable Museum of African American History. 346-3278.

Chicago Auto Show: This purports to be the world's largest and best-attended auto show, exhibiting upward of 800 domestic and foreign cars, trucks, and previews of concept cars, at McCormick Place. 698-6630.

Chinese New Year Parade: This dizzying display of colors, lights, music, and food is celebrated with great panache, at Wentworth Avenue and Cermak Road. 326-5607.

Lincoln State Cat Club Show: In Villa Park. 528-2209.

MARCH

African Violet Show: This show is sponsored by the Radiant African Violet Club of Rockford and St. Charles, in St. Charles. 377-3355.

Brookfield Zoo Easter Parade and Bonnet Contest: When Easter Sunday falls in March. 242-2630.

Lithuanian Easter Egg Decorating Workshops and Display: Learn the scratch-carve method of decorating. 582-6500.

Maple Syrup Festival: An old-fashioned pancake-and-sausage breakfast highlights this day of maple syrup demonstrations and tree tapping. 583-8970.

Medinah Shrine Circus: Aerialists, clowns, and wild animals are the highlights of this three-week extravaganza to benefit the Shriners Crippled Children's Hospital. 266-5000.

Midwest Boat Show: More than 120 boat and boat accessory dealers exhibit at O'Hare Expo Center. 299-3131.

Annual Events

St. Patrick's Day Parade: The Chicago River is dyed greener than usual while the Irish and near-Irish parade through the Loop and politicos jockey for position. 744-4691.

Winnetka Antiques Show: This show features American and English furniture, antique jewelry, period silver, folk art, nautical brasses, vintage clothing, and much more, in Winnetka. 446-0537.

APRIL

Brookfield Zoo Easter Parade and Bonnet Contest: This event takes place Easter Sunday. 242-2630.

Chicago Cubs opening day: One of the biggest days of the year at Wrigley Field. 878-2827.

Chicago Latino Film Festival: 327-3184.

Chicago White Sox opening day: A similarly big day at Comiskey Park for Sox fans. 559-1212.

Hispanic Festival of the Arts: 684-1414.

International Kennel Club Dog Show: This is an all-breed show that includes demonstrations and tests. 237-5100.

International Theater Festival of Chicago: This biennial event hosts a score of productions from countries around the world. 664-3370.

O Punning Day: The annual international Save the Pun Foundation dinner, usually held on April Fool's Day. 973-3523.

Spring and Easter Flower Show: The lily is the featured flower at this annual favorite held at the Lincoln Park and Garfield Park conservatories. 294-2493.

Very Special Arts Festival: Different hosts every year sponsor several thousand artists in this annual event. It offers a noncompetitive, integrated showcase for the artistic creations and talents of those with disabilities. 890-8363.

Volvo Tennis/Chicago: This tournament benefits the *Chicago Tribune* Charities. 977-0977.

MAY

Buckingham Fountain: Chicago's famous fountain and its surrounding lights in Grant Park at Congress and Lake Shore drives — often called the most beautiful illuminated fountain in the country — kick off the summer season, drawing crowds of sightseers, lovers, and other city denizens every night at 9 p.m.

Chicago International Art Exposition: More than 150 art dealers and galleries in the United States, Europe, and elsewhere gather at Navy Pier in this city's annual art gala. 787-6858.

Chicago International Festival of Flowers and Gardens: Modeled on famous European floral events, this ten-day festival focuses on the art of floral, landscape, and interior design. 787-6858.

Greek Independence Day Parade: 565-0111.

Israel Independence Day Celebration: In Skokie. 346-6700.

Nabisco Mayor's Cup Bike Race: Professional cyclists compete for big cash prizes in this event specifically designed for maximum spectator thrills. 670-BIKE.

Norwegian Independence Day Parade: In Park Ridge. 364-5654.

Polish Constitution Day Parade: 286-0500.

Tour of Historic Churches: This is a five-hour tour of seven churches, sponsored by the Landmarks Preservation Council of Illinois. 922-1742.

Walk with Israel: Walks, family miniwalks, and jogging and bike-a-thon events commemorate Israel's statehood and benefit that country's needy. 675-2200.

JUNE

Body Politic Street Festival: A celebration of music and art, with nonstop entertainment at two bandstands, scores of juried artists, street performers, and great eating, is sponsored by this local theater. 871-3000, 348-7901.

Brandeis University Used Book Sale: It's billed as the world's largest used-book sale, with over 400,000 books in 40 categories. 446-6177.

Chicago Blues Festival: Scores of international blues performers descend on Chicago and turn Grant Park's Petrillo Music Shell into a sea of tears. 744-3315.

Chicago Book and Memorabilia Fair (Printers Row Book Fair): Historic Dearborn Station and Dearborn Street are the site for thousands of rare, new, old, and antiquarian books for sale and on display by publishers and booksellers from the Midwest. Demonstrations, readings, special children's programs, music, and food

Annual Events

add to the fun. 663-1595.

Chicago Gospel Festival: Gospel recording artists and contemporary celebrities praise the Lord at the Petrillo Music Shell in Grant Park. 744-3315.

Chicago International Wooden Boat Festival and Sailboat Show: This event is devoted exclusively to boats and boating-related activities. Scheduled events include demonstrations of boat building, marlin-spike seamanship, lofting, semaphore signaling, and lectures on boating and boat safety. 787-6858.

Farm Visit Day: Working farms open to visitors to see how our food is produced. Tours of facilities, animals, and machinery are given by farm families. 815-288-3361.

57th Street Art Fair: This outdoor art extravaganza held in the block bounded by 56th and 57th streets and Kenwood and Kimbark avenues offers more than 300 artists exhibiting all types of media.

Gay and Lesbian Pride Week Parade: This annual parade culminates an entire week's worth of Pride events and includes thousands of participants, both in the parade and on the sidelines. There are floats and marching bands and, afterward, a rally and music fest. 348-8243.

Latino Film Festival: Films (with English subtitles) by Latino filmmakers from around the globe are screened at the Getz Theater of Columbia College. 327-3184.

Old Town Art Fair: This Old Town institution is the Midwest's oldest juried art fair and includes an auction, kids' activities, and garden tours. 337-5962.

Save-A-Pet Adoption Days: This nonprofit organization known for its no-euthanasia policy brings adoptable dogs and cats to the Old Orchard Mall in Skokie in an effort to find them homes. 934-7788.

JULY

Air and Water Show: An aerial and aquatic spectacle, this event includes performances both on and above the water off North Avenue Beach. 294-2494.

Bastille Day Celebrations: 787-5359.

Chicago Distance Classic: Runners and walkers can go the distance in this benefit for the Chicago Lung Association. 243-2000.

Chicago-Mackinac Island Yacht Race: Long before the America's Cup hysteria, the Mackinac race was one of the world's most popular sailing competitions. The race starts east of Monroe Street Harbor and can be viewed either from shore or from cruise boats. 861-7777.

Fourth of July Celebrations: Chicago celebrates the holiday July 3 with a concert in Grant Park, followed by state-of-the-art fireworks. The following day — also in Grant Park — there's a flea market, arts and crafts fair, games, water show, jazz and marching bands, bagpipers, and more fireworks. 294-2420.

Graceland West Garden Walk: This is an annual horticultural tour. 478-5908.

Greek Festival: Music, dancing, food, and games highlight this celebration of Greek culture sponsored by St. Andrew's Greek Orthodox Church. 334-4515.

Howard Street Alive! Ethnic entertainment, food, and crafts are featured on Chicago's northern boundary. 508-5885.

Illinois Storytelling Festival: Storytellers from across the United States gather in Spring Grove Village Park, Spring Grove, Illinois, with stories and old-time music. 815-648-2039, 815-385-1974.

Neighborhood festivals: Almost all of Chicago's neighborhoods host a festival. Find out about the one in your area by calling the Mayor's Office of Special Events. 744-3315.

Sheffield Garden Walk and Festival: Discover urban gardens, garage sales, music by some of the city's top bands, and lots of food and drinks at this annual neighborhood event. 327-4148.

Taste of Chicago: An eating extravaganza that grows year by year, this annual pig-out event includes food from nearly 100 Chicago-area restaurants, in Grant Park. 744-3315.

Taste of Lincoln Avenue: This annual eat-a-thon featuring food from area restaurants even has a mini-health fair. 472-9046.

AUGUST

All-Midwest Hunting and Outdoor Show: Displays of sporting arms, archery equipment, taxidermy and wildlife art, hunting-dog breeders,

Annual Events

clubs, and conservation groups are the highlights at this Grayslake, Illinois, event. It will next be held in 1989. 299-3131.

Broadway Art Fair: More than 150 artists participate in this late-summer event. 248-8285.

Chicago RiverFest: Not normally used as a parade route, Chicago's river now gets festival treatment with music, food, river cruises, and a full river regatta. 922-4020.

Chicago Triathlon: Four thousand contestants start the day with a bracing dip in Lake Michigan, looping the Aquarium and Planetarium, then bike 40 kilometers and run 10 kilometers along Lake Shore Drive, finishing at the Daley Bicentennial Plaza. 761-6311.

Manufacturers Hanover Corporate Challenge: This is a 3.5-mile road race open to full-time employees of corporations, businesses, and other institutions, which starts and ends at Michigan Avenue and Harrison Street. 664-8257.

Medieval Fair in Oz Park: This fair features a large cast of entertainers, including jugglers, mimes, magicians, musicians, singers, dancers, and puppeteers, as well as gourmet food tastings. 880-5200.

Venetian Night: A parade of decorated boats that bobs from Monroe Street Harbor to the Planetarium and finishes with a grand fireworks finale. 294-2200, 744-3315.

SEPTEMBER

Chicago Federation of Labor Parade: 263-6612.

Chicago International Folk Fair: A celebration of the city's ethnic diversity —

food, performances, arts and crafts, and film. 744-3315.

Chicago International New Art Forms Exposition: Twentieth-century decorative arts, including furniture, sculpture, and utilitarian works of art, are featured in this Navy Pier extravaganza. 787-6858.

Chicago Jazz Festival: International and local stars converge on Chicago's Petrillo Music Shell to celebrate the music that made this city great. 744-3315.

Mexican Independence Day Parade: Equestrian riders, bands, and floats march through the Loop. 674-5838.

Steuben Day Parade: United German-American Societies of Chicago celebrate German culture and heritage with this march honoring General von Steuben, who served General Washington during the Revolutionary War. 478-7915.

OCTOBER

Antiques Show: The Women's Club of Wilmette hosts dealers from all over the Midwest. 251-0527.

Apple Fest: Fresh apples, cider, and fall edibles from local restaurants, plus live bands and other entertainment, ring in autumn in Lincoln Square. 878-7331.

Chicago International Antiques Show: Dealers from England, France, Belgium, and the United States converge on Navy Pier for the biggest juried antiques show held in Chicago. 787-6858.

Chicago International Film Festival: This festival brings films and directors from around the globe to Chicago. In addition to screenings, there are lectures and a FestCafe adjacent to the theaters. 644-3400.

Columbus Day Parade: This giant parade celebrates Italian culture and heritage with bands, floats, marching groups, and, of course, food. 372-6788.

Dinosaur Days: Weekends at the Field Museum are filled with games, stories, and crafts celebrating dinosaurs. 922-9410.

Graceland Cemetery Walking Tour: Monuments and sculptures are only part of what you'll see when you take a tour of this famous cemetery, home to many of Chicago's most illustrious citizens. Walks are also given in August and September. 922-3432.

Morton Arboretum Bonsai Society Show: Bonsai on parade in Lisle. 968-0074.

Multimedia's Chicago International Festival of Children's Films: The films, from more than 25 countries, include shorts and feature-length animated movies, television specials, and live-action features. Children serve on the jury to select films for screening, and choose the most popular film of the festival. 281-9075.

Park Forest Earth Science Club Gem and Mineral Show: Exhibits of members' collections of rocks, minerals, gems, fossils, and artifacts, plus demonstrations, in Park Forest. 448-1997.

Ringling Bros. & Barnum & Bailey Circus: The circus performs under the big top at the Chicago Stadium. 733-5300.

NOVEMBER

Arts Expressions: Held in the atrium of the State of Illinois Center, this event is filled with exhibits and demonstrations. 895-3710.

Christmas Around the World: Held at the Museum of Science and Industry, this is a Chicago tradition. 684-1414.

Christmas Tree Lighting: This much-anticipated event is held in the Daley Center Plaza, usually on the Friday after Thanksgiving.

Chrysanthemum Show: A wide array of flowers is on view at the Garfield Park and Lincoln Park conservatories. 533-1281.

Lithuanian Christmas Straw Ornament Workshops: Each Friday during the month, the Balzekas Museum of Lithuanian Culture presents a demonstration in the folk art of making straw ornaments. 582-6500.

Veterans Day Parade: 744-3515.

Virginia Slims Tennis Tournament: 647-0505.

DECEMBER

A Christmas Carol: This holiday tradition is performed at the Goodman Theater. 443-3800.

Brookfield Zoo's Christmas Party: Brunch with Santa and the elves at the Safari Lodge, followed by a party at the children's zoo. 242-2630.

Christmas Flower Show: Varied display of traditional Christmas flowers from many lands, starring the poinsettia, at the Lincoln Park and Garfield Park conservatories. 294-2493.

In the Spirit: A month-long celebration of Christmas, Hanukkah, and Kwanzaa, sponsored by the Chicago Public Library Cultural Center. 346-3278.

***Nutcracker* ballet:** This Yuletide ballet is danced at the Arie Crown Theater and benefits the *Chicago Tribune* Charities. 791-6000.

NEIGHBORHOODS

The Loop and Environs

VISITORS TO CHICAGO always want to know why locals call this part of the city the "Loop." Usually they're told that the name stems from the elevated tracks encircling the city's center. Actually, it's more due to the convergence of cable-car lines that formed a loop around the business section in the 1890s. Historical niceties aside, though, the central business area within and without the el's circle makes up the Loop.

The Loop is Chicago's nucleus: City street numbers begin at the intersection of State and Madison streets; La Salle Street's canyons are the Midwest's financial focus; Clark and Dearborn streets boast a complement of local, state, and Federal government buildings; department stores and specialty shops line State Street and Wabash Avenue; and Michigan Avenue offers an unmatched cultural complex. In addition, the entire downtown is shot through with architectural masterpieces that chronicle Chicago's seminal role in the development of the modern high-rise.

The Loop and its environs are approximately bounded by the Chicago River on the north and west, the lake on the east, and Roosevelt Road on the south. Within this area, though, are various neighborhoods and environments. The central Loop is crammed with skyscrapers; by day its streets are bustling with business and service people; by night it's virtually dead. South Dearborn Street has been revitalized with loft conversions, boutiques, and restaurants, while Michigan Avenue is lined on one side with elegant old office towers and cultural institutions and on the other by Grant Park.

HISTORY

Indians massacred Fort Dearborn's garrison during the War of 1812. Within four years, however, the fort was rebuilt at what is now Michigan Avenue and Wacker Drive. Canal-building schemes attracted new settlers, and, by 1837, four thousand people celebrated the city's incorporation.

Early Chicagoans clustered around the fort. In the 1830s, businesses flourished on South Water Street (now Wacker Drive), while manufacturing, warehousing, and shipping spread along the North Branch's banks. By 1850, retailers had moved a block south to Lake Street. Chicago's political center was fixed in 1853 when the city and county erected a combined office building-courthouse on the site of the present City Hall-County Building, a neoclassical colossus covering a square block at Clark and Randolph streets. La Salle Street became the financial center when the Board of Trade moved there in 1865.

The great Chicago Fire of 1871 turned the thriving downtown into a pile of ashes, leveling elegant new commercial buildings and squalid back-alley housing with egalitarian thoroughness. Hindered only by a nationwide business depression, downtown

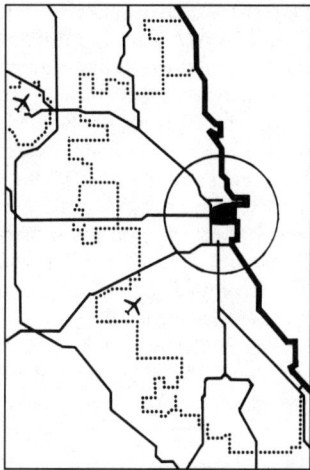

The Loop and Environs

Chicago, save for the slums, rebounded with amazing speed. Rebuilding followed old patterns of activity, but everything was, and still is, bigger, taller, more assertive.

State Street became the center for discriminating shoppers, a position it held for almost a century. Today, though, the street has lost much of its glamour. Many shoppers have taken their business to North Michigan Avenue's Magnificent Mile and suburban shopping malls. Restaurants folded or shortened their evening hours, which further discouraged State Street shoppers. Once-grand movie theaters have fallen on hard times and rely on exploitation films for sustenance.

State Street's merchants responded by supporting the State Street Transit Mall, a dismal, barren misconception that accomplished little more than ridding the strip of ugly lampposts. Fast-food outlets and bargain-basement stores began to dot the west side of the street, which didn't help attract the sort of clientele to which the street's merchants had been accustomed.

Still, Marshall Field's remains in all its glory on the street, as do several other old stalwarts. Plans for revitalizing State — dubbed "That Great Street" — are always afloat, keeping the dream of its old glory, as well as that of the Loop, alive.

Interesting Places

American Police Center and Museum
1705 S. State St.
431-0005
Displays of police uniforms from around the world, Chicago Police Department memorabilia, and crime-prevention information fill this interesting place.

Amoco Building
200 E. Randolph Dr.
This marble-clad 80-story monolith was designed in 1974 by Edward Durell Stone and the Perkins and Will Partnership. Despite trees, fountains, and a rather pleasant sunken plaza with a reflecting pool and Harry Bertoia's *Sounding* sculpture of slender bronze rods, the building (formerly the Standard Oil Building) lacks any human scale and seems to stand in isolation.

ArchiCenter
Monadnock Building
330 S. Dearborn St.
782-1776
This organization is more than just a starting point for tours. In addition to a well-stocked store selling posters, books, and architectural memorabilia, it offers films, lectures, and exhibits.

Art Institute of Chicago
Michigan Ave. at Adams St.
443-3500
(see Museums)

Auditorium Building and Theater
50 E. Congress Pkwy.
922-4046
This first major fruit of a fortunate collaboration combined Dankmar Adler's engineering expertise with Louis Sullivan's decorative genius and is deservedly a city landmark. The theater inside was saved from destruction and reopened in 1967. Under the direction of Harry Weese, the sweeping 4,000-seat hall, enhanced by gilt, mirrors, and stained glass, maintained its glorious acoustics and sight lines. The most advanced theater of its day remains one of

the world's finest. It was Chicago's first electrically lit commercial building and the first "air-conditioned" house. It even sported complex hydraulic stage machinery that could lower the entire stage to create an 8,000-person ballroom.

Brunswick Building
69 W. Washington St.
The small plaza here is home to Joan Miró's *Chicago*.

Carbide and Carbon Building
230 N. Michigan Ave.
This black and dark-green gem was designed in 1929 by Burnham Brothers.

Carson Pirie Scott & Company Building
1 S. State St.
This big department store moved from Lake Street to the five-year-old, Louis Sullivan-designed Schlesinger and Mayer store in 1904. The Carson's building's lightness and warmth are exemplified by Sullivan's intricate iron ornamentation and wood-paneled rotunda, all lovingly restored under the direction of John Vinci.

Chicago Board of Trade
141 W. Jackson Blvd.
435-3500

Chicago Board Options Exchange
400 S. La Salle St.
786-5600
Many of the temples of commerce forming La Salle Street's financial canyon are in the classical mode, but the street's focus is the Board of Trade's Holabird & Root-designed art deco building topped with a statue of Ceres, the Greek goddess of grain, who stands 609 feet above the ground below. Visitors can view the action immortalized in Frank Norris's *The Pit* from a fifth-floor visitors' center, or just enjoy the sleek, three-story marble lobby. In 1982, the firm of Murphy/Jahn designed a sleek glass addition, and, the following year, Skidmore, Owings & Merrill designed the Options Exchange building across the street.

Chicago Loop Synagogue
16 S. Clark St.
346-7370
Bronze-and-brass *Hands of Peace* by Henri Azaz grace the façade; Abraham Rattner's stained-glass windows illuminate the interior. Opened in 1958, this temple was designed by Loebl, Schlossman and Bennett.

Chicago Mercantile Exchange
30 S. Wacker Dr.
930-1000
Founded in 1919, "the Merc" is the world's leading financial futures exchange, dealing in 33 futures and options on futures contracts ranging from frozen pork bellies to Japanese yen.

Chicago Public Library Cultural Center
78 E. Washington St.
744-6630
(see Museums)

Chicago Temple
(First United Methodist Church of Chicago)
77 W. Washington St.
236-4548
Dedicated in 1924, this church's Chapel in the Sky is the world's loftiest at four hundred feet above ground. At the ground level, stained-glass windows trace the history of the church.

Chicago Theater
175 N. State St.
236-4300
Called "The Wonder Theater of the World" when it opened in 1921, Rapp and Rapp's baroque fantasy even had lavish, Arc de Triomphe-inspired light displays. Richly ornamented outside and in the grand lobby, it has recently been lovingly restored and is among the last examples of Chicago's rococo movie-palace architecture.

City Hall-County Building
Randolph to Washington streets, Clark to La Salle streets
744-4000
This massive, somber, neoclassical building was designed by Holabird & Roche and constructed between 1906 and 1911. Mayoral mandates emanate from the fifth floor (La Salle Street side), while the City Council holds forth on the second. The vaulted ceilings of the spacious lobby are covered with mosaics.

Continental Illinois National Bank and Trust Company of Chicago
231 S. La Salle St.
828-2345
The handsomest of La Salle Street's bank buildings, Continental Illinois has a marvelous block-long, high-ceilinged banking floor built on the grand scale of a railway station waiting room. The 1924 building (it was then the city's tallest) is the work of Graham, Anderson, Probst & White, who are also responsible for Union Station, the Civic Opera House, the Merchandise Mart, and the La Salle National Bank Building, the last art deco tower built in Chicago and the last major Loop undertaking before a 20-year hiatus forced by the Depression and World War Two. Continental maintains a visitors' center in the La Salle Street lobby.

Richard J. Daley Center
Randolph St. between Dearborn and Clark streets
443-7980
This 1965 Cor-Ten steel tower was designed by C. F. Murphy Associates. The upper reaches house city and county offices and civil courts; the lobby, an information booth loaded with helpful maps and booklets, a changing art display, and lunch-time concerts. In the summer, performances move out into the (Richard J. Daley) plaza, which houses the giant, Cor-Ten steel "Chicago Picasso."

Dearborn Station
Polk and Dearborn streets
Designed by Cyrus L. W. Eidlitz and built in the mid-1880s, this National Register property has been converted into stores, offices, and restaurants.

Delaware Building
36 W. Randolph St.
This recently renovated building was designed in 1874 by Wheelock and Thomas.

Federal Center and Plaza
Dearborn St. between Adams St. and Jackson Blvd.
The plaza of this 1964 Mies

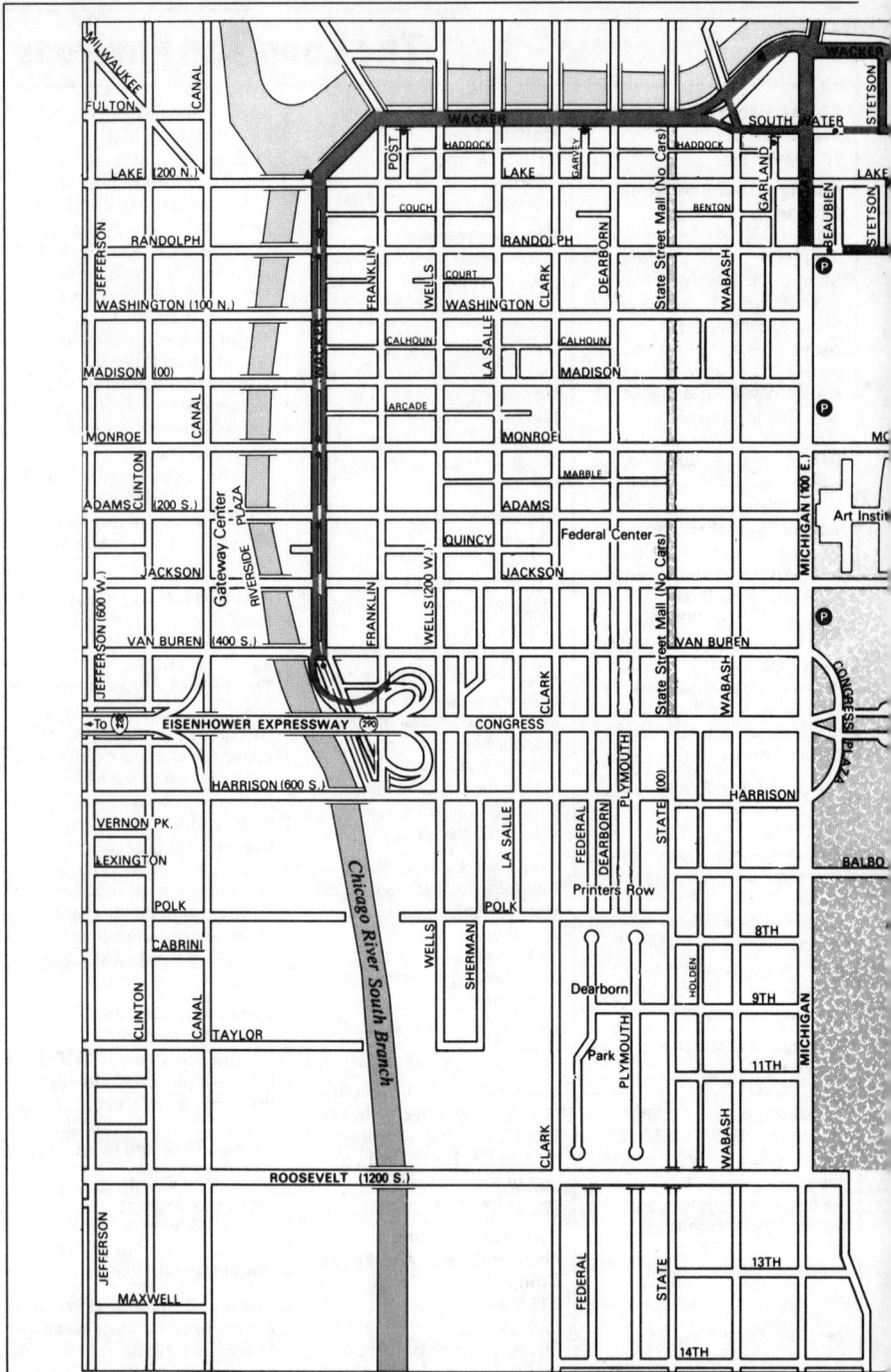

MILWAUKEE

FULTON

CANAL

WACKER

SOUTH WATER

STETSON

WACKER

LAKE (200 N.)

POST

HADDOCK

LAKE

GARVEY

HADDOCK

STETSON

BEAUBIEN

LAKE

JEFFERSON

RANDOLPH

COUCH

RANDOLPH

DEARBORN

State Street Mall (No Cars)

BENTON

GARLAND

WABASH

P

WASHINGTON (100 N.)

FRANKLIN

WELLS

COURT

WASHINGTON

CLARK

MADISON (00)

CALHOUN

LA SALLE

CALHOUN

MADISON

P

MONROE

CANAL

ARCADE

MONROE

MO

CLINTON

MARBLE

MICHIGAN (100 E.)

ADAMS (200 S.)

Gateway Center

PLAZA

ADAMS

Art Instit

JEFFERSON (600 W.)

JACKSON

RIVERSIDE

QUINCY

Federal Center

JACKSON

P

FRANKLIN

WELLS (200 W.)

JACKSON

VAN BUREN (400 S.)

State Street Mall (No Cars)

VAN BUREN

WABASH

CONGRESS PLAZA

To (N) ← EISENHOWER EXPRESSWAY (290)

CONGRESS

CLARK

CONGRESS

HARRISON (600 S.)

PLYMOUTH

STATE (00)

HARRISON

VERNON PK.

LA SALLE

FEDERAL

DEARBORN

BALBO

LEXINGTON

POLK

Printers Row

Chicago River South Branch

CABRINI

WELLS

SHERMAN

POLK

8TH

CLINTON

CANAL

Dearborn

HOLDEN

9TH

TAYLOR

Park

PLYMOUTH

11TH

MICHIGAN

WABASH

CLARK

ROOSEVELT (1200 S.)

JEFFERSON

FEDERAL

STATE

13TH

MAXWELL

14TH

The map on the left side shows labels:

icago River

nter

ANDOLPH

ard J. Daley
centennial
Plaza

P

s C. Petrillo
usic Shell

KSON

Chicago Harbor

kingham
untain

LAKE SHORE DRIVE

Shedd Aquarium

Field Museum
of
Natural History

ACL

MC FETRIDGE

Soldier Field

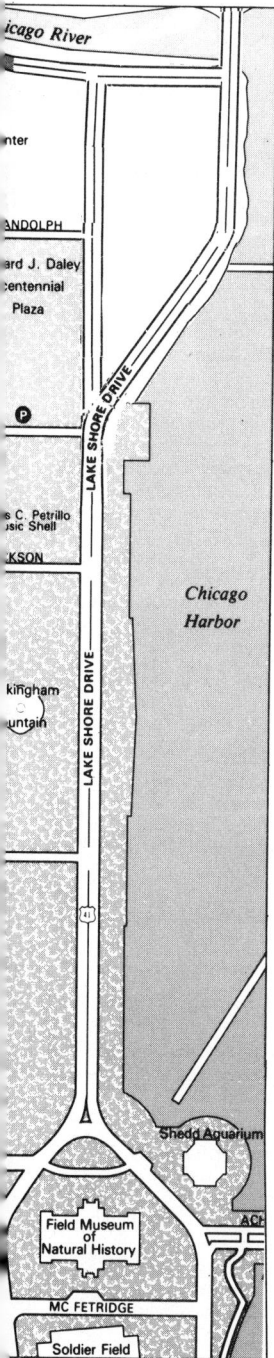

van der Rohe building is enlivened by Alexander Calder's hot red *Flamingo*.

Fine Arts Building
410 S. Michigan Ave.
427-7602
The Fine Arts Building is an official city landmark, designed by Solon S. Beman for the Studebaker brothers' carriage business in 1885 and converted to Chicago's equivalent of Carnegie Hall in 1898. Behind the Romanesque façade, with the motto ALL PASSES — ART ALONE ENDURES carved inside the entrances, the marble-and-wood interior is rich with ornament and history. Early tenants included Frank Lloyd Wright and Lorado Taft. William W. Denslow and Frank L. Baum collaborated on *The Wizard of Oz* here, and drama teacher Ann Morgan staged the first American performances of plays by George Bernard Shaw and Henrik Ibsen. *Poetry: A Magazine of Verse* was published here, introducing sizable audiences to Carl Sandburg, T. S. Eliot, and Ezra Pound. Also published here was Margaret Anderson's avant-garde literary journal, *The Little Review*. Both *The Dial* and the *Saturday Evening Post* were among other publi-

cations with offices in the building. The two first-floor theaters were converted in 1982 into four movie theaters that show independent and foreign films.

First National Bank of Chicago
Monroe St. between Clark and Dearborn streets
732-6204
The plaza here is graced with Marc Chagall's joyful mosaic, *The Four Seasons*. Beneath the gently tapering curtain wall designed by the Perkins and Will Partnership and C. F. Murphy Associates, there's a lot of space, plus ledges for perching, an outdoor café, food vendors, and occasionally music, all of which make this the Loop's best summertime people-watching spot.

Fisher Building
343 S. Dearborn St.
This Gothic-ornamented building was designed by D. H. Burnham and Company in 1896.

Heald Square Monument
Wacker Dr. and Wabash Ave.
Lorado Taft's last sculpture was completed in 1941 by Leonard Crunelle. It portrays George Washington flanked by Revolutionary War financiers Haym Salomon and Robert Morris.

Illinois Center
Wacker Dr. to Randolph St., Michigan Ave. to Lake Michigan
The plans here call for a 21st-century city-within-a-city stretching along Michigan Avenue from Randolph Street to Wacker Drive. Fujikawa, Conterato, and Lohan's Illinois Center is planned as a mixed-use complex linked by through streets, parking, shopping arcades, and, supposedly, park land. Nevertheless, what's been built is windy,

---

MAP LEGEND

▦ Underground road system

● Passage to and from underground road system

▲ One-way passage from underground to street level

▼ One-way passage to underground from street level

🅿 Underground parking access

The Loop and Environs

barren, and sterile. The raised plazas are spurned by pedestrians except on the nicest days. Bustling with people, the subterranean walkways are reminiscent of airport corridors. Most of the arcade shops solely offer nine-to-five essentials, giving little reason for anyone to patronize them for other purposes.

Inland Steel Building
30 W. Monroe St.
This is the first major postwar Loop building. Designed in 1957 by Skidmore, Owings & Merrill, the stainless-steel tower emphasizes the curtain wall by putting supporting members outside the skin. All the mechanical facilities are in a separate shaft.

Manhattan Building
431 S. Dearborn St.
Though renovated as upscale apartments, when built in 1890 it was the first tall office building to use iron-and-steel skeletal construction throughout. It was designed by William Le Baron Jenney.

Marquette Building
140 S. Dearborn St.
The functional austerity of Holabird & Roche's 1894 building is softened by bronze reliefs above the entrance and dazzling lobby mosaics that depict scenes from the explorations of Marquette and Joliet.

Metropolitan Correctional Center
71 W. Van Buren St.
322-7457
Harry Weese brought all his innovative and humanistic talent to this 1975 Federal jail, which doesn't offend the streetscape that much and (apparently) is considerate of inmates' needs.

Monadnock Building
53 W. Jackson Blvd.
This building's north half was designed in 1891 by Burnham and Root, while its south half was done in 1893 by Holabird & Roche. The Monadnock, named for a New England mountain, is the tallest masonry wall-bearing structure in Chicago, with walls six feet thick at its base. Recently and lovingly restored, the building houses numerous restaurants and the Chicago Architecture Foundation's ArchiCenter.

Old Colony Building
407 S. Dearborn St.
This building was designed by Holabird & Roche in 1893.

Old St. Mary's Church
*Wabash Ave. and
Van Buren St.*
922-3444
This is the fifth location of Chicago's oldest Catholic parish. The original church at Lake and State streets was organized in 1833.

One South Wacker Drive
1 S. Wacker Dr.
Helmut Jahn's building reinforces the street's position as one of the city's most important office-tower rows.

Orchestra Hall
220 S. Michigan Ave.
Theodore Thomas, organizer of the Chicago Symphony Orchestra, complained so vehemently about the Auditorium's size that Orchestral Association trustee Daniel Burnham contributed his design services for a more intimate hall. The 1904, Georgian Orchestra Hall isn't the acoustic equal of the Auditorium but is one of a spate of World's Columbian Exposition-inspired, neoclassical buildings that transformed Michigan Avenue in the early years of the century.

Prairie Avenue Historic District
*Mainly Prairie Avenue
between 18th and Cullerton
streets*
After the Chicago Fire, the city's barons built splendid mansions along Prairie Avenue, near the site of the Fort Dearborn Massacre, creating Chicago's first Gold Coast. By the turn of the century, the street was passé. Only a few houses remain, including Glessner House, Chicago's only surviving residential work by H. H. Richardson. The Widow Clarke House, the city's oldest, was moved back near its original location in 1977 and has been beautifully restored (see Museums).

Prudential Building
130 E. Randolph Dr.
Built in 1958, it was once the city's tallest building.

Reliance Building
32 N. State St.
Designed in 1894 by Charles Atwood of D. H. Burnham and Company, the glass-and-terra-cotta-sheathed building was remarkable for its time and remains a tribute to graceful, turn-of-the-century functionalism. Though the building is hideously disfigured on its lower floors, the interior is virtually unchanged higher up. Notice the striking reliefs on the lobby-level brass elevator doors.

Rookery Building
209 S. La Salle St.
The lobby of this 1886 Burnham and Root building was designed by Frank Lloyd Wright for a 1905 remodeling. Wrapping around a fanciful iron-and-glass light well, it's

one of the most beautiful public spaces in any major Chicago building.

Sears Tower
233 S. Wacker Dr.
875-9696 (Skydeck)
Towering over Wacker Drive at 1,488 feet (110 stories), the world's tallest building was designed by Skidmore, Owings & Merrill in 1974. The building consists of nine 75-foot-square tubes and houses the corporate headquarters of Sears, Roebuck and Company. From the Skydeck the views of the entire city and beyond can either be breathtaking or induce vertigo. The boring ground-floor lobby is enlivened somewhat by Alexander Calder's *Universe.*

Second Presbyterian Church
Michigan Ave. and 20th St.
225-4951
James Renwick, the New Yorker who designed both the Main Building at Vassar College and the Capitol in Washington, D.C., created this 1874 neo-Gothic gem. In 1901 the interior was redone by Howard Van Doren Shaw. The cream of Prairie Avenue society — from the Armours to Mrs. Abraham Lincoln — worshiped in light filtered through 14 Tiffany windows.

Seventeenth Church of Christ, Scientist
Wacker Dr. and Wabash Ave.
236-4671
In 1968, Harry Weese designed this small semicircular gem in Heald Square. Just east is a seven-story triangular building that houses offices, meeting rooms, and other amenities.

State of Illinois Center
Randolph to Lake streets, Clark to La Salle streets
Everyone has an opinion of this 1985 Helmut Jahn work; people either hate it or love it, with few opinions in between. Inside is a huge multistory rotunda surrounded by retail space and restaurants on the lower levels and state offices for more than 50 agencies on the upper floors. The exterior is clad in red, white, and blue glass. Dubuffet's ten-ton *Monument with Standing Beast* rests in front of the building.

Stone Container Building
360 N. Michigan Ave.
Designed in 1923 by Alfred S. Alschuler as the London Guaranty Building, this structure is a fanciful flurry of neoclassicism, vaguely trapezoidal in shape. The building's entrance is flanked by four grand columns, while the roof is topped by a column-supported dome.

35 East Wacker Drive Building
35 E. Wacker Dr.
Once the Jewelers Building, this 1926 rococo structure has a fine cream-colored terracotta façade. Tenants drove from lower Wacker Drive right into an elevator, which took them to the proper floor of the interior 22-story central garage.

333 North Michigan Avenue Building
333 N. Michigan Ave.
Based on Eliel Saarinen's second-prize-winning entry in the 1922 *Tribune* contest, this 1928 Holabird and Root art deco masterpiece exemplifies a more refined treatment of style. The fifth-floor windows are flanked by carvings illustrating Chicago's early history.

United States Gypsum Building
101 S. Wacker Dr.
The Perkins and Will Partnership's 19-story steel, marble, and slate building, erected in 1963, is set at a 45-degree angle to the street and suggests a giant gypsum crystal.

Unity Building
127 N. Dearborn St.
Clarence Darrow and Edgar Lee Masters had their offices in this building, in which Rotary International was founded.

Major Institutions

American Conservatory of Music
17 N. State St., 18th floor
263-4161
The conservatory trains students from around the world and offers free concerts and recitals as well.

Chicago-Kent College of Law
77 S. Wacker Dr.
567-5000
This school — founded in 1888, it's the second-oldest law school in Illinois — became a division of the Illinois Institute of Technology in 1969.

Columbia College
600 S. Michigan Ave.
663-1600
This college, which traces its roots to 1890, specializes in the arts and media. It has thriving undergraduate and graduate schools combining liberal arts and technical training.

The Loop and Environs

**DePaul University
Loop Campus**
*Jackson Blvd. and
Wabash Ave.*
341-8000
This downtown campus
includes colleges of law and
commerce and the adult-edu-
cation School for New Learning, in three buildings.

**Harold Washington
College**
30 E. Lake St.
781-9430
Formerly Loop College, this
school changed its name to
honor the late mayor, Harold
Washington. It is one of nine
City Colleges of Chicago.

John Marshall Law School
315 S. Plymouth Ct.
427-2737
This is Chicago's principal
unaffiliated law school.

Roosevelt University
*Auditorium Building
430 S. Michigan Ave.*
341-3500
Roosevelt is located in
Adler and Sullivan's 1889
masterpiece.

**School of the Art
Institute of Chicago**
280 S. Columbus Dr.
443-3700
This is home to both a world-
renowned school of fine arts
and the Film Center, which
has public screenings of an
extraordinary variety of films,
from classic to experimental.

**Spertus College
of Judaica**
618 S. Michigan Ave.
922-9012

Hotels

Ascot Hotel
1100 S. Michigan Ave.
922-2900
There are bargain bed-and-
breakfast rates here.

Blackstone Hotel
636 S. Michigan Ave.
427-4300
This is where the phrase
"smoke-filled room" was
coined when cigar-puffing
politicians masterminded
Warren Harding's nomination
in 1920. The ballroom and
lobby of this 1910 Marshall
and Fox Second Empire masterpiece have been restored.

**Chicago Hilton
and Towers**
720 S. Michigan Ave.
922-4400
Opened in 1927 as the Stevens
Hotel — with 3,000 luxurious
guest rooms, an 18-hole roof-
top golf course, its own hospital, and a 1,200-seat
theater — it was the world's
largest. In 1951, then-owner
Conrad Hilton named it after
himself. Over the years, the
hotel had its ups and downs,
but today, after completion of
a $185-million top-to-bottom
renovation, it shines anew.
With magnificent views of
Lake Michigan and Grant
Park, this is one of Chicago's
great hotels. For a real treat,
reserve the $4,000-a-night
Conrad Hilton Suite, a duplex
that comes complete with a
private butler and maid, three
bedrooms, five bathrooms,
and a dining room that
seats 12.

Congress Hotel
520 S. Michigan Ave.
427-3800
Built as an annex to the Auditorium Hotel, Clinton J. Warren's 1893 façade remains one
of the city's handsomest.

Essex Inn
800 S. Michigan Ave.
939-2800
This modest hotel has
weekend bed-and-breakfast
rates.

Executive House
71 E. Wacker Dr.
346-7100
This nicely situated, modern
hotel mostly services the
traveling business community.

Fairmont Hotel
200 N. Columbus Dr.
565-8000
Overlooking Lake Michigan
and opened in 1987, this 45-
story hotel is the newest addition to the Illinois Center
complex. It houses 700 rooms,
numerous restaurants, and the
Moulin Rouge, a supper club
that offers both dancing and
big-name entertainment.

Hyatt Regency Chicago
151 E. Wacker Dr.
565-1000
Most of the activity here is in
the East Tower, around the
glass atrium lobby's huge
fountain. There are numerous
restaurants and bars here, as
well as huge numbers of con-
ventioneers.

Hotel Morton
500 S. Dearborn St.
663-3200
Housed in an elegantly restored building, this hotel
is just south of the Loop
in the burgeoning Dearborn
Park area.

Palmer House
17 E. Monroe St.
726-7500
Refurbished at a cost of $35
million, the Palmer House has

a grand second-floor lobby with towering ceilings and marble accents; beneath it is a block-long shopping arcade.

Shopping and Services

DEPARTMENT STORES

Carson Pirie Scott & Company
1 S. State St.
744-2000
Housed in Louis Sullivan's masterpiece, Carson's caters successfully to a middle-class market with high-quality, reasonably priced fashions, accessories, and products that appeal to a wide spectrum of people. In an effort to reach the upper end of the scale, though, it has expanded services in recent years with its home-accessories store, called Level 6, and, on the second floor, Metropolis, which sells high-fashion sports and casual wear, such as Generra and Esprit. In addition, the Corporate Level, located in the basement, is a wood-toned upscale shopping arcade oriented toward the professional person. Offering both a fine (and pricey) selection of business and weekend clothes for men and women, the Corporate Level also has hair salons, a cleaner, and luggage, shoe, and optical departments.

Marshall Field & Company
111 N. State St.
781-1000
This store embodies everything State Street was, as well as a hopeful sign of what it could be again. One of the world's great department stores, Field's takes the title seriously. Some 450 depart-

ments surround the skylit courts. Whether or not the original Marshall Field really commanded, "Give the lady what she wants," that's what the company has been doing for well over a century. On the main floor alone, cosmetics glisten with enviable selections, the luggage and silver departments know few peers, and the city's largest candy section overflows not only with the famed Frango mints but also with luxury imported chocolates, delightful trompe l'oeil marzipans, and top-quality bonbons turned out by squads of hand-dippers in Field's kitchens. Boutiques devoted solely to such designers or brands as Louis Vuitton, Fendi, Chanel, Bottega Veneta, and Ralph Lauren vie for space.

Equally outstanding merchandise fills the other floors, as do numerous restaurants, such as the proper Walnut Room, where hordes of Christmas shoppers often wait hours for a table. Impressive services range from the expected, such as the Bridal Registry, fur storage, gift wrapping, and Personal Shopping Service, to the rare: children's birthday reminders and interpreters for more than 20 languages.

BOOKS

China Books and Periodicals
55 E. Washington St.,
Suite 1003
782-6004
Books, magazines, and artworks from the People's Republic are on sale here.

B. Dalton Bookseller
129 N. Wabash Ave.
236-7615
This is the national chain's Chicago flagship store.

I Love a Mystery Bookstore
55 E. Washington St.,
Suite 616
236-1338
This store offers the city's largest selection of paperback mysteries, domestic and imported.

Illinois Labor History Society
28 E. Jackson Blvd.
663-4107
The books here offer labor's side of history and contemporary issues. There's also a selection of labor-oriented audio-visual material that can be purchased or rented. Call first, though, because appointments to visit are required.

Kroch's & Brentano's
29 S. Wabash Ave.
332-7500
Of the many bookstores in the Loop, Kroch's is the biggest and best-known. Carl Kroch, the very active president, has made his store a superb full-service bookstore. Astute buyers stock the shelves with all but the most obscure books, from best sellers to children's books, from foreign-language volumes to technical tomes, from books on art and architecture to others on sports and religion. Services include nominally priced book searches, extensive back lists, autograph parties, one-day delivery to branches, and deliveries anywhere in the world.

Marshall Field's Rare Book Department
111 N. State St.
781-4299
In Chicago, only Field's would make room in a department store for this fine antiquarian book operation. All that keeps it from being competitive with the city's best booksellers is the absence of catalogues. In

The Loop and Environs

addition to the antiquarian books, Field's has a full-stocked bookstore and magazine section.

Kenneth Nebenzahl, Inc.
333 N. Michigan Ave., 28th floor
641-2711
Regarded by many as Chicago's finest rare-book dealer, Nebenzahl sells great maps, as well as the finest of books.

Powell's Book Warehouse
1020 S. Wabash Ave., 4th floor
341-0748
Rickety shelves hold remaindered texts, art books, and scholarly and academic books, as well as bargain-priced paperbacks.

Prairie Avenue Bookshop
711 S. Dearborn St.
922-8311
Located in the middle of Printing House Row, Marilyn Hasbrouk's store is devoted to new and used books about architecture, design, and urban planning.

Rand McNally Map Store
23 E. Madison St.
332-4628
Maps, atlases, and globes, as well as guides and travel books, are available at this outlet store.

Sandmeyer's Bookstore
714 S. Dearborn St.
922-2104
This well-designed store specializes in top-quality hardbacks, with an emphasis on travel books. There's also a nice children's book department.

Savvy Traveler
50 E. Washington St.
263-2100
A multitude of travel books, maps, guides, travel-oriented literature, and travel accessories is available at this sprightly second-floor shop.

CLOTHING

Attitudes
122 S. Michigan Ave.
427-7932
This store caters to upscale men and women looking for the latest clothes from the hottest designers. Mixed in with jackets, pants, shirts, and (mini) skirts, there's also a nice selection of funky ties and sunglasses.

Jos. A. Bank Clothiers
25 E. Washington St.
782-4432
This private-label, traditional-clothing store offers a huge selection of men's suits, sport coats, slacks, shirts, sportswear, and sundries, as well as a respectable collection of women's wear.

Baskin
137 S. State St.
346-3363
Hart Schaffner & Marx, which began as a retailing and tailoring partnership in 1887 and grew into a national brand, produces men's clothing. Retail outlets include several old-line stores brought under the corporate umbrella. Baskin is one, a favorite source for fairly traditional clothing, with Hickey-Freeman and Austin Reed both made by the parent company.

Eddie Bauer, Inc.
123 N. Wabash Ave.
263-6005
If you're looking for durable backpacks, rugged field boots, or hunting, fishing, and camping equipment — even a canoe — head to Eddie Bauer. Prices aren't low, but an unconditional guarantee backs everything. The salespeople are helpful, knowledgeable, and enthusiastic.

Brooks Brothers
74 E. Madison St.
263-0100
This store, a branch of the nation's oldest clothing retailer, favors conservative styles. Although the store is nothing special to look at, the racks are crammed with Ivy League-looking clothes, and expert tailoring has been the chain's hallmark since 1818.

Capezio Dance Theater Shop
50 E. Washington St.
236-1911
Here ballet slippers, tap shoes, leotards, calf warmers, and the like are not only an invitation to dance but also very much in style.

Capper & Capper, Ltd.
1 N. Wabash Ave.
236-3800
Gentlemen of distinction shop here, a handsome, old-fashioned store with knowledgeable salespeople offering conservatively styled, expensive clothes. Hickey-Freeman and Oxxford suits top the line, and custom-cut orders can be placed from a library of swatch books. There's also a selection of appropriate shirts, hats, and accessories.

Fashionette Swimwear
17 N. State St.
332-2802
Fashionette can fit all sizes from an enormous year-round collection of beachwear. The shop also carries men's and women's racing suits, goggles, ear plugs, and swim caps.

Handmoor
70 E. Randolph St.
726-5600
For bargains in the latest women's fashions, locals and out-of-towners head here. Dresses, suits, separates, and sportswear fill a sea of racks.

Lane Bryant, Inc.
9 N. Wabash Ave.
621-8700
Of an increasing number of
stores specializing in hard-to-
fit sizes, this may be the oldest
and best-known.

Mallard's
*50 E. Washington St.,
2nd floor*
444-9295
Casual clothes in traditional
styles for men are the specialty
here, though there are coats
and slacks as well.

Mother's Work
*50 E. Washington St.,
2nd floor*
332-0022
This store specializes in
clothes for pregnant women
who work and want to
maintain a professional
appearance.

Mysels Furs
108 N. State St., 10th floor
372-9513
Many Loop furriers are hidden on upper floors of old
buildings, go unnoticed by
window-shoppers, and draw
their customers by word of
mouth. One that does get
noticed is Mysels. Many furs
are sold at this high-volume
operation for half the price
charged by other salons.

Nierman's Tall Girl Shoes
17 N. State St., 12th floor
346-9797
High-fashion shoes for
women with hard-to-find sizes
and unusual widths have been
sold here for more than
50 years.

**Pendleton Woolen Mills
Products Stores, Inc.**
*Palmer House Arcade
17 E. Monroe St.*
372-1699
This tiny shop is full of famous woolen plaids and other
men's and women's casual
wear.

Riddle-McIntyre, Inc.
175 N. Franklin St.
782-3317
Frank Hee Kong custom-
makes shirts from your choice
of fabric; there's a three-shirt
minimum initial order.

Chas. A. Stevens
25 N. State St.
630-1500
The store offers seven levels of
fashions and services for
women, from the petites in the
basement to the sixth-floor
Directive beauty salon with
the Adrien Arpel spa.

Tall Girls Shop
17 N. State St., 8th floor
782-9867
This shop stocks everything
from uniforms to quality on-
the-town clothes for women
between five feet seven and
six feet five.

MUSIC

Beautiful Sound
333 N. Michigan Ave.
726-7911
This is the exclusive retailer of
elite Bösendorfer pianos; Kim-
ball pianos are also available.

Bein & Fushi, Inc.
*410 S. Michigan Ave.,
10th floor*
663-0150
Bein & Fushi has one of the
city's largest violin-repair
facilities and also sells rare
bowed instruments to an
international clientele.

Carl Fischer of Chicago
312 S. Wabash Ave.
427-6652
Don't be surprised if music
fills your ears at the intersection of Wabash Avenue and
Jackson Boulevard. This was
once the center of Chicago's
music row. The golden days
are past, but there is still
plenty of activity, anchored
primarily by this store, where
you'll find the world's largest

inventory of published music.
The first floor contains vocal
music, rock, jazz, and specialty instrumentals — from
balalaika to zither; the second
floor serves bands and orchestras; and the third is devoted
to choral scores, including
complete operas. Nothing's
ever thrown away at Carl
Fischer, so it's a gold mine for
collectors; music of the 1920s
and '30s is big right now. If
you can't remember a title, try
humming a few bars; a member of the expert staff can
probably identify it. Fischer
also carries books about
music, musical games, and
musical accessories.

Kagan & Gaines Music Co.
207 S. Wabash Ave., 6th floor
939-4083
Kagan & Gaines carries a full
line of musical instruments
that are geared more toward
orchestras and bands than to
jazz and studio musicians.

Schilke Music Products
529 S. Wabash Ave., 8th floor
922-0230
Renold Schilke has been making and repairing brass instruments — mostly trumpets —
since 1929. He is one of the
few high-quality instrument
makers left in America, and
back orders run from about
six months for trumpets to
about a year and a half for
piccolos. Horn makers still
apprentice with Schilke.

GENERAL

**American Floral Art
School**
539 S. Wabash Ave., 2nd floor
922-9328
Visitors are welcome here,
where you can learn everything necessary to open up
a flower shop.

The Loop and Environs

Bachrach, Inc.
218 E. Ontario St.
236-1991
Bachrach is the photographer of some of the city's most prominent people.

Boy Scouts of America Scout Supply Center
128 S. Franklin St.
726-4085
Everything you need to BE PREPARED.

Carteaux, Inc.
31 N. Wabash Ave.
782-5375
The Jewelers Club meets in the basement of the Pittsfield Building, with its handsome lobby arcade and wonderful elevator brasswork. Besides scores of dentists' offices, the Pittsfield is home to Carteaux, which specializes in gold: traditional, classic, and precious jewelry plus top-of-the-line watches.

Chicago Trunk & Leather Works, Inc.
12 S. Wabash Ave.
372-0845
The Levine family has been selling trunks, suitcases, and travel accessories in the Loop since 1911. There's a good selection of business cases and women's handbags; free monogramming comes with the purchase of luggage by makers such as Hartmann, Lark, French, and Skyway.

Corrado Cutlery
26 N. Clark St.
368-8450
Corrado has been sharpening and selling fine knives since 1905.

Crate & Barrel
101 N. Wabash Ave.
372-0100
In addition to the first floor's relatively inexpensive but stylish dishes, glasses, stemware, silverware, and cooking utensils, the downstairs floor offers even-less-expensive housewares. There's also a good selection of utensils for various sorts of ethnic cooking, from woks and wok supplies to the proper things with which to make Mexican food or deep-dish pizzas.

Favor Ruhl Co.
23 S. Wabash Ave.
782-5737
Weekend artists and students from nearby schools frequent Favor Ruhl, one of the city's oldest and most prestigious art-supply houses. The store carries a full range of material for commercial artists; and the atmosphere is youthful and exuberant, rather than businesslike.

Flax Co.
52 E. Randolph St.
346-5100
Another art-supply house, though this is geared more toward the commercial artists.

Girl Scout Shop
55 E. Jackson Blvd., 14th floor
435-5500
Like the shop catering to a Girl Scout's male counterpart, this store sells everything a scout needs.

Hirk Company
125 N. Wabash Ave., 14th floor
346-0194
This store specializes in monogramming furs and linens. Skilled operators using special machines initial shirt cuffs, safeguard sables, and run off emblems for softball teams. The shop will embroider almost anything.

House of Williams
37 S. Wabash Ave.
236-6320
This place retins copperware and repairs, replaces, and cleans silver.

International Importing Bead and Novelty Company
17 N. State St., 12th floor
332-0061
Dancers, chorus girls, period-costume designers, Chicago Historical Society clothing conservators, and everyone else have been frequenting this shop for more than 60 years. The store is stacked floor-to-ceiling with baubles, bangles, and beads; rhinestones, sequins, and sequined patches; intricately carved wood beads; painted porcelain ones; others of faceted crystal; shells, and many other accessories are sold by the scoop or by the piece.

K. Matsumoto Art Repair Shop
226 S. Wabash Ave., 7th floor
922-4110
For 64 years this store has been fixing damaged porcelain, glass, ivory, jade, and most other delicate objects except dinnerware and broken hearts. The owner and several assistants also grind down chipped lips on crystal goblets and do wonders with broken antique lamps. Their museum-quality restorations don't come cheap, nor should you expect overnight service.

Old Chicago Smoke Shop
169 N. Clark St.
236-9771
Here find cut-rate cigars from the Canary Islands, Jamaica, the Philippines, and other far-off places.

C. D. Peacock Jewelers
101 S. State St.
630-5700
Elijah Peacock sold watches and clocks even before Chicago got its charter. Today, C. D. Peacock is the city's oldest store. Behind bronze peacock doors, it's the picture of Old World elegance, with cof-

fered green marble ceilings, crystal chandeliers, and polished wood cabinets displaying the big names in crystal, silver, china, timepieces, jewelry, and porcelain.

Otto Pomper Inc.
109 S. Wabash Ave.
372-0881
Cutlery has been the stock in trade here since 1890. Knives by Henckels, Case, Chicago Cutlery, Marks, and Wüsthof Trident share the space with a related but odd assortment of devices, both useful and whimsical: straight razors, electric ones, and converters for foreign travel; kitchen gadgets as diverse as silver corncob holders and bean stringers; bird feeders and foot relaxers.

Iwan Ries & Co.
19 S. Wabash Ave., 2nd floor
372-1306
A Loop fixture since 1857, this is the world's highest-volume tobacco store, renowned for its stock of more than 25,000 pipes and its best-selling Three Star smoking fixture. Catalogues go to more than 300,000 people; mail orders account for more than half the retail business. Cigar smokers flock to the refrigerated walk-in humidor to select house brands that can be warmed in the store's microwave oven. The Pipe Museum has a recorded commentary describing rare and intricately carved pieces, and tools and buffing machines are on hand for cleaning and polishing your favorite calabash.

Scriptorium Benedictine Artistic Lettering
410 S. Michigan Ave., 6th floor
427-2428
Here they make illuminated books and presentation scrolls on parchment and vellum.

Universal Bowling and Golf Corporation
619 S. Wabash Ave.
922-5255
Billiard supplies, bowling balls, and golf clubs at low prices in a no-nonsense atmosphere are the specialties here.

Universal Pen Hospital
17 N. State St.
332-5373
Sam Himoto personalizes pens here, but his real forte is reshaping points to fit individuals, and doctoring pens with broken points, dried-out pads, and worse.

Word City
703 S. Dearborn St.
663-4242
This is a nonprofit graphic-design and typesetting operation staffed by artists and does work for other artists and nonprofit groups at about half the going commercial rate.

Restaurants

Benchers Fish House
Sears Tower
233 S. Wacker Dr.
993-0096
This handsome restaurant offers free limo service (book ahead), making it the ideal pre-opera or -theater choice. Try peppery Cajun shrimp or cheese-sprinkled toasted ravioli for starters. Fish are fresh and carefully cooked — usually over charcoal — and come with a choice of sauces. Meat courses include a 19-ounce rib steak.

Berghoff
17 W. Adams St.
427-3170
This oak-paneled landmark still bustles with tourists and regulars. The food is hearty, no-nonsense, and reasonably priced. German standards,

such as sauerbraten, schnitzel, and ragout à la Deutsch, vie for attention with seafood, steaks, and delectable chops. Rich root beers and specially brewed light and dark draft beers are highlights as well.

Buckingham's
Chicago Hilton and Towers
720 S. Michigan Ave.
294-6600
This expensive, clubby room offers interesting "new American" dishes. There's a tempting seasonal menu as well as nightly specials from which to choose. The selection of game is broad, with squab, duck, venison, and pheasant on the winter menu, for instance.

Everest Room
The La Salle Club
440 S. La Salle St.
663-8920
Though the décor and cityscapes here are very appealing, it's the food that truly stands out. A complimentary starter, such as cold vegetable mousse, is brought to you shortly after you're seated. First-course specials may include a flaky filo sachet of fresh shrimps with leeks and wild mushrooms or, perhaps a meltaway dish of sautéed foie gras. Dessert includes a pear crème brûlée, a Champagne sabayon, and sorbets.

Nick's Fishmarket
First National Plaza
Monroe and Dearborn streets
621-0200
Dining here is a relaxing and private experience, with dim lighting, soft music, and well-spaced tables. The seafood is consistently fresh; oysters Rockefeller and clams casino are as good as you'll find. Ambrosia is a light dessert of papaya with ice cream and strawberries; candy-crusted cappuccino mousse cake is more sinful.

The Loop and Environs

Printer's Row
550 S. Dearborn St.
461-0780
Talent and imagination keep
this comfortable, subdued
American place from ever
being stodgy. Beautiful first
courses include flavorful carpaccio rolled around chopped
olives, gherkins, and capers,
served with vinaigrette and a
colorful confetti of vegetables.
Poultry, fish, and venison are
always good choices for main
courses, and homemade ice
creams and sherbets are mem-
orable desserts.

Don Roth's River Plaza
405 N. Wabash Ave.
527-3100
The second-floor dining room
of this American restaurant
offers window-side diners one
of the more appealing views of
the river and cityscape. The
menu is wide-ranging: prime
ribs, barbecued spare ribs, and
Boston scrod as well as Cajun
and Creole dishes.

Near West Side

CHICAGO'S FIRST SETTLEMENTS quickly spread to the Near West Side from the factory-, lumberyard-, and shipyard-lined banks near the mouth of the Chicago River. The city limits reached Ashland Boulevard in 1837 and extended as far as Western Avenue by 1851. Although the far reaches were suburban in the early years, the area close to what is now downtown filled with immigrants. In the 1850s, Germans organized **St. Francis of Assisi Church**, and the Irish founded **St. Patrick's** — Chicago's oldest church building — and **Holy Family Church**. The beautiful brick buildings towered over the meanest of wood shacks. Bohemians followed the early settlers in such numbers that by 1870 the community centered at Roosevelt Road and Halsted Street was known as Praha (Prague).

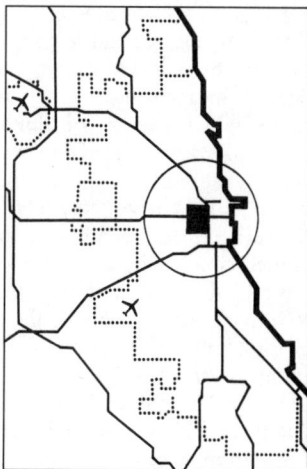

The 1871 Chicago Fire, which allegedly started at De Koven and Jefferson streets, treated the riverside to its first urban-renewal program but left most of the Near West Side unscathed. Post-Fire refugees swelled the neighborhood's population, and, over the next four decades, waves of Italian, Jewish, and Greek immigrants crowded into the already-dilapidated housing stock.

Jane Addams and Ellen Gates Starr moved into this area of urban desperation and squalor in 1889 with a pioneer concept — the settlement house. For the next 70 years, almost no aspect of life in the neighborhood was divorced from **Hull House**. The list of Hull House's Chicago firsts is staggering: the social settlement; public facilities such as baths, a playground, a swimming pool, a gymnasium, and a kitchen; little theater; a Boy Scout troop; college extension courses; citizenship classes; art exhibits.

At the turn of the century, **Maxwell Street** was the center of the Jewish community, which by then numbered more than 20,000. The ferocity of the local merchants was so notorious that the City Council passed a law in the 1930s outlawing "pullers," men who literally dragged customers into the stores and made getting out without buying almost impossible.

To the north of the Jewish neighborhood was a teeming Italian community. Construction of the University of Illinois campus truncated this neighborhood, removing Halsted Street's tenements and leaving only a few blocks of neat, turn-of-the-century houses and apartments west of Morgan Street that once represented the good life for Italians.

"Greektown" is another Near West Side ethnic pocket. From 1900 to the onset of World War Two, Greeks settled in the "Delta" — a triangle formed by Halsted Street, Blue Island Avenue — and beyond. They established the country's first Greek Orthodox parish, Holy Trinity, in 1897 (it has since moved) and purchased the Anshe Sholom edifice, christening it **St. Basil**. In the 1950s the Eisenhower Expressway cut a huge swath through the community, and, in the early 1960s, the university claimed the rest

Near West Side

after a spirited but futile battle. No homes survived: Two blocks of commercial buildings alongside Halsted Street north of the expressway are all that remain.

One by one, the old Jewish, Italian, and Greek ghettos have fallen to institutional use, leaving only a few stores and restaurants as reflections of their former life. Once one of Chicago's most densely populated neighborhoods, by day it bustles with businesspeople, University of Illinois students, and Medical Center personnel. At night, except for the tourists at Italian and Greek restaurants, it's a ghost town.

So, what did Chicago get when two of its vibrant ethnic neighborhoods were bulldozed for the **University of Illinois at Chicago** (UIC) campus? Skidmore, Owings & Merrill created a complex you either love or hate, but can't fail to notice. Most of the poured-concrete buildings are low and have a suburban industrial-park feel. The campus probably looked great on the model board, but there's a sterile, unyielding quality to it that's relieved only by the playful Behavioral Sciences and the Science and Engineering buildings — multilevel boxes stacked at angles, where finding particular classrooms is almost impossible.

Medical schools and hospitals lie just west of the campus in the **Medical Center District**. This unique 365-acre tract was set aside for health-care institutions by the Legislature in 1941. The district includes 60 health-care institutions. Some, such as Cook County Hospital (built in 1873) and the UIC hospitals, preceded the designation; the Rush-Presbyterian-St. Luke's Medical Center merger and the West Side Veterans Administration Hospital came after 1941. The buildings span a century of styles from baroque to ultramodern.

Homes in the increasingly desirable enclave between the university and the medical center reflect the same diversity. New developments are beginning to sprout up on Ashland Boulevard, and Lexington Street between Lytle and Ada streets displays well-maintained Victorian row houses, showing what middle-class sections of the Near West Side looked like in the 19th century.

Founded in 1864, **Notre Dame de Chicago Parish** serves the local French Canadian community. Notre Dame outgrew its first building on the corner of Halsted Street and Congress Parkway and built the present church at Flournoy and Ada streets in 1888. Grégoire Vigeant designed the unusual Romanesque, domed structure, which is listed on both the Illinois and the National Register of Historic Places as the only extant example of French church architecture in Chicago.

Though much of the Near West Side was composed of working-class communities, the area once had an upper crust as well. Ashland Boulevard and Adams, Monroe, and Washington streets were all fashionable thoroughfares in the second half of the 19th century. Florenz Ziegfeld was raised at 1448 West Adams Street, and Theodore Dreiser lived overlooking Union Park at Ashland and Washington boulevards, where his sister Carrie aspired to move. Only one block remains intact today: the **Jackson Boulevard Historic District**. The streetscape, a pleasing blend of Italianate, Queen Anne, and Second Empire styles, evokes a gentler age.

After the area fell from favor, its proximity to downtown led to a variety of commercial and institutional uses. Ashland Boulevard north of the expressway is "Union Row," with regional headquarters of the Teamsters, Amalgamated Clothing Workers, and many more.

Other interesting and historic sites on the Near West Side include the present-day incarnation of **Maxwell Street**. Though Maxwell Street and its environs were crammed after the turn of the century with peddlers, pushcarts, and overflowing clothing stores, it has since deteriorated greatly. Still, on Sundays some of the old magic returns. Starting very early in the morning, a coterie of regulars stakes out favorite spots for a weekly open-air market. By 8 a.m. the blocks west of Halsted Street and south of Roosevelt Road are filled with bargain hunters searching for antiques or used clothing.

There's also **Haymarket Square** at Randolph and Desplaines streets, scene of the 1886 riot and the first use of a dynamite bomb by U.S. "terrorists." A monument to the 176 policemen (seven of whom were killed) who charged the workers' rally was repeatedly blown up in the 1960s and finally moved to the central police headquarters in 1972.

SHOPPING

Before World War Two, Roosevelt Road was solid with tenements from State Street past Morgan Street, and the Halsted-Roosevelt intersection was an exciting jumble of streetcars, wagons, and pushcarts. Halsted Street was filled with high-pressure ladies' clothing stores, and Jefferson Street was the center of the clothing jobber trade. Successors to a few of the hundreds of local merchants are still going strong east of the Dan Ryan Expressway, in factorylike 1950s buildings constructed after "slum clearance."

Chernin Shoes has grown into what may be the city's largest outlet for brand-name shoes. The pace is hectic and the atmosphere harried in both the men's and women's sections, but the enormous selection and discounted prices make shopping here worthwhile. **Fishman's Fabrics** boasts bolt after bolt of fabrics from around the world, all at reasonable prices. Three levels are filled with sewing supplies.

A forest of double-hung racks fills the football-field-sized sales floor at **Benjamin's Clothing**. They're loaded with menswear from name-brand manufacturers in mostly traditional styles, all at substantial discounts. **Rottapel Clothes**, which has been around for three-quarters of a century, sells at retail to individuals while it wholesales job lots of new clothing, although the used-clothing business that once was a local mainstay has since evaporated. Two more good sources for bargains are **Morris & Sons** and **Meyerson Associated Clothing Company**, both in the Jeffro Plaza, a lackluster series of shops with its own parking lot south of Roosevelt Road.

C & C Florists Supplies maintains a show room at its warehouse as well as at the Merchandise Mart. One of the country's largest wholesalers of silk and dried flowers, plumes, preserved foliage, containers, and baskets, C & C welcomes retail customers. Many of Chicago's galleries and private collectors turn to **Frederic's Frame Studio** for museum-quality framing. This is one of the country's last sources for gold- and silver-leaf work, and the other frames are almost as precious: hand-carved rococo antique reproductions, art deco, art nouveau, curved corner, Tokyo corner, ribbon corner, and a staggering array of plainer ones of most woods and finishes.

At **Conte di Savoia**, an international food market, the Italian offerings in particular are exhaustive: pastas of every description, imported tomatoes and olive oils, a full deli counter with meats and cheeses, olives and artichoke salads, and candies.

Of the few food outlets that remain on Taylor Street, the **Original Ferrara, Inc.**, stands out. This huge bakery may have the largest selection of Italian cookies, pastries, and cakes in the city. Ferrara supplies local restaurants and does a big wedding-cake business. If an in-home Greek meal is more to your taste, go to **Athens Grocery**. In the deli case, half a dozen types of olives glisten in tubs next to cheeses, mounds of halvah, and jars of fish-roe spread. There are loads more of olives in jars, smoked fish, dried herbs, nuts, pastas, and a whole shelf of olive oils. On top of this, Athens is a full American grocery store. The **Mediterranean Pastry Shop** is equally delightful with Greek and French pastries, cookies, and candies.

N & G Produce always has a good selection ranging from ginger to Mexican peppers, and nothing's prepacked in plastic wrap. **Quality Supermarket Products** is a full-scale wholesale-retail supermarket-butcher. Large sizes of packaged goods and half-case lots of canned ones predominate, some at very attractive savings. Prices are also good at the **Columbus Meat Market**, where the wide variety of meats includes goat.

The city's large wholesale produce jobbers moved out to the **South Water Market** when Wacker Drive cut through its namesake in 1925. Past Lake Street's machinery row, however, Fulton Street is still a meat and fish wholesale center. **Pick Fisheries**, just east of the Kennedy Expressway, sells a wide variety of fresh and frozen fish at low prices in a lovely old building.

RESTAURANTS

With remnants of so many different ethnic communities around, it's not surprising that there are more than a few heady dining experiences.

No trip to Maxwell Street is complete without a nosh. Try **Nate's Delicatessen**, known to many as Lyon's, which sells corned-beef sandwiches and herring from a grubby basement shop. And then there's **Manny's Coffee Shop**, a pale reflection of the glitzy Jewish restaurants like Baron's that once lined Roosevelt Road, but the food's not too different. Lamb shanks, prune tsimmes, baked chicken and fish, dairy dishes, and cold plates are served in cafeteria style. And such corned-beef sandwiches!

With no surviving tradition like the Maxwell Street market, Taylor Street's main draws are restaurants: old-line Southern Italian spots such as **Gennaro's** and **Mategrano's** where pizza and pasta are the main fare, the music is likely to be Sinatra, the red wine chilled, and the help gruff.

Florence Restaurant provides a charming alternative to mediocre food and indifferent service. With a high tin ceiling and antique woodwork rescued from Hull House buildings, the room is delightful. Although the menu is limited, the food's prepared with a sensitivity usually reserved for more expensive spots.

For a wider choice of restaurants, and to see what the area looked like before urban renewal, visit "Little Italy," a section that grew up around the post-Fire McCormick reaper works at 26th Street and Western Avenue. Cermak Road traces the little quarter's northern edge. There are about half a dozen good, modestly priced restaurants here. Basically, the similarities are greater than the differences among these places, so individual favorites are usually the result of happy experiences. **Bruna's Ristorante** is a classic neighborhood spot with a small, aging dining room behind the bar. Everything is cooked to order with great care, and veal dishes and fettuccine stand out. At **La Fontanella**, perhaps the best-known restaurant, fried and baked chicken Fontanella is a specialty, as are the green-noodle casserole and arancini — breaded, meat-filled, deep-fried balls of rice.

For more home-style Italian cooking, check out **Febo**, which offers a lengthy menu, friendly service, and generally high-quality food. The many pastas are cooked *al dente*, and the veal's pretty good.

Danilo's has an atypically short menu featuring pastas — the tortellini are excellent — and properly prepared veal dishes.

Restaurants are the main attractions in "Greektown" as well. In spite of the dismantling of the community, or perhaps because of it, the Halsted Street restaurants have become big, main-line businesses. Years ago, **Diana Grocery and Restaurant** was just a little dining room in the back of a Greek grocery. With the original building and all the Greek clientele gone, the owners embarked on a promotional campaign to draw in customers. Thousands of hand kissings, saganaki flamings, and ouzos later, the dining room is of supermarket size, while the grocery has shrunk to an excuse for the name.

Most of the nearby spots offer similar fare in big, noisy rooms decorated with mu-

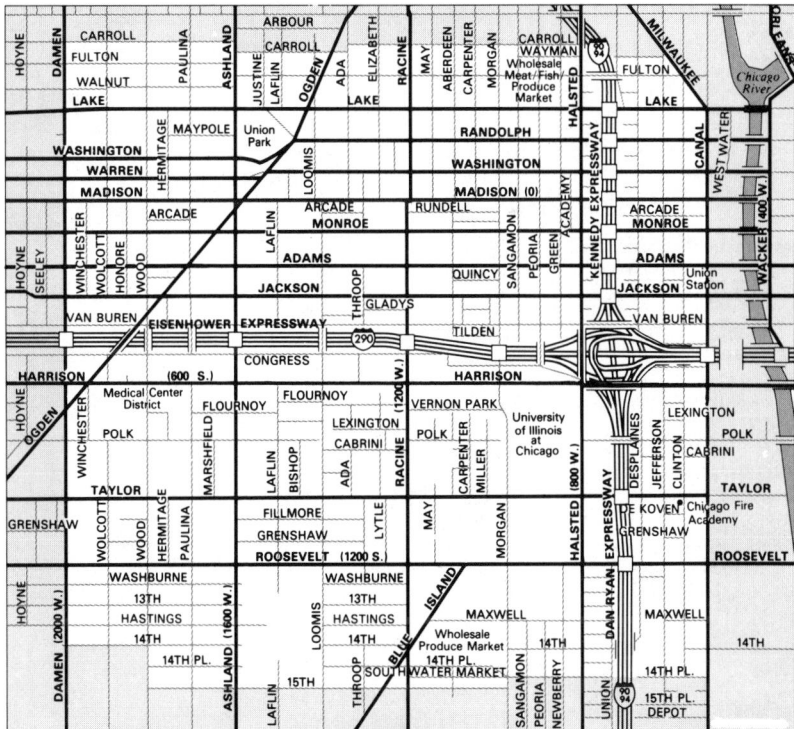

Near West Side

rals, hanging plastic grapevines, and the like. A whole pig or lamb roasting in the window of the **Parthenon** presages the treats inside. The large menu includes roast, fried, baked, boiled, and barbecued meats; seafood, such as a fine, cold octopus salad, and shrimp cooked in saganaki style; and the familiar gyros, dolmades, moussaka, and so forth. The darker and often noisier **Greek Islands** is a favorite with Chicago authors such as Saul Bellow and sells many of the same dishes as "de luxe" choices. Egg-lemon soup and spinach-cheese pie are topnotch, as are desserts.

Dressed-up décor, live music, and embellished service make the **Courtyards of Plaka** Greektown's most upscale spot. The menu offers nice varieties of standards, as well as less familiar dishes. Broiled meats go beyond shish kebab to lamb, pork chops, and strip steak, and the best desserts are baklava and tart yogurt with honey and walnuts.

No exotic treats grace the menu at **Lou Mitchell's**, but the canny owner has made this big lunchroom a Chicago landmark. The breakfast — served all day — keeps people coming back. Fresh butter and double-yolked eggs, fluffy omelets served in skillets, and what may be Chicago's best coffee aren't cheap, but you always get your money's worth.

Interesting Places

▶ **Jane Addams Hull House and Dining Hall**
800 S. Halsted St.
996-2793

▶ **Haymarket Square**
Randolph and Desplaines streets

▶ **Holy Family Church**
Roosevelt Rd. and May St.
243-7207

▶ **Jackson Boulevard Historic District**
1500 block of Jackson Blvd.

▶ **Maxwell Street Market**
Centered at Peoria and 14th streets

▶ **Medical Center District**
Ashland Blvd. to Oakley Blvd., Congress Pkwy. to 13th St.

▶ **Notre Dame de Chicago Church**
Flournoy and Ada streets
243-7400

▶ **St. Basil Greek Orthodox Church**
Ashland Blvd. and Polk St.
243-3738

▶ **St. Francis of Assisi Church**
Roosevelt Rd. and Newberry Ave.
226-7575

▶ **St. Patrick's Church**
Desplaines and Adams streets
782-6171

▶ **University of Illinois at Chicago**
University Hall
601 S. Morgan St.
996-3000

Shopping

▶ **Athens Grocery**
324 S. Halsted St.
332-6737

▶ **Benjamin's Clothing**
1150 S. Clinton St.
922-1536

▶ **C & C Florists Supplies**
1245 W. Washington Blvd.
421-1500

▶ **Chernin Shoes**
606 W. Roosevelt Rd.
922-4545

▶ **Columbus Meat Market**
906 W. Randolph St.
829-2480

▶ **Conte di Savoia**
555 W. Roosevelt Rd.
666-3471

▶ **Fishman's Fabrics**
1101 S. Desplaines St.
922-7250

▶ **Frederic's Frame Studio**
1230 W. Jackson Blvd.
243-2950

▶ **Mediterranean Pastry Shop**
308 S. Halsted St.
332-1771

▶ **Meyerson Associated Clothing**
555 W. Roosevelt Rd.
421-5580

▶ **Morris & Sons Company**
555 W. Roosevelt Rd.
243-5635

▶ **N & G Produce**
904 W. Randolph St.
942-9432

▶ **Original Ferrara, Inc.**
2210 W. Taylor St.
666-2200

▶ **Pick Fisheries**
702 W. Fulton Market
226-4700

▶ **Quality Supermarket
Products**
924 W. Randolph St.
421-1887

▶ **Rottapel Clothes**
531 W. Roosevelt Rd.
942-0816

▶ **Mategrano's**
1321 W. Taylor St.
243-8441

▶ **Lou Mitchell's**
563 W. Jackson Blvd.
939-3111

▶ **Nate's Delicatessen**
807 W. Maxwell St.
421-9396

▶ **Parthenon**
314 S. Halsted St.
726-2407

Restaurants

▶ **Bruna's Ristorante**
2424 S. Oakley Ave.
847-8875

▶ **Courtyards of Plaka**
340 S. Halsted St.
263-0767

▶ **Danilo's**
1235 W. Grand Ave.
421-0218

▶ **Diana Grocery and
Restaurant**
130 S. Halsted St.
263-1848

▶ **Febo Restaurant**
2501 S. Western Ave.
523-0839

▶ **Florence Restaurant**
1030 W. Taylor St.
829-1857

▶ **La Fontanella**
2414 S. Oakley Ave.
927-5249

▶ **Gennaro's**
1352 W. Taylor St.
243-1035

▶ **Greek Islands**
200 S. Halsted St.
782-9855

▶ **Manny's Coffee Shop**
1141 S. Jefferson St.
939-2855

Pilsen

OF ALL THE 19TH-CENTURY South and West Side residential neighborhoods that were once near the Loop, only Pilsen has survived. Industrial development in the 1920s claimed some; Depression-era public housing replaced others. Highway and institutional construction added to the neighborhoods' destruction in the 1950s and '60s and, finally, HUD policies finished what neglect had missed. Pilsen, which was surrounded by railroad tracks and edged by industry, managed to endure and continues to provide housing to recent immigrants as it has done throughout its history.

In fact, English has been the second language here for a hundred years. By the 1890s, Pilsen's side streets were lined with frame houses, as well as two-, three-, and four-story brick buildings housing numerous Czech families each. Eighteenth Street, lined with small commercial buildings and with grander graystones, catered to the area's stockyard and factory workers.

Travel the side streets: Almost every block harbors fanciful, brightly colored façades. Lintels, elaborate cornices, cast-iron storefronts, and hammered-tin-covered bays are painted in contrasting colors, highlighting their ornamental patterns. Reminders of the past are everywhere, including an old-time photographer's studio at 1439 West 18th Street. The two-story, stone-front building houses a barbershop behind the unaltered vintage storefront, and the slanted north wall of the second story is all glass to admit the light necessary for pioneer photography. There may be no architectural masterpieces in Pilsen, but there's plenty to see nonetheless.

Of the many churches that dot the neighborhood, four stand out. Designed by Paul Huber and dedicated in 1883, **St. Procopius Church** is one of the city's oldest and has a traditional Gothic vaulted interior. The South Side's oldest Polish parish, founded in the mid-1870s, built **St. Adalbert's Church**, a white-brick, Beaux Arts masterpiece with clock towers and pink Corinthian marble columns, in 1914. On 18th Place, the Victorian **St. Vitus** sports handsome, figural stained-glass windows. Equally exciting stained glass adorns the Shrine of St. Jude, **St. Pius V Church**.

There are more than 20 exterior murals in Pilsen, created in the past 15 years by such artists as Aurelio Diaz and Ray Patian, often with itinerant local assistants. The paintings make strong comments in the Mexican tradition of Rivera. Colors are bold; perspectives are distorted; decorative elements draw heavily on Aztecan and Mayan themes; and subjects range from the sociopolitical and religious to pop culture.

Pilsen muralists flaunt their work, but the presence of another group of artists is just barely evident from the street. Although more than 200 painters, sculptors, potters, weavers, and other artisans have studios in the vicinity of Halsted and 18th streets, no sign heralds a Pilsen artists' colony, and there are no Friday-night gallery openings. Every year, though, there's the Pilsen Artists' Open House, when many locals open their studios to the public and sell their work.

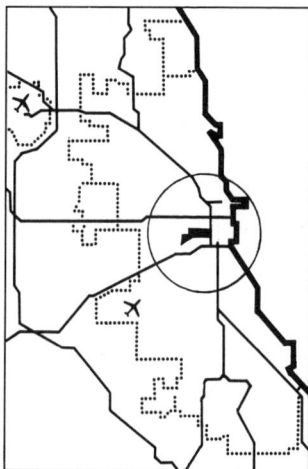

82

Pilsen

SHOPPING AND RESTAURANTS

The shopping streets — Ashland and Blue Island avenues and 18th Street — have all the familiar Mexican-neighborhood fare: bodegas crammed with tropical imports; little, old-fashioned department stores; outlets for imported pottery and religious artifacts; record stores spilling music into the street; lots of seedy taverns; and bakeries.

Half a dozen bakeshops offer traditional unfilled sweetened bread, puff-dough pastries topped with granulated sugar or glaze, giant cookies, fried doughnuts, and loaves of dense, crusty bread. One of the best, **Nuevo León**, displays them all in handsome wood cabinets and, like many, is set up for self-service. Other good bakeries include **Laredo Bakery**, **Diana's Bakery**, and **La Mexicana Bakery**.

La Casa del Pueblo is a big grocery store, selling both Mexican and American foodstuffs. It also has a luncheonette.

There's one old-style department store in the neighborhood, **Zemsky Brothers**, which has a wide selection of clothing and shoes. For records and tapes, try the **Librería Girón**.

Modest restaurants serving enchiladas, flautas, tacos, bistec, and eggs ranchero are common in Pilsen. Another **Nuevo León** has authentic treats like breaded fried brains, while the rustic **Cuernavaca** features a braised-goat dinner. **Sabinas** offers a weekend Mexican barbecue as well as half a dozen other fish dishes in a clean, bright storefront, while the menu at **Ostionería Playa Azul**, a plastic-and-Formica place enlivened by a few nautical accents, lists only seafood.

If your taste for Mexican food goes only as far as chili, head to **Chicago's Original Bishop's Famous Chili**, which for more than 50 years has been serving what many Chicagoans consider to be the world's finest in a no-nonsense storefront atmosphere. The chili is also packed to go.

Pilsen

Interesting Places

▶ **St. Adalbert's Church**
17th and Paulina streets
226-0340

▶ **St. Pius V Church**
19th St. and Ashland Ave.
226-0074

▶ **St. Procopius Church**
18th and Allport streets
226-7887

▶ **St. Vitus Church**
18th Pl. and Paulina St.
226-0380

Shopping

▶ **La Casa del Pueblo**
1810 S. Blue Island Ave.
421-4640

▶ **Librería Girón**
1335 W. 18th St.
829-2697

▶ **Laredo Bakery**
1540 W. 18th St.
733-9293

Marxist-Leninist Books
1631 W. 18th St.
243-5302

▶ **La Mexicana Bakery**
1339 W. 18th St.
666-3395

▶ **Nuevo León Bakery**
1634 W. 18th St.
243-5977

▶ **Zemsky Brothers Department Store**
1700 W. 18th St.
226-6230

Restaurants

▶ **Chicago's Original Bishop's Famous Chili**
1958 W. 18th St.
829-6345

▶ **Cuernavaca Restaurant**
1160 W. 18th St.
829-1147

▶ **Nuevo León Restaurant**
1515 W. 18th St.
421-1517

▶ **Ostionería Playa Azul**
1514 W. 18th St.
421-2552

▶ **Sabinas Restaurant**
2022 S. Ashland Ave.
829-9256

Chinatown

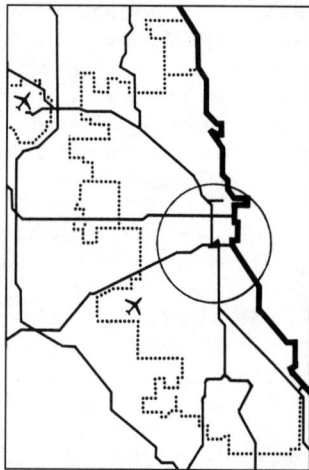

THE CITY'S FIRST CHINATOWN was centered at Clark and Van Buren streets shortly before World War One. Then the On Leong tong, one of the two fraternal organizations in the area, created a settlement at Cermak Road and Wentworth Avenue in a complicated series of real estate deals. While this association is responsible for the fanciful chinoiserie of the On Leong Merchants Association building on South Wentworth Avenue, its longtime rival, the Hip Sing Association, remained in the South Loop until the Federal Detention Center replaced its building in 1970. The Hip Sing, under the guidance of restaurateur Jimmy Wong, embarked on creating another Chinatown at Broadway and Argyle Street, which has been somewhat slow in catching on, though the area has attracted many Vietnamese residents and businesses.

Although Chinatown's roots stretch back 75 years, the community has remained fairly isolated from the city at large. Assimilation has been difficult for the Chinese, but even those who don't enter the mainstream often leave Chinatown's crowded, deteriorating housing, returning to join their less-fortunate cousins only for shopping and religious festivals. Still, an ever-increasing flow of new arrivals keeps Chinese not just the first language but, in many cases, the only language of a significant portion of the area's population.

The **ornamental gate**, built in 1975 over South Wentworth Avenue at West Cermak Road, is inscribed with quotations from Chiang Kai-shek and Sun Yat-sen, indications of the area's staunchly nationalistic bent.

The Chinese who moved to South Wentworth Avenue joined an Italian community then of 20 years' standing. **St. Therese Chinese Catholic Mission**, an intimate, yellow-brick church with handsome stained-glass windows, was built in 1904 as Madonna Incoronata, and it served an Italian congregation until 1964. Even today, the Italian enclave in Bridgeport reaches as far north as West 24th Street, so Chicago's Chinatown, like New York's and San Francisco's, abuts a Little Italy, yielding a rich cultural mélange.

SHOPPING

The Wentworth Avenue strip is crammed with stores peddling gifts to tourists. Though most are ordinary, a few stand out. The **Chinese Trading Company** is a wholesale noodle company with an attached spacious store cluttered with gifts, including good dishes, vulgar little statues, jardinières, and those fanciful lanterns so popular in Chinese restaurants. Elaborately embroidered silk kimonos are displayed at **Far East Fashions**, which also sells less opulent clothes for kids and adults. The **Oriental Boutique** mixes much of the same with slippers, decorative combs, other accessories, and kung fu supplies.

Chinatown

For a microcosm of the quintessential, old-line Chinatown, spend some time in the pagoda-roofed **On Leong Merchants Association** building's ground-floor shops. **Chinatown Books and Gifts** bursts with cheap jewelry, cookbooks, paper lanterns, and other tourist favorites, as well as a selection of Chinese periodicals.

The stock and the wooden store fixtures at **Sun Chong Lung**, a food store catering to Asians, look as if they haven't changed since the building was erected. For baked goods, check out **Happy Garden Bakery**, which has a full line of cookies and sweets, or **Dong Kee**, where the more limited selection includes excellent fortune cookies and good almond cookies.

At **Woks 'n' Things Oriental Cookware**, you'll find woks in all sizes as well as their accompanying utensils, cookbooks, and basic hardware.

RESTAURANTS

Though Chinatown's shops draw many visitors, the restaurants are really the main attraction. In keeping with the conservative bent of the area, most serve Cantonese food. Nevertheless, several are worthwhile, and Chinatown still remains the city's best source for dim sum.

At **Hong Min**, a no-frills storefront, it hardly matters what you order: Virtually everything is delicious, especially the seafood. Also, try the Chinese eggplant or the deep-fried tofu in a ginger-infused sauce. The outstanding dim sum lunch offers more than three dozen items. Dim sum is also served at **Three Happiness**, a popular spot that tends to be noisy, crowded, and fun.

For Mandarin or Szechwan, try **Mandar-Inn**, one of the more refined restaurants in the area. The menu covers all bases, with several standouts, including plump pot stickers, moist bon bon chicken in a velvety sesame sauce, and a richly flavored moo shu pork. The **Chinese Deli** serves unique won tons, noodles, and seafood specialties to a knowing, mostly Asian crowd in modest surroundings. Another good spot for a bite to eat is **King Wah**.

To satisfy the late-evening munchies, chow down with cops, cabbies, and other night people at **Chinatown Chop Suey**, where egg foo young, chop suey, chow mein, and a few other standards are served until the wee hours.

Chinatown

Interesting Places

▶ **Chinatown Gate**
Wentworth Ave. and Cermak Rd.

▶ **On Leong Merchants Association**
2216 S. Wentworth Ave.
225-5751

▶ **St. Therese Chinese Catholic Mission**
218 W. Alexander Pl.
842-6777

Shopping

▶ **Chinatown Books and Gifts**
2214 S. Wentworth Ave.
326-1761

▶ **Chinese Trading Company**
2263 S. Wentworth Ave.
842-2820

▶ **Dong Kee Chinese Bakery**
2252 S. Wentworth Ave.
225-6340

▶ **Far East Fashions**
2219 S. Wentworth Ave.
326-2076

▶ **Happy Garden Bakery**
2358 S. Wentworth Ave.
225-2730

▶ **Oriental Boutique**
2262 S. Wentworth Ave.
842-3798

▶ **Sun Chong Lung**
2220 S. Wentworth Ave.
225-6050

Ten Ren Tea & Ginseng Company of Chicago
2247 S. Wentworth Ave.
842-1171

▶ **Woks 'n' Things Oriental Cookware**
2234 S. Wentworth Ave.
842-0701

Restaurants

▶ **Chinatown Chop Suey**
207 W. Cermak Rd.
326-2265

▶ **Chinese Deli**
225 W. Cermak Rd.
326-3171

▶ **Hong Min**
221 W. Cermak Rd.
842-5026

▶ **King Wah**
2225 S. Wentworth Ave.
842-1404

▶ **Mandar-Inn**
2249 S. Wentworth Ave.
842-4014

Moon Palace Restaurant
2206 S. Wentworth Ave.
842-2390

▶ **Three Happiness**
2130 S. Wentworth Ave.
791-1228

Bridgeport/Canaryville

MANY CHICAGOANS ENVISION BRIDGEPORT as an almost legendary land where neat, political-poster-festooned bungalows line very, very clean streets, and hardworking Hibernians alternate between their city jobs and Democratic Organization obligations. That Bridgeport isn't entirely mythical. The streets and homes are tidy, most residents are Democrats, and for 46 years one Chicago mayor or another did live in Bridgeport. But the myth, like all myths, is misleading. It obscures a rich, 100-year, multiethnic history that has made Bridgeport and adjoining Canaryville quintessential Chicago working-class neighborhoods.

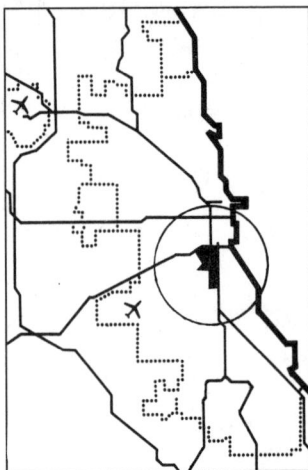

Lithuanians, Germans, Italians, and Poles have long outnumbered the Irish here. Many are second- and third-generation Bridgeporters. They work all over, but often live their entire lives in the community, maintaining strong church and family ties.

Bridgeport began as Hardscrabble (named after the first resident's farm), a shantytown for workers on the Illinois and Michigan Canal in the 1830s and '40s. Completion of the canal in 1848 brought new industries, notably meat slaughtering and packing. Following the 1865 consolidation of South Side slaughterhouses into the Union Stock Yards, successive waves of Eastern European immigrants poured in. Each group clustered in a small section and built a church and school where classes and services were held in its own language. Seen from the Stevenson Expressway, Bridgeport looks old-world, with dozens of spires towering above low houses.

While **Holy Cross Lutheran Church**, which still has services in German, is a smallish, single-steeple, German-style building, **All Saints St. Anthony Padua Church** is much grander. In 1913, construction was underwritten by the Western Indiana Railroad, which had expanded its yards onto the congregation's church property at 24th and Canal streets. With all the bills paid, the parish adorned the building with mosaics and stained glass imported from Munich.

Equally impressive, especially for its beautifully painted interior, magnificent dome, towers, and stained-glass windows, **St. Mary of Perpetual Help Church** was opened in 1889 as an offshoot of St. Adalbert's in Pilsen, the South Side's first Polish parish. The octagonal **St. Barbara Church** was built two decades later to handle the overflow of an expanding Polish population. It rests on a floating base, which protected it from blasting at a nearby quarry.

Chicago's first Lithuanian church, **St. George**, was built in 1886 and is a handsome Gothic structure with a stonework bas-relief over the entrance showing St. George slaying the dragon.

Other churches of note in the area include **St. Gabriel**, built by the Irish in Canaryville, and **Nativity of Our Lord**, duh Mayor's old church.

Between 1890 and 1933, the stockyards processed about 13 million animals a year, but marketing and technological advances, as well as the increased use of trucks rather than of trains, closed them by 1971. Today only a few firms and Burnham and Root's **Union Stock Yards Gate** remain as memorials to the teeming activity immortalized by Carl Sandburg and Upton Sinclair.

Another area tradition is **Comiskey Park**, the nation's oldest major-league ballpark. An athletic field since the 1860s, the land purchased for the park from "Long John" Wentworth's estate just barely fulfilled an agreement with the Cubs that the White Sox should never play north of 35th Street.

Bridgeport/Canaryville

The 35th Street exit from the Dan Ryan Expressway puts you right at the park, and the rest of Bridgeport is only a few blocks west. Just to the east are the **Illinois Institute of Technology** campus, designed by Mies van der Rohe, and **De La Salle Institute**, training ground for generations of local politicians.

SHOPPING AND RESTAURANTS

For blue jeans and khakis of every description, mosey over to the **Pants Shop** on what may be the most interesting block of the neighborhood shopping strip along Halsted Street between 30th and 36th streets. The store claims to have some of the lowest prices in the city and cuffs your purchases free while you wait.

Turn-of-the-century displays in the windows of **Greifenstein's Pharmacy** hint at the wonderful stuff inside: antique oak cabinets, brass fixtures, old ceiling fans, and lots of apothecary jars filled with mysterious medicines. **Henry's Sports and Bait Shop** is open long hours and all night on weekends during the fishing season. The adjoining marine store is open regular business hours.

There are a couple of good bakeries in the area, including **Ace Bakeries**, where kugelis, soft Lithuanian rye bread, cookies, and pies are reasonably priced. Also, **Granata Bakery** offers breads, including an unusual pork-crackling loaf; homemade Italian-beef and sausage sandwiches; and pizza by the slice.

Buy a copy of the *Bridgeport News*, take it to the **Ramova Grill**, and join the locals for a very thin, freshly ground hamburger or bowl of chili in this archetypal greasy spoon.

Walk a few blocks north to Halsted and 32nd streets for a taste of Lithuanian Bridgeport. The **Healthy Food Restaurant** serves breakfasts, sandwiches, and about two dozen Lithuanian and American entrées with Lithuanian side dishes, as well as first-rate breads, blynai (blintzes), koldunai (dumplings), and kugelis (fried potato-pudding slices) in a pleasant, wood-paneled room.

The northeast quadrant of Bridgeport, an Italian bailiwick for generations, is heaven for street-food fans. Inexpensive Italian-beef, sausage, meatball, and breaded-steak sandwiches are joined by poor boys. Lines of double-parked cars in front of **Ricobene's Pizzeria** attest to the popularity of this take-out spot's Italian-beef and terrific breaded-steak sandwiches.

Interesting Places

▶ **All Saints St. Anthony Padua Church**
28th Pl. and Wallace St.
842-2744

▶ **Comiskey Park**
324 W. 35th St.
924-1000

▶ **De La Salle Institute**
3455 S. Wabash Ave.
842-7355

▶ **Holy Cross Lutheran Church**
31st Pl. and Racine Ave.
523-3838

▶ **Illinois Institute of Technology**
3300 S. Federal St.
567-3000

▶ **Nativity of Our Lord Church**
37th St. and Union Ave.
927-6263

▶ **St. Barbara Church**
Throop St. between Archer Ave. and Lyman St.
842-7979

▶ **St. Gabriel Church**
45th St. and Lowe Ave.
268-9595

▶ **St. George Church**
33rd St. and Lituanica Ave.
376-2141

▶ **St. Mary of Perpetual Help Church**
33rd St. between Morgan and Aberdeen streets
927-6646

▶ **Union Stock Yards Gate**
Exchange Ave. and Peoria St.

Restaurants and Shopping

▶ **Ace Bakeries**
3202 S. Halsted St.
225-4973

▶ **Granata Bakery**
3520 S. Halsted St.
847-8306

▶ **Greifenstein's Pharmacy**
3659 S. Union Ave.
847-5656

▶ **Healthy Food Restaurant**
3236 S. Halsted St.
326-2724

▶ **Henry's Sports and Bait Shop**
3130 S. Canal St.
225-4364

La Milanese Pizza
3156 S. May St.
254-9543

▶ **Pants Shop**
3513 S. Halsted St.
247-4364

▶ **Ramova Grill**
3510 S. Halsted St.
847-9058

▶ **Ricobene's Pizzeria**
250 W. 26th St.
225-9811

Back of the Yards

BACK OF THE YARDS is a by-product of the livestock industry, which dominated every aspect of past residents' lives — even the foul air they breathed. It's the neighborhood Upton Sinclair depicted in *The Jungle*, and, though he may have exaggerated some, life was brutal for the Poles, Lithuanians, and Slovaks who followed the Germans and Irish into the area to work in the stockyards. Violence flared during the Knights of Labor's unsuccessful organizing efforts in the packing houses of 1886 and at a 1921 mass meeting in Davis Square Park; martial law was even imposed during the 1894 railroad strikes and the 1919 race riots.

Workers had more than job conditions to protest. Tiny homes and sordid boarding houses were woefully overcrowded. In 1900, ten years after its annexation to Chicago, Back of the Yards had no electric lights and only a few paved streets.

Inadequate water and sewer systems, an open dump along 47th Street, and runoffs from the stockyards resulted in staggering infant-mortality and tuberculosis rates. The situation was so bad that the bureaucrats excluded the neighborhood from a 1901 housing survey to avoid dragging down citywide averages!

Today, though, Back of the Yards is the kind of family neighborhood where any holiday brings window decorations to homes and stores. Now that the Union Stock Yards are gone, Ma-and-Pa groceries, bakeries, and churches nestle quietly on side streets among small, frame houses. On the main shopping streets, SE HABLA ESPAÑOL increasingly replaces MÓWIMY PO POLSKU in shop windows.

Back of the Yards continues to attract recent immigrants, and services in many tongues fill turn-of-the-century churches, though some Eastern European congregations are dwindling. Polish masses are still celebrated at **St. Joseph Church**, which was built in 1913. Inside the ornate Romanesque building are plenty of trompe l'oeil "marble" work and "mosaics," heavily carved confessionals, and impressive statuary; the towers loom large over the surrounding streets. Polish and Spanish masses are also held at **St. John of God Church**, a 1905 graystone, Beaux Arts monolith facing Sherman Park. Behind metal doors enhanced with carved stonework, the Lithuanian **Holy Cross Church**, built the same year as St. Joseph, reveals green-marble Corinthian columns, "rock" grotto shrines, high-relief Stations of the Cross, stained-glass portraits of the saints, and outstanding transept windows.

With **Nativity of the Blessed Virgin Mary Church**, neighborhood Ukrainians and Croatians re-created in miniature the onion-domed churches of their homelands, and the Byzantine rite is still followed in the beautiful, intricately painted church capped by a central dome. **St. Basil's Church**, a big, barrel-vaulted, domed basilica with intricate rose windows and marble trim, was built by an Irish congregation in 1904. Constructed in 1896, the charming, modest, red-brick **St. Martini Lutheran Church** used to have masses in German, but now has them in English only. Spanish and English masses alternate at **Immaculate Heart of Mary Church**, a cleverly remodeled storefront with a California-Spanish, yellow-brick façade.

SHOPPING AND RESTAURANTS

Stores radiate in four directions from **Goldblatt's** at Ashland Avenue and 47th Street. They include branches of almost all the lower-priced clothing and shoe chains and furniture outlets. Two large, local department stores survive; tiny to huge *super-mercados* abound; bridal salons and photographers' studios flourish; and the record shops stock an unusual assortment.

If square dancing is your speed, swing over to **Gibson Music Store**. With more than 100,000 different 45-rpm titles in stock, thousands of LPs, and guitars and other paraphernalia, it may be the nation's largest country-and-Western music store.

As in many of the city's ethnic neighborhoods, exotic foodstuffs beckon from groceries, meat markets, bakeries, and delis. **Central Bakery** prepares an unusually wide selection of Mexican pastries. No display heralds the **Baltic Bakery** retail outlet adjoining the wholesale operation, but this wonderfully disorganized shop is worth a special trip. Besides fresh breads, there are pastries, topnotch pierogi, great Polish sausage straight from the bakery's ovens, sauerkraut, pickles, spices, grains, and even Lithuanian and Polish newspapers. Almost as eclectic, **Bobak's** sells its own sausages made in a nearby factory, as well as pastries from a few North Side bakeries.

The friendly staff makes **Elvia's** one of the neighborhood's more inviting Mexican restaurants. The menu offers conventional tacos, burritos, flautas, and tostadas, as well

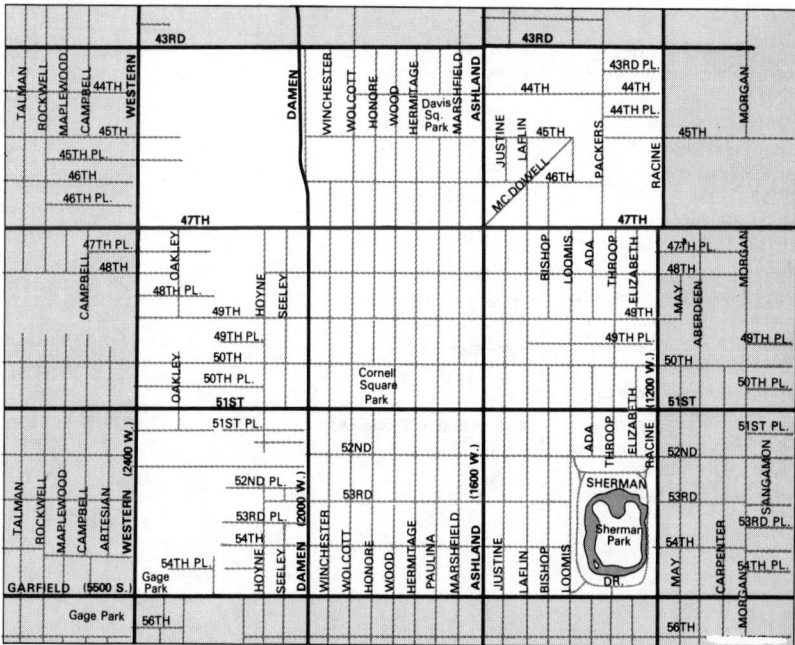

Street map of Back of the Yards. Streets labeled include: 43RD, 43RD PL., 44TH, 44TH PL., 45TH, 45TH PL., 46TH, 46TH PL., 47TH, 47TH PL., 48TH, 48TH PL., 49TH, 49TH PL., 50TH, 50TH PL., 51ST, 51ST PL., 52ND, 52ND PL., 53RD, 54TH, 54TH PL., 55TH (GARFIELD, 5500 S.), 56TH. North-south streets: TALMAN, ROCKWELL, MAPLEWOOD, CAMPBELL, ARTESIAN, WESTERN (2400 W.), OAKLEY, HOYNE, SEELEY, DAMEN (2000 W.), WINCHESTER, WOLCOTT, HONORE, WOOD, HERMITAGE, PAULINA, MARSHFIELD (1600 W.), ASHLAND, JUSTINE, LAFLIN, BISHOP, LOOMIS, ADA, THROOP, ELIZABETH, RACINE (1200 W.), MAY, ABERDEEN, CARPENTER, MORGAN, SANGAMON, PACKERS, MCDOWELL. Parks/landmarks: Davis Sq. Park, Cornell Square Park, Sherman Park (Sherman Dr.), Gage Park.

Back of the Yards

as a few dinners and breakfast plates. There are also other full-menu, modestly priced Mexican spots along Ashland Avenue.

Interesting Places

Berean Memorial Baptist Church
44th and Paulina streets
376-0637

Davis Square Park
4430 S. Marshfield Ave.
927-1983

▶ **Holy Cross Church**
46th St. and Hermitage Ave.
376-3900

▶ **Immaculate Heart of Mary Church**
4545 S. Ashland Ave.
376-3900

▶ **Nativity of the Blessed Virgin Mary Church**
50th and Paulina streets
737-0733

Sacred Heart Church
Wolcott Ave. and Honore St.
523-1041

St. Augustine Church
Laflin St. between 50th and 51st streets
254-4455

▶ **St. Basil's Church**
Garfield Blvd. and Honore St.
925-6311

St. Cyril and St. Methodius Church
50th St. and Hermitage Ave.
778-4044

▶ **St. John of God Church**
52nd and Throop streets
285-6008

▶ **St. Joseph Church**
48th St. and Hermitage Ave.
254-2366

▶ **St. Martini Lutheran Church**
51st St. and Marshfield Ave.
776-7610

Restaurants and Shopping

Archer Tinning & Re-tinning
1019 W. 47th St.
927-7240

▶ **Baltic Bakery**
4627 S. Hermitage Ave.
523-1510

Bobak's
1658 W. 47th St.
847-4845

▶ **Central Bakery**
4523 S. Ashland Ave.
523-0293

▶ **Elvia's**
1738 W. 47th St.
376-4513

▶ **Gibson Music Store**
1956 W. 51st St.
776-0700

▶ **Goldblatt's**
4700 S. Ashland Ave.
247-0773

Martinez Shoes
4604 S. Ashland Ave.
254-8874

Paradise Hall
1758 W. 48th St.
247-6775

South Side Knitting Mills
5036 S. Ashland Ave.
776-7949

Universal Candies
5056 S. Ashland Ave.
778-9580

The Yards Inn
1139 W. 47th St.
254-4882

McKinley Park/Brighton

MCKINLEY PARK AND BRIGHTON are so ordinary, they're special: In the days when Chicago's reputation rested on industrial output, the stockyards, and gangsters, when State Street was unchallenged as "that great street," much of the city was like these two neighborhoods — Eastern European, blue-collar, staid. Somehow, the changes of the last 40 years — for better and for worse — have missed large parts of the Southwest Side, an anomaly that's nowhere more apparent than here, where the slickest stores are fast-food joints along Archer Avenue.

Like so many of the 19th-century villages surrounding Chicago in its infancy, McKinley Park and Brighton owe their growth to fortuitous geographic accidents. Located along the first routes into the city from the southwest, they were natural sites for early development, at least until they were surpassed by areas closer to what became the city's center.

By 1870, former Chicago mayor "Long John" Wentworth had no better use for his portion of the once-flourishing Brighton Park racetrack than to lease it to farmers as a cabbage patch; for three decades, it produced raw material for the sauerkraut industry. The land was eventually incorporated into the Chicago park system and named McKinley Park in honor of the recently assassinated President.

Similarly, the consolidation of the Union Stock Yards in 1865 killed the livestock business at the Brighton Stock Yards just north of the racetrack. Other industries, however, quickly filled the gap: steel mills, brick works, explosives factories, and a cotton mill. These are all gone now, too. The present character of the area was established before World War One by the Central Manufacturing District, Crane Manufacturing Company's giant Corwith Works on Kedzie Avenue, and industrial development along 47th Street.

Naturally, residential growth came with industrial expansion. The Poles and Lithuanians who followed the Irish and German settlers into McKinley Park after the turn of the century built the brick bungalows and two-flats that today line the side streets with rarely relieved monotony. The streetscape is a little more varied in Brighton, though.

One significant exception to the modest scale of these neighborhoods is a mansion built by John Dolese, a contractor whose firm paved the major South Side boulevards. Originally set in formal gardens along Western Avenue, the house was moved in the 1920s to 3558 South Artesian Avenue, where it forlornly sits today. Another antique house sits on Campbell Avenue's dead end, just north of the intersection of Archer Avenue and 38th Street. At the other end of the spectrum, the squalid tenement row houses on the 3500 block of South Honore Street, built in 1866 for industrial workers, were known as Outhouse Alley because of the line of outdoor privies that once stood behind them.

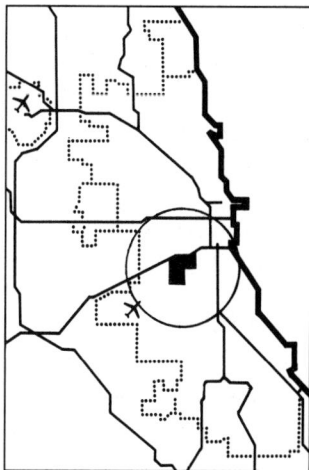

McKinley Park/Brighton

Brighton's most handsome church is **St. Joseph and St. Anne**. Erected by a small local French colony in 1891, it is the National Shrine to St. Anne, a center of French Catholic religious life in this country. Its plain exterior gives little indication of its Gothic interior, done in "French" blue and gilt with a highly ornate apse enlivened by striking paintings, rich stained glass, trompe l'oeil "marble" Corinthian columns, and beautifully executed, surprisingly naturalistic bas-relief Stations of the Cross.

Brighton is the most solidly Polish neighborhood in Chicago, still often called the second largest Polish city.

SHOPPING

Take the area's pulse with a shopping excursion on Archer Avenue, the former cattle route that skewers Brighton and McKinley Park as it slants toward the Loop. **Santo Sport Store** has all the paraphernalia to get your body in shape. Santo does a big business in trophies, custom-drilled bowling balls, and team uniforms.

Nothing goes better with sports than hot dogs. You can get old-fashioned wieners, as well as other sausages, potato dumplings, blintzes, Polish baked beans, and salads,

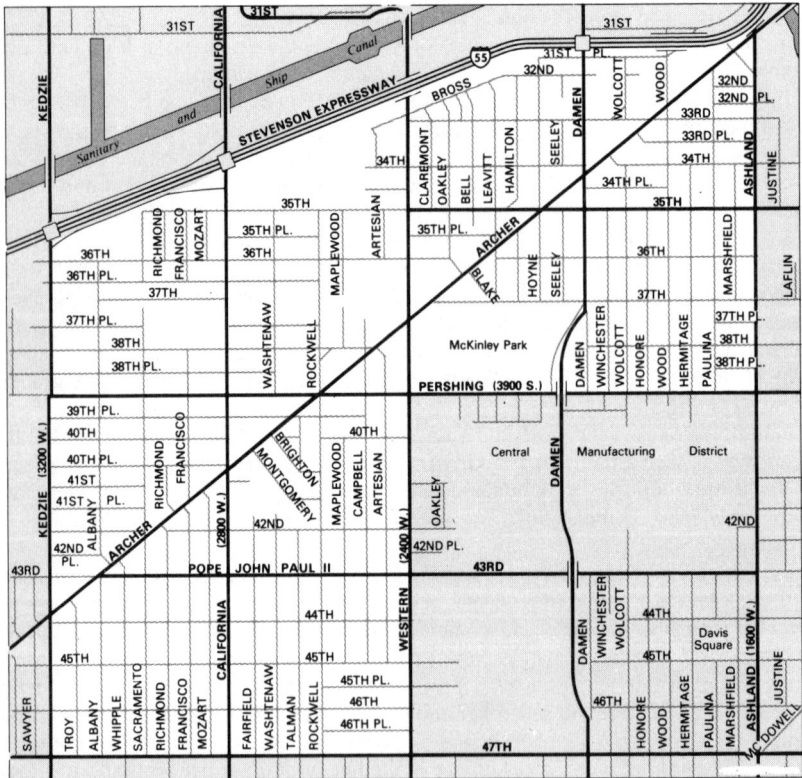

McKinley Park/Brighton

at **Sliz's Delicatessen**, just off Archer Avenue. Sliz's and **Matthew's** are just two of the many Polish sausage shops in the neighborhood. The **Archer Fish Mart**'s fish-shaped business card says, "If it swims we will get it." The store stocks a variety of fresh and smoked fish, and also sells fish and chips to go.

All the usual clothing and shoe stores also dot this strip of Archer, as do fast-food places and auto dealerships.

For everything from a tuna sandwich to dessert, check out **Gertie's Candies**, next to the Brighton Theater. What may well be the city's finest hot-fudge and butterscotch sundae toppings are two of the joys at this 1930s luncheonette cum ice-cream parlor and candy store. Owner Tony Jeropke makes all the ice cream, toppings, and candy.

At **Julia's Restaurant**, the trucks parked outside are a clue to the hearty, inexpensive food served within. The menu changes daily and offers such things as roast pig, pot roast, stuffed cabbage, and homemade sausages, as well as sandwiches.

Interesting Places

Five Holy Martyrs Church
Pope John Paul II Dr. and Richmond St.
254-3636

Immaculate Conception Church
44th St. and California Ave.
523-1402

International Polka Association Polka Music Hall of Fame and Museum
4145 S. Kedzie Ave.
254-7771

► **McKinley Park**
Pershing Rd. and Western Ave.
523-3811

St. Agnes Church
Pershing Rd. and Washtenaw Ave.
247-5356

St. Andrew's Lutheran Church
37th and Honore streets
523-0130

► **St. Joseph and St. Anne Church**
38th Pl. and California Ave.
927-2421

Sts. Peter and Paul Church
38th and Paulina streets
523-3410

Restaurants and Shopping

► **Archer Fish Market**
4311 S. Archer Ave.
523-3429

Avalon Galleries
4243 S. Archer Ave.
247-6969

Brighton Park Arts and Hobby Centre
4238 S. Archer Ave.
523-3334

Crafts by Claudia
4300 S. Archer Ave.
247-4387

Hal's Bakery
2025 W. 35th St.
847-2121

Kozy's Cyclery
1610 W. 35th St.
523-8576

► **Matthew's Supreme Homemade Sausage**
4328 S. Archer Ave.
523-2809

► **Santo Sport Store**
4270 S. Archer Ave.
927-1125

► **Sliz's Delicatessen**
3116 W. 43rd St.
523-9533

Tropicana Living Things
3879 S. Archer Ave.
254-2131

Biolo Izba — Polish food
4808 S. Archer Ave.
523-7632

► **Gertie's Candies**
4231 S. Archer Ave.
247-3060

► **Julia's Restaurant**
4440 S. Western Ave.
523-4922

Lindy's Chili
3685 S. Archer Ave.
927-7807

Gage Park/Marquette Park

GAGE PARK AND MARQUETTE PARK were the last of the pre-World War Two neighborhoods to grow organically from the stockyards. They have few institutions to attract outsiders' attention. Instead, lurid newspaper accounts of racial confrontations set the pattern for the area's reputation. While integration was far from smooth at Gage Park High School and the ravings of a few nuts in Nazi regalia may articulate widely-held fears, these communities behind Western Avenue's Maginot Line of car lots have an evocative texture apart from their occasional notoriety.

First settled by German farmers in the 1840s, Gage Park experienced a speculative real-estate boom in the 1870s in anticipation of a railroad along Central Park Avenue and the South Park Commission's land purchases for its boulevard and park system. Development didn't take off, however, until the 20th century. During the first three decades, the Kenwood Manufacturing District opened; industries spread along Western Avenue; German, Irish, Polish, Czech, and Balkan workers, escaping the congestion of the stockyards communities and attracted by new factories, moved in.

The neighborhood's ethnic diversity is unusual for the older Southwest Side. While each ethnic group had its own church in nearby communities, **St. Gall**, Gage Park's oldest parish, has always served a multilingual congregation. It has been in its present location since 1916. Volunteers helped build what is known as the crypt church: Foundations for a large structure were laid, then covered with a low roof as a temporary expedient until a traditional soaring church could be raised. Temporary can be a long time. Not until 1958 was the present structure built, and it's quite different from what was originally planned. It's worth a look, particularly the bronze Stations of the Cross. Across the street is another institution central to Gage Park, the home office of **Talman Home Federal**, Illinois's largest savings and loan association.

The neighborhood of Marquette Park appears, at first glance, to be an extension of Gage Park. But a solidly Lithuanian enclave surrounding both the park proper and the 63rd Street-Kedzie Avenue area is quite different.

John E. Eberhart subdivided the area in 1873. (Eberhart is said to have introduced Stephen Douglas to Abraham Lincoln.) He built his house at **3415 West 64th Street**, where it stands today — the oldest for miles around. More houses from the pioneer area are nearby, mixed in with brick bungalows and small apartment buildings.

Chicago's Lithuanian population is America's largest concentration. South of Marquette Road, Lithuanians moving from Bridgeport, Back of the Yards, and Brighton early in the century formed a tight little village now served by a neighborhood of Lithuanian institutions. One of the most important includes the **Sisters of St. Casimir Mother House**, which was built in 1911 and maintains a Lithuanian

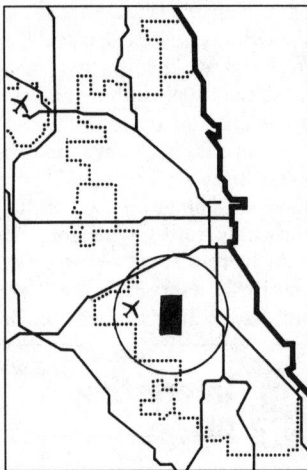

museum. A striking Lithuanian baroque structure recalling Old World churches, **Nativity of the Blessed Virgin Mary** incorporates both Christian and pagan themes in the dramatic bell towers and detailing. Exterior mosaic materials by noted Lithuanian artist Adomas Varnas depict scenes from Lithuanian history, while the murals and centuries-old artifacts inside are also inspired by a combination of religious, military, and pagan themes.

Dominating an entire block, **St. Rita** is a huge Byzantine church with massive transepts. It is completely marble-lined, has a sweeping, barrel-vaulted nave, and boasts fine stained glass.

Another interesting site is the **Darius Girenas Monument**, which was erected in 1935 to honor two flyers who were killed on a goodwill trip to Lithuania.

SHOPPING

With the busy shopping strips on Archer Avenue in Brighton to the north and on West 63rd Street in Marquette Park to the south, Gage Park itself never developed a major commercial center, but a few inviting shops are scattered through the neighborhood. Perhaps the best known is **Gertie's Own Ice Cream**, an old-fashioned, wood-paneled, corner shop. Started in 1901, the city's oldest ice-cream parlor serves good, homemade, 14-percent-butterfat ice cream in sodas and sundaes.

Of several bakeries in Gage Park, **Kolatek's** may be the most popular. This cheerful, friendly shop sells Polish, Bohemian, Hungarian, French, and Danish pastries, as well as cakes and breads.

Baltic Blossoms is a florist, but also a gallery for limited-edition woodblocks by East Coast artist Vytautas Ignas, an old friend of the store's employees. **Talman Grocery and Deli** stocks ingredients for Lithuanian cuisine and sells wonderful ready-to-eat food. The little corner shop is crammed with sausages; fresh sour cream guaranteed not to curdle in hot soup; salads; meats in aspics; whole roast duck; and prune-stuffed duck rolls.

The 63rd Street shopping strip may be the South Side's most inviting. A broad, bustling business area, it offers the usual panoply of neighborhood shops as well as the unexpected.

Marquette Park's Teutons (and others) keep **Hoeffken's Bakery** hopping. The sign says THE BUSY BAKERY, and no billing was ever truer. As many as six people work the counters of this community institution. Standard sweet rolls are nothing special, but the pound cake is terrific, and the German and Eastern European pastries are quite good, as are the breads. Near Eastern goodies can be found at **Eastern Bakery and Grocery**, a much smaller operation.

Driftstone Wedding Cake-A-Rama offers only made-to-order nuptial creations. Neither time nor changing fashion can induce Sy and Ben Kopersmith to vary their mother's 50-year-old recipe. Samples are available during the wedding season.

You might get the ice cream to go with your cake at **Cupid Candies**. Cupid's counter and window displays are wonderfully tempting, and the store looks like a 1940s movie set. Although the candy for this small chain is made in a large factory farther south on Western Avenue, all the ice cream is produced in the rear of the shop. Virtually the equal of Gertie's, for some reason it's not as popular or as crowded.

What can even be said about **Dove Candies and Ice Cream** that hasn't been heard before? Any night of the week is a good time to stop in for what may be the city's largest sundaes and sodas. Owner Mike Stefanos is a CPA, but portions show no signs of cost control. The 1950s place is a find: Whipped cream is the real stuff, mint meltaways rival the best, and the sublime ice-cream bars put Good Humor to shame.

Marzano's Miami Bowl has 80 lanes and is open 24 hours a day, 365 days a year. If your interests are a little more staid, check out **Chicago Law Book Company**,

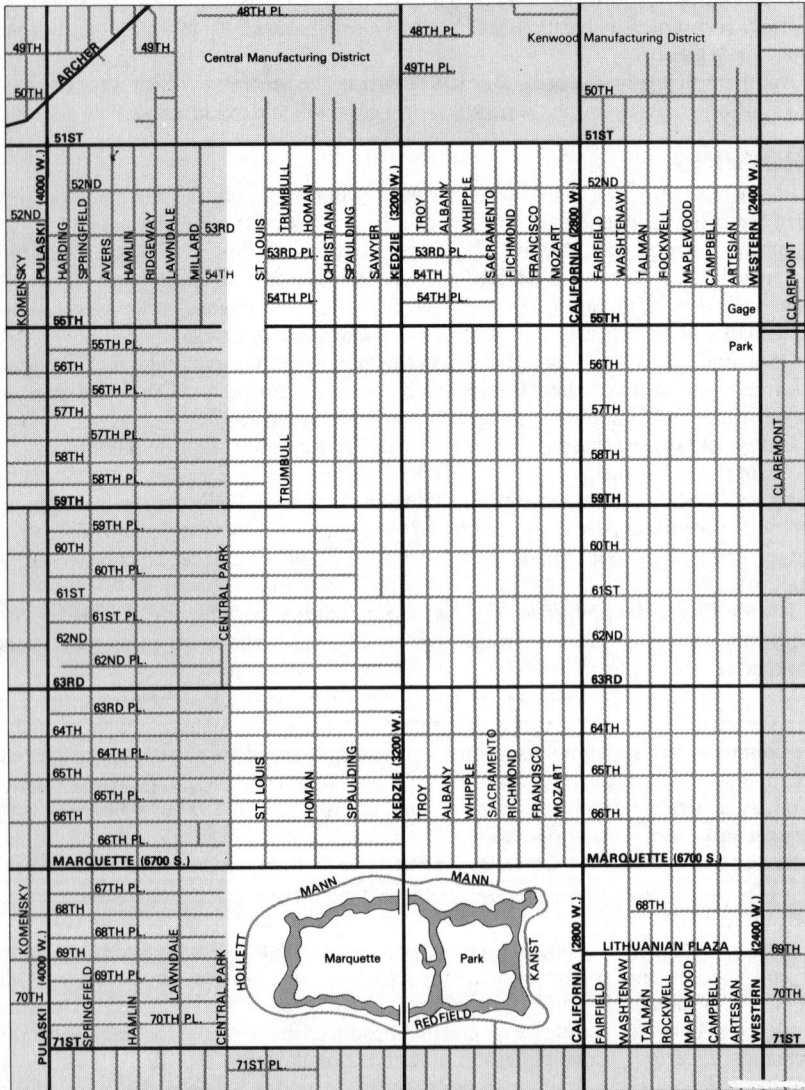

Map of Gage Park/Marquette Park area showing streets from 48TH PL. to 71ST PL., including Central Manufacturing District, Kenwood Manufacturing District, Central Park, Gage Park, Marquette Park, and Lithuanian Plaza. North-south streets include Komensky, Pulaski (4000 W.), Harding, Springfield, Avers, Hamlin, Ridgeway, Lawndale, Millard, St. Louis, Trumbull, Homan, Christiana, Spaulding, Sawyer, Kedzie (3200 W.), Troy, Albany, Whipple, Sacramento, Richmond, Francisco, Mozart, California (2800 W.), Fairfield, Washtenaw, Talman, Rockwell, Maplewood, Campbell, Artesian, Western (2400 W.), Claremont. Archer Avenue runs diagonally. Marquette (6700 S.) runs east-west. Mann, Hollett, Kanst, and Redfield border the park lagoons.

which specializes in books for lawyers, police officers, paralegals, and law students. **Trost Hobby Shop** stocks everything for the armchair athlete. Model trains are big here (repairs, too), as are slot cars and plastic scale models. **Something From Knotting** is devoted to — naturally — macramé supplies. At **Gowdy Leather Works**, Vida and Tom Marshall will teach you leather crafting or sell you finished, hand-tooled purses, belts, wallets, photo album covers, and more, as well as commercially manufactured deerskin accessories.

There's a strip of Pulaski Road that isn't really in Gage Park or Marquette Park but is worth exploring. **Izzy Rizzy's House of Tricks** is probably the largest store of its kind in Chicago, with loads of magic tricks, gag items, and more. **Irish Treasures and Imports** stocks a nice selection of goods from the Emerald Isle, including men's wool caps and hats and fisherman's-knit sweaters, as well as kitsch bumper stickers, pottery, jewelry, china, and crystal.

RESTAURANTS

Many Gage Park restaurants cater to factory workers, are closed by dinner, and have little to offer visitors. There are a few Polish restaurants that are exceptions, though. While **Polonia Inn** serves old favorites in comfortable surroundings at reasonable prices, at **Olympic Inn**, an all-you-can-eat place, you can taste them all in one sitting. It offers good salads, stuffed cabbage, pierogi, sauerkraut-and-meat casseroles, sliced-to-order baked ham and roast beef, and daily specials such as roast duck. The **Europejska Lounge** serves Polish dinners and à la carte specialties in a huge banquet-hall-like room. Unlike many of the area's ethnic restaurants, it has a liquor license and stays open late.

Nearby Lithuanian restaurants differ subtly from the Polish establishments. Besides rye, the breadbaskets offer eggy, raisin-studded bread; soup choices often include lightly spiced sauerkraut, which is served with boiled potato on the side. Entrées range from familiar roast duck, pork, and chicken, to dumplings and potato pancakes, to lighter selections such as fruit-filled pancakes.

At **Nida Delicatessen and Restaurant**, stuffed cabbage, dumplings, and excellent filled pancakes are always on the menu in the cozy, seven-table dining room. **Neringa Restaurant** may well be the area's largest and busiest. The quality and bounty of the food easily explain the restaurant's popularity. The potato pancakes are a crisp delight.

Tulpé is a tiny, eight-table place, where an entrée, dessert, and beverage will cost less than five dollars. Try the coleslaw or soup, or any of the 16 daily posted selections. Roasted meats are generally moist and flavorful, and they typically arrive with boiled potato, delicious sauerkraut, and vegetables.

Since winning *Chicago* magazine's pizza taster's plaudits, **Giordano's** has come into its own. This local institution deep-dishes up terrific double-crusted 'zas in a slick subterranean area of a strikingly renovated vintage building. Outlets have sprouted up all over, but devotees swear that the original is still the most satisfying.

Gage Park/Marquette Park

🏛 Interesting Places

▶ **Darius Girenas Monument**
*California Ave. and
Marquette Rd.*

▶ **John E. Eberhart House**
3415 W. 64th St.

▶ **Nativity of the Blessed
Virgin Mary Church**
*Lithuanian Plaza Ct.
and Washtenaw Ave.*
776-4600

▶ **St. Gall's Church**
55th St. and Kedzie Ave.
737-3113

▶ **St. Rita Church**
63rd St. and Fairfield Ave.
434-9600

▶ **Sisters of St. Casimir
Mother House**
2601 W. Marquette Rd.
776-1324

▶ **Talman Home Federal
Savings and Loan
Association**
5501 S. Kedzie Ave.
434-3322

🏷 Shopping

▶ **Baltic Blossoms**
2451 W. Lithuanian Plaza Ct.
434-2036

▶ **Chicago Law Book
Company**
4814 S. Pulaski Rd.
376-1711

▶ **Cupid Candies**
7637 S. Western Ave.
925-8193

▶ **Dove Candies and
Ice Cream**
6000 S. Pulaski Rd.
582-3119

▶ **Driftstone Wedding
Cake-A-Rama**
3135 W. 63rd St.
737-3331

▶ **Eastern Bakery and
Grocery**
2943 W. 63rd St.
476-2814

▶ **Gertie's Own Ice Cream**
5858 S. Kedzie Ave.
737-7634

▶ **Gowdy Leather Works**
2849 W. 63rd St.
434-4822

▶ **Hoeffken's Bakery**
3044 W. 63rd St.
737-0390

▶ **Irish Treasures and
Imports**
5536 S. Pulaski Rd.
581-5911

▶ **Izzy Rizzy's House of
Tricks**
6034 S. Pulaski Rd.
735-7370

▶ **Kolatek's Bakery**
5405 S. Kedzie Ave.
737-2113

▶ **Marzano's Miami Bowl**
5023 S. Archer Ave.
585-8787

▶ **Something from Knotting**
6405 S. Kedzie Ave.
778-0661

▶ **Talman Grocery and Deli**
2624 W. Lithuanian Plaza Ct.
434-9766

▶ **Trost Hobby Shop**
3111 W. 63rd St.
925-1000

✕ Restaurants

▶ **Europejska Lounge**
2524 W. 51st St.
476-3037

▶ **Giordano's**
3214 W. 63rd St.
436-2969

▶ **Neringa Restaurant**
2632 W. 71st St.
476-9026

▶ **Nida Delicatessen
and Restaurant**
2617 W. 71st St.
476-7675

▶ **Olympic Inn**
5111 S. Kedzie Ave.
776-0795

▶ **Polonia Inn**
2735 W. 55th St.
737-3044

▶ **Tulpé**
2447 W. Lithuanian Plaza Ct.
925-1123

Hyde Park/Kenwood

LIVE AMONG GIANTS" was the lure of the locally celebrated ad trumpeting Hyde Park housing. It conjured up intellectual colossi like Enrico Fermi, Saul Bellow, and 40 other Nobel laureates who have made this neighborhood their home. The massive, steel-strapped oak door pictured in the ad also evoked Hyde Park's formidable stock of institutions: the University of Chicago, half a dozen theological and professional schools, the Museum of Science and Industry, the Oriental Institute, the David and Alfred Smart Gallery, the DuSable Museum of African American History, and the Morton B. Weiss Museum of Judaica.

But contrary to popular misconceptions, Hyde Park isn't merely an academic fortress surrounded by slums. Hyde Park is Chicago's most successfully integrated community, and an increasingly affluent one at that. The only independent ward during the Daley years, it maintains a reputation for political activism.

The pastoral, middle-class, residential suburb Paul Cornell envisioned when he bought 300 acres of South Side lakefront land in 1853 so flourished that, 36 years later, when Hyde Park was annexed to Chicago, it was called the Evanston of the South Side. The predominance of large, older homes and the presence of major universities in both communities make the sobriquet equally apt today.

Founded in 1892 by John D. Rockefeller as a Baptist bastion, the **University of Chicago** is well worth seeing. The first building on campus, **Cobb Hall**, opened two weeks before the adjacent World's Columbian Exposition in 1893 and, like the other Gothic or Tudor halls, illustrates the school planners' desire to imitate the great English universities. While **Hitchcock Hall** combines neo-Gothic architecture with indigenous "prairie" detailing, the **Mandel Hall-Mitchell Tower-Reynolds Club** complex demonstrates real Anglomania. The exterior was modeled on the Great Hall of Crosby Place; the tower was copied from Magdalen College; and Hutchinson Commons, the wood-paneled dining hall, is a Christ Church Commons replica.

Carved bosses, vibrant stained-glass windows, dark woodwork, and a copper strip bearing Biblical quotations — in a gothic face so ornate that deciphering it often distracts frequenters of medieval-music concerts — decorate tiny **Bond Chapel**, hidden inside the quadrangle behind the Divinity School's Swift Hall. **Rockefeller Memorial Chapel** hosts free concerts during the school year on one of the country's finest concert organs. The chapel also maintains a choir and orchestra that give several annual concerts. Elaborate woodwork carved *in situ*, vaulted ceilings, and Norman Laliberte's liturgical banners created for the Vatican Pavilion at the 1965 World's Fair adorn the interior.

Traditional and modern sculptures dot the campus. Henry Moore's *Nuclear Energy*, on the old Stagg Field site next to Regenstein Library, marks the site of humanity's first controlled, self-sustaining chain reaction, while Ruth Duckworth's ceramic mural,

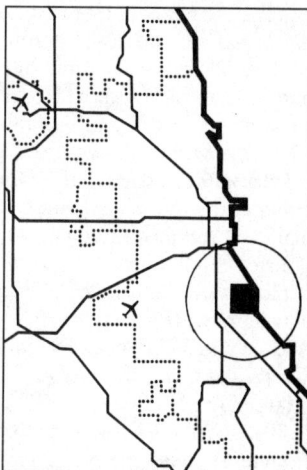

Hyde Park/Kenwood

Earth, Water, and Sky, enlivens the lobby of the striking Geophysical Sciences Building. A statue of celebrated Swedish botanist Carl von Linné (Carolus Linnaeus), holding one of the books he wrote and a flower he discovered and named, graces the Midway Plaisance just south of Harper Library. The Tomáš Masaryk Monument, a tribute to Czechoslavakia's first president, who once taught at the university, stands at the Midway's east end, and Lorado Taft's famous *Fountain of Time* is on the west end where the Midway flows into Washington Park.

Midway Studios, Taft's workplace and home until his death in 1936 and now the home of the university's fine-arts department, is one of four National Historic Landmarks on campus. Another is Frank Lloyd Wright's 1909 **Robie House**, the ultimate Prairie-school statement.

Homes on the residential streets to the north and east of the campus represent an unusually wide variety of styles from pre-Fire Italianate villas (5630 South Kimbark Avenue and 5714 South Dorchester Avenue) to urban-renewal town houses by Harry Weese, I. M. Pei, and others. Pullman architect Solon Beman designed Rosalie Villas (Harper Avenue between 57th and 59th streets) as a planned community in the mid-1880s, and the Victorian and Queen Anne houses form an evocative streetscape free from modern intrusions. The list of architects who designed homes on University Avenue reads like a *Who's Who* of American architecture: Henry Ives Cobb (5855), Hugh Garden (5735), Arthur Maher (5629), Howard Van Doren Shaw (5533), Borst & Hetherington (5327). Those on Woodlawn Avenue complete the picture: Rapp & Rapp (5725), Dwight Perkins (5711), Holabird & Roche (5637), Tallmadge and Watson (5605-9), J. M. Van Osdel (5548), Pond & Pond (5533), W. F. Shattuck (5127), and, of course, Wright's Robie House (5757) and the 1897 Heller House (5137).

Many of these architects were also designing revival Elizabethan, Romanesque, Georgian, and Colonial residences in adjoining **Kenwood**, which became the choice of Chicago's elite after Prairie Avenue fell from grace. Woodlawn, Greenwood, and Ellis avenues, between East Hyde Park Boulevard and 47th Street, boast one of the city's highest concentrations of grand mansions uninterrupted by high-rises or commercial development. Meat packers T. E. Wilson and Gustavus Swift; lumber merchants Martin Ryerson and William Goodman, benefactors of the Art Institute and the Goodman Theater; Sears, Roebuck executive Julius Rosenwald; and Marshall Field's president John Shedd, who endowed the Museum of Science and Industry and the aquarium, all moved to Kenwood within ten years of 1900. They spared no expense, and the houses, set on huge lots, are palatially equipped with ballrooms, coach houses, greenhouses, and more.

Both Hyde Park and Kenwood are on the National Register of Historic Places, and the latter has been designated a Chicago Landmark District.

If you've a taste for monumental architecture, tour Hyde Park's churches. Ten of them form a compact group centered on 57th Street and Woodlawn Avenue. Aside from Rockefeller and Bond chapels, don't miss the **First Unitarian Church**, with its grand nave and wood-paneled chapel, and **St. Thomas the Apostle Church**, a neo-Moorish building designed in 1922 by Barry Byrne. The Victorian graystone **United Church of Hyde Park** offers a fan-shaped sanctuary with a striking dome and outstanding stained-glass windows. The home of the Midwest's oldest Jewish congregation, **K.A.M. Isaiah Israel**, is an official city landmark. Alfred A. Alschuler designed the Byzantine-tile-and-stone building in 1924 with recently excavated Mesopotamian temples in mind.

The pioneer Hyde Park-Kenwood urban renewal plan of the mid-1950s changed the neighborhood substantially. Not only were scores of "deteriorating" homes demolished to be replaced by town houses, and the streets turned into a maze of one-ways to reduce traffic flow, but the major commercial strips — Lake Park Avenue and 55th Street — were almost totally dismantled. An additional casualty was the 57th Street "artists' colony." This collection of clapboard shacks left over from the World's Columbian Exposition was a hangout for Theodore Dreiser, Edgar Lee Masters, Carl Sandburg, Sherwood Anderson, and other greats early in the century. In 1965, a few of the colony tenants moved into **Harper Court**, a unique urban-renewal complex built to house artists' workshops, with rent subsidized by adjoining conventional stores.

SHOPPING

Numerous excellent bookstores share the 57th Street strip between Kimbark and Harper avenues with an unimpressive selection of groceries, cleaners, and restaurants. Browsing at **Powell's** can easily occupy several days. Perhaps the largest used-book store in the city, it's bursting with shelves of literary criticism, foreign language, ancient history, modern poetry, drama, fiction, scholarly works, and children's books; thousands of paperbacks; bargain-table clearances; stacks on the floor; and occasionally even boxes of freebies outside. **O'Gara and Wilson** also has an extensive, excellent selection of used hardbacks and paperbacks, especially in history, the arts, philosophy,

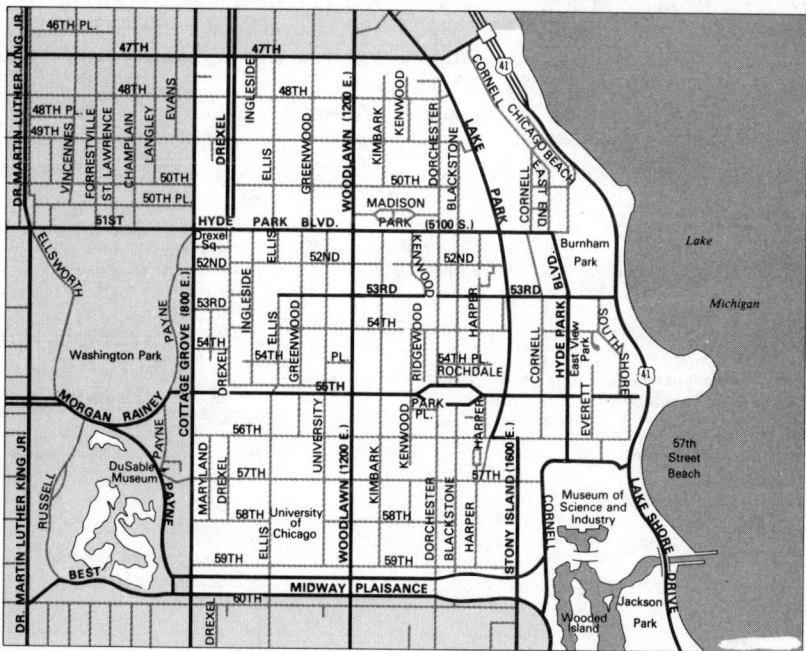

Hyde Park/Kenwood

and theology. Well-lit and orderly, the store looks like a movie version of a secondhand-book shop.

For new books, try **Harper Court Bookstore**, **Scholar's Bookstore**, **57th Street Books**, **Seminary Co-op Books**, and the **University of Chicago Bookstore**.

Supplies for all sorts of arts from painting and calligraphy to wood working and framing are available at **Art Directions**. If your creativity tends more toward the edible, try **Freeling Pot and Pan**, a well-stocked kitchenware store with everything from appliances to tiny gadgets. There are lots of quality pots and pans, too. And if cooking and eating really are your hobby, then exercise and sports are a good idea. At **Harper Court Sports** you'll find all the clothes and shoes you'll need, as well as custom-strung racquets.

The kids will love **Toys Et Cetera**, where their whims can be indulged (at their parents' expense) with what seems like almost any toy known. There are also kites, plastic-model kits, and role-playing and fantasy games.

Plants Alive is crammed full of lush greenery. Even the weeds outside look cared for! Also crammed full of items is the **Sewing Circle**, where the prices for fabrics are more reasonable and the stock is broader than one might expect.

RESTAURANTS

The Green Door Bookstore used to be in front of the **Medici Gallery and Coffeehouse** but, years ago, the Medici expanded to specialize in pan pizza. The restaurant also serves excellent hamburgers and a variety of hot coffee drinks. Art on the walls and some of the old coffeehouse atmosphere remain, making it a popular local hangout. A branch of **Edwardo's** down the block, a whitewash-and-planty sort of place, serves good deep-dish pizza and stuffed pizza.

At the least expensive end of the spectrum, **Valois**, a cafeteria, has been dishing up hearty, just-like-Mom-used-to-make, all-American grub at rock-bottom prices for about 65 years. Cops and cabbies eat here; the Hopperesque place looks grubbier than it really is; and the motto is "See Your Food."

Interesting Places

▶ **First Unitarian Church**
5650 S. Woodlawn Ave.
324-4100

▶ **K.A.M. Isaiah Israel Congregation**
1100 E. Hyde Park Blvd.
924-1234

▶ **Midway Studios**
6016 S. Ingleside Ave.

▶ **Robie House**
5757 S. Woodlawn Ave.
702-8374

▶ **St. Thomas the Apostle Church**
55th St. and Kimbark Ave.
324-2626

▶ **United Church of Hyde Park**
1448 E. 53rd St.
363-1620

▶ **University of Chicago Administration Building**
5801 S. Ellis Ave.
702-1234

Shopping

▶ **Art Directions**
5211 S. Harper Ave.
493-6158

▶ **Freeling Pot and Pan**
1365 E. 53rd St.
643-8080

▶ **57th Street Books**
1301 E. 57th St.
684-1300

▶ **Harper Court Bookstore**
5211 S. Harper Ave.
947-0165

▶ **Harper Court Sports**
5225 S. Harper Ave.
363-3748

▶ **O'Gara and Wilson**
1311 E. 57th St.
363-0993

▶ **Plants Alive**
5210 S. Harper Ave.
667-2036

▶ **Powell's Book Store**
1501 E. 57th St.
955-7780

▶ **Scholar's Bookstore**
1379 E. 53rd St.
288-6565

▶ **Seminary Co-op Books**
5757 S. University Ave.
752-1959

▶ **Sewing Circle**
5225 S. Harper Ave.
363-5237

▶ **Toys Et Cetera**
5206 S. Harper Ave.
643-4777

▶ **University of Chicago Bookstore**
970 E. 58th St.
702-8729

✕ Restaurants

▶ **Edwardo's**
1321 E. 57th St.
241-7960

▶ **Medici**
1450 E. 57th St.
667-7394

▶ **Valois**
1518 E. 53rd St.
667-0647

South Shore

I N SOUTH SHORE'S HEYDAY, when the South Shore Country Club was the private playground of the privileged, the future seemed to hold unending prosperity. No one could foretell the ravages that racial change and white flight would bring. Enviably situated along the lakefront and served by rapid transportation to the Loop, the neighborhood developed strong community organizations and a healthy commercial base. By 1930, it had experienced three decades of astonishing growth. Not even the Depression dampened local boosters' spirits. While Chicago's population doubled between 1900 and 1940, South Shore's increased eightfold to 80,000.

South Shore's early development paralleled much of Chicago's. The Illinois Central Railroad station at 71st Street and Jeffery Boulevard was opened in 1881 to accommodate the hamlet of Bryn Mawr's 30-odd homes. A few years later, pioneer developer Frank Bennett bought the Ferdinand Rohn farm and built the first subdivision, which he called South Kenwood. Many of the houses still stand on Euclid Avenue between 71st and 73rd streets. At the turn of the century, most of South Shore was still rural. The Windsor Park Country Club occupied an 80-acre tract from Colfax to Yates avenues between 75th and 79th streets, the amusement pier brought day-trippers to the beach at 75th Street, and East 79th Street remained farmland.

By 1930, however, South Shore was one of the South Side's most desirable upper-middle-class communities. Although the population was cosmopolitan, a countrywide mania for things Tudor dictated subdivision names like Chatham Field, Avalon Highlands, and Cheltenham — originally called Hoboken! Many of the homes were English-style cottages. The grandest legacies of the feverish construction activity are the **Jackson Park Highlands** and the lakefront high-rises (the one at 7321 South South Shore Drive, designed by De Goyler, is the city's only residential tower on the National Register of Historic Places).

The Highlands are an ironically named plot between Jeffery Boulevard and Stony Island Avenue overlooking Jackson Park. They were a low-lying marsh until early in the century. The first residents were a diverse lot, ranging from successful business owners to acclaimed artists. In a studio behind the house at **7209 South Euclid Avenue**, Edward Kemeys sculpted the lions that guard the Art Institute's portals. Today, the same sorts of people live in these large, elegant homes lining Euclid, Constance, and Bennett avenues, between 67th and 71st streets. Though built a bit later and on smaller lots, many of the houses rival Kenwood's and are South Shore's most valued properties.

Four local institutions testify to South Shore's meteoric rise, even more rapid decline, and present arduous stabilization. The **South Shore Country Club**, organized in 1906 by Prairie Avenue resident Lawrence Huyworth, quickly became the center of activity for South Shore's, if not the South Side's, social set. The main structure of its

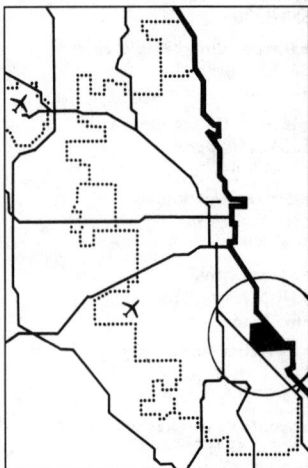

handsome neo-Spanish, stucco-covered complex, designed by Marshall and Fox, dates from 1916. Suffering from declining membership throughout the 1960s, the club folded in 1974. Now everyone can play the links and wander in awe through the clubhouse, although the opulent furnishings were auctioned off before the property was purchased by the Chicago Park District. The renovated gates may look forbidding, but drive on in — it's all ours.

The **Bryn Mawr Community Church** attracted many of the same local luminaries as the country club. The first church building, patterned after a northern Italian Protestant one, was built in 1916. For the next decade Bryn Mawr was South Shore's nondenominational Protestant church, attracting a very affluent congregation, including the chairman of the board of Standard Oil and many Illinois Central executives. In 1926, the original building was moved to the back of the lot and the present, beautiful English Gothic church was erected.

The **Church of St. Philip Neri** was completed in 1926 to open for the International Eucharistic Congress held in Chicago that year. The magnificent structure, styled after the grand English cathedrals, can seat more than 1,500. The Stations of the Cross are exquisite mosaics executed in Rome by P. Dachiardi in 1920; the stained-

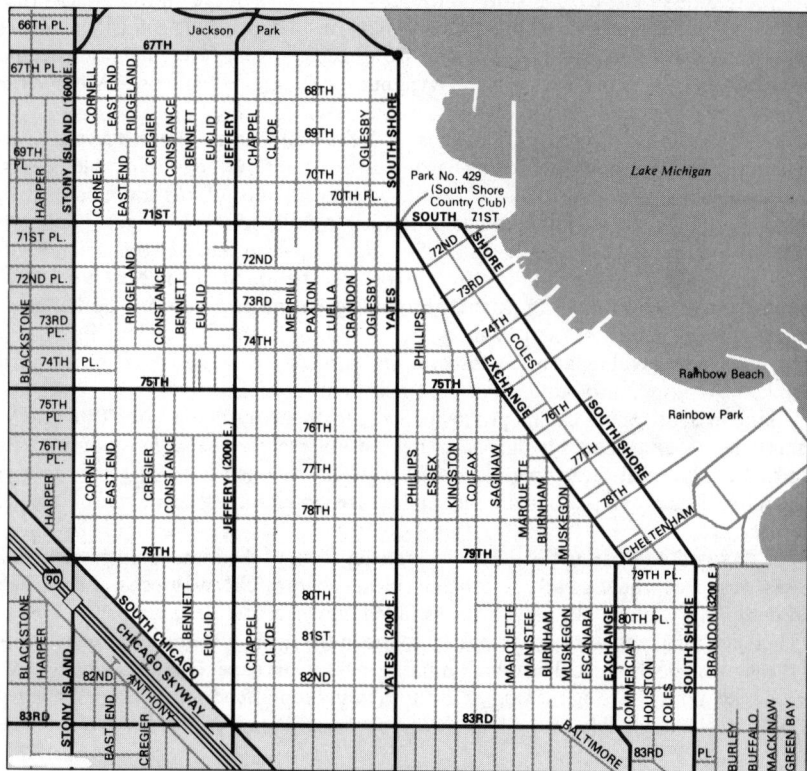

glass windows, above the oak wainscoting, pair male and female saints; the ornate altar and painted, beamed ceiling are masterpieces.

For years, South Shore was mistakenly considered to be a Jewish neighborhood. It has, in fact, always been predominantly Christian, although the Jewish population was substantial until the 1960s. The South Shore Congregation was established in the early 1920s and held services in a small, wooden house at 72nd Street and Jeffery Boulevard until 1928, when the temple was built on the site. The congregation continued to swell through the 1950s. But the 1960s and early '70s brought a virtual exodus from South Shore: Younger families moved to the suburbs, and older residents with stronger South Side loyalties moved to Hyde Park. The temple building is now the **Old Landmark Church of Holiness in Christ**.

Postwar population shifts on the South Side also increased South Shore's Greek community, which built the magnificent Byzantine SS. Constantine and Helen Church structure in 1946. Twenty-six years later, the church followed its congregation to Palos Hills, and the old church building became **Masjid Honorable Elijah Muhammad**.

SHOPPING AND RESTAURANTS

The South Side's most elegant stores once lined both sides of the railroad tracks running along East 71st Street, but the specialty shops, restaurants, and professional offices that attracted shoppers from miles around are all gone. In their place, and often behind metal grates, are bars, record stores, and neighborhood service businesses. More of the same is along 75th and 79th streets.

There is, however, some wheat mixed in with the chaff. At the **Workbench**, Kiyoshi Tanouye has been custom-crafting hardwood bookcases, dining room tables, desks, and cabinets for more than a quarter century. Although most of it is contemporary in feel, he is dedicated to building things people can't find elsewhere.

Drew Sales is the only store outside the Loop to specialize in Masonic lodge regalia. African masks, baskets, and other artwork can be found at the **Native Shop**. Founded in 1916, **WGN Flag and Decorating Company** has four buildings of flags, flagpoles, pennants, and banners for every business and occasion. Bring in a design and WGN will make a flag for you. The company, which is run by the original founder's grandson, also builds floats and sells float material.

Dining in South Shore can be problematical, mostly because there aren't that many restaurants. **Alexander's** is the last of the old-line places. The large room, with its handsome 1950s bar stretching along one wall, is crammed with overstuffed vinyl banquettes. Steaks and seafood are the staples here, and standing prime rib roast is the specialty.

The **Essex Restaurant** is the soul-food equivalent of the Lithuanian places a few blocks west in Marquette Park. Smothered chicken, ham hocks and greens, and chicken and dumplings are casually served at this faded, luncheonette-style place.

There are also quite a few take-out rib joints in the neighborhood. **Thomas Bar-B-Q** may well be the best. The owner minds the pit while supervising his young crew, which is kept busy passing the smoky, meaty ribs and topnotch fried chicken to hungry crowds on the other side of the bulletproof partition. Phoning ahead will reduce the wait.

South Shore

🏛 Interesting Places

► **Bryn Mawr Community Church**
70th St. at Jeffery Blvd.
324-2403

► **Church of St. Philip Neri**
72nd St. and Merrill Ave.
363-1700

► **Jackson Park Highlands**
Constance, Bennett, and Euclid avenues between 67th and 71st streets

► **Masjid Honorable Elijah Muhammad**
7351 S. Stony Island Ave.

► **South Shore Country Club**
7059 S. South Shore Dr.
753-0640

South Shore Historical Society Museum
7651 S. South Shore Dr.
375-5379

Restaurants and Shopping

► **Alexander's Steak House**
3010 E. 79th St.
768-6555

► **Drew Sales**
2414 E. 75th St.
978-4500

► **Essex Restaurant**
1652 E. 79th St.
734-0032

Leon's Bar-B-Q
1640 E. 79th St.
731-1454

► **Native Shop**
2606 E. 79th St.
221-3577

Shirley's Hallmark Shop
1944 E. 71st St.
363-1944

► **Thomas Bar-B-Q**
2347 E. 75th St.
221-4265

► **WGN Flag and Decorating Company**
7984 S. South Chicago Ave.
768-8076

► **Workbench**
7048 S. Stony Island Ave.
363-1957

Southeast Side

FROM THE CHICAGO SKYWAY'S relatively antiseptic heights, the city's southeast section — part of the country's largest concentration of steelworks — is a wasteland akin to murky hinterlands like Gary. But for a historical accident, the remote-seeming Southeast Side might have become Chicago's center. In its natural state, the mouth of the Calumet River was very similar to the Chicago River's. The Federal Government survey party sent to select a fortification site at Lake Michigan's edge in the early 1800s considered both locations and observed that the Calumet region even offered an interior harbor — Lake Calumet. Legend has it that the love felt by one of the team's army officers for an Indian maiden determined Fort Dearborn's Chicago River location.

While Chicago grew, the Calumet region stagnated. George Ewing bought a huge chunk of it from an Indian woman for $1,000 in 1851, but by 1860 only five houses had been built. Development didn't take off until the Federal Government dredged the harbor in 1870. Within three years, railroads crisscrossed the area, and James Bowen's Calumet and Chicago Canal and Dock Company platted the land to the west of the river's mouth in 1875.

The first steelworks opened at 109th Street and the river the following year, a harbinger of the heavy industry that would eventually span thousands of acres all the way to Indiana. Sparked by the Chicago Fire's destructiveness and spurred by the Illinois Central commuter line that reached 91st Street in 1883, the neighborhood of South Chicago and the 91st Street-Commercial Avenue shopping area were firmly established by the turn of the century.

More than the Calumet River separates the "East Side" from her sister mill communities. Although early German and Swedish settlers built large houses in the 1880s, and one of the largest sections resembles other 19th-century, working-class areas, much of the neighborhood could be part of Hammond, Indiana, which it abuts.

The years have taken their toll on "Millgate" and "The Bush," the oldest sections of South Chicago. The Poles who flocked to work at what is now the **United States Steel South Works** in the 1890s built inexpensive homes. The community's creative energy seems to have been lavished on **St. Michael's Church**. The common-brick façade of this former bishopric belies a magnificent, European-style cathedral interior. St. Michael's lush stained glass, carved altars, intricate ribbing, and detailed ceiling frescoes all command attention. The **Immaculate Conception of the Blessed Virgin Mary Church** is also worth a visit. The oval nave's walls, arches, and ceiling are richly polychrome in pastels, and the arcades are lined with figural stained glass.

There are many other churches of note in the area, including **St. Francis de Sales**, the East Side's oldest Catholic parish. The present church was incorporated into the school building after its magnificent predecessor burned in 1925. The 5,500-pound bell, which had been sitting in the priest's yard for years, was then mounted in the

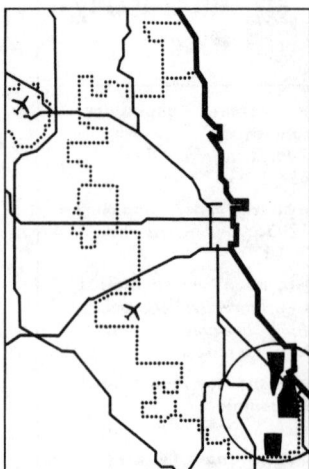

school's tower.

Across from the scene of the 1937 Memorial Day march is the **United Steel Workers of America Local 1033** hall. A small plaque on the adjoining flagpole commemorates the MARTYRS — HEROES — UNIONISTS SHOT DOWN MAY 30, 1937... The hall is used for both social and business occasions.

SHOPPING AND RESTAURANTS

South Chicago's main business strip, which begins at 87th Street and continues along Commercial Avenue to 92nd Street, is a bit run-down. The **Polka Home Style Sausage Company** is a good place to stock up on homemade sausages, cold cuts, and the raw ingredients for duck-blood soup.

There are also various specialty stores in the area, including **East Side Archery**, which caters to bow hunting and also has a small indoor range to test bows before buying them, and **Calumet Fisheries**, on the bridge from the East Side to South Chicago. Load up on topnotch shellfish, frog legs, and fish and chips, excellent trout, sable, and chubs.

The **Continental Bakery** roasts whole lambs and pigs on Sundays; ordering ahead is a good idea. Its koláčky and thick-crusted Italian bread are good, too. A visit to **Banner Liquor and Tap** provides a good selection of Yugoslavian wines and spirits.

The best-known restaurant is the **Golden Shell**, in an old, rambling frame building with several dining rooms and a bar. The wide-ranging menu includes Yugoslavian, American, and Italian entrées. Except for good bread and real mashed potatoes, the food isn't exceptional, but large portions, moderate prices, weekend entertainment, and long serving hours make this a popular local hangout. **Giappo's** serves stuffed pizza and sandwiches in fairly slick surroundings.

There are several Mexican spots in the area; the best is **Mexican Inn**, a small but bustling restaurant that does good business with inexpensive, well-prepared tacos, tostadas, and enchiladas. Another choice for Mexican is **Cocula Restaurant**. A huge, naive mural above the

Southeast Side

door hints at the selection, which includes goat, brains, tripe, tongue, and al pastor (Mexican gyros).

Interesting Places

▶ **Immaculate Conception of the Blessed Virgin Mary Church**
88th St. and Commercial Ave.
768-2100

Sacred Heart Croatian Church
96th St. and Escanaba Ave.
768-1423

▶ **St. Archangel Michael Serbian Orthodox Church**
98th St. and Commercial Ave.
375-3848

▶ **St. Francis de Sales Church**
102nd St. between Ave. J and Ewing Ave.
734-1383

St. George Church
96th St. and Ewing Ave.
734-0554

▶ **St. Michael's Church**
83rd St. and South Shore Drive
734-4921

▶ **United Steel Workers of America Local 1033**
11731 S. Ave. O
646-0800

Restaurants and Shopping

▶ **Calumet Fisheries**
3259 E. 95th St.
933-9855

▶ **Cocula Restaurant**
9811 S. Commercial Ave.
374-3214

▶ **Continental Bakery**
3522 E. 95th St.
721-5940

▶ **East Side Archery**
3711 E. 106th St.
721-0115

▶ **Giappo's Pizza**
4000 E. 106th St.
734-4700

▶ **Golden Shell Restaurant and Bar**
10063 S. Ave. N
221-9876

▶ **Mexican Inn**
9510 S. Ewing Ave.
734-8957

▶ **Polka Home Style Sausage Company**
8753 S. Commercial Ave.
221-0395

Pullman

PULLMAN, ON THE FAR Southwest Side, was voted the "most perfect" town in the world at the Prague International Hygienic and Pharmaceutical Exposition of 1896. Visiting the Pullman Historical District vividly recalls 19th-century political and social history. Designed in the 1880s by architect Solon S. Beman and landscaper Nathan Barrett for George Pullman around his Pullman Palace Car Works, this company town was unique in its attention to the workers' health and comfort. More than 80 percent of the original 1,800 buildings stand today, providing a lasting model of what was then Solomon-like community planning.

The town and its amenities were not a philanthropic venture. Not only did Pullman believe that well-housed workers would be more productive, long before social scientists "proved" it, but also he intended the development to show a modest profit as part of a pioneer vertical industrial organization.

All did not go well in this utopia, though. In 1889, over Pullman's objections, dissatisfied residents voted for annexation to Chicago. The company reacted to the depression of 1893 with wage cuts and layoffs but didn't lower rents or utility charges. Intolerably burdened, many workers joined Eugene V. Debs's American Railway Union, which struck in 1894. After Pullman refused arbitration, the strike spread nationwide and became brutal. It was ultimately broken by Federal troops; Debs was jailed and the ARU was immeasurably weakened. Shortly afterward, however, public outrage led to a court order, forcing the company to divest itself of all nonindustrial property (and streets were redesignated to expunge Pullman family names).

The company no longer manufactures railroad cars, but social history is still being forged in Pullman. The Historic Pullman Foundation, housed in the **Florence Hotel**, which it owns and is restoring, has acquired major historic sites for restoration, is spearheading adaptive reuse of dilapidated factory buildings, and is aiding in the rehabilitation of adjoining North Pullman.

The Florence Hotel, which is open for both lunch and dinner, is the best place to begin a neighborhood tour. Opened in 1881, the four-story, 51-room, Queen Anne masterpiece boasted elegant public rooms, as well as a palatial owner's suite, and had many unusual features for its day: a servant-call and fire-alarm bell system, indoor plumbing, gas lights, and central heating supplied by the town's Corliss steam engine.

Armed with a walking-tour map, take to the streets to see Pullman.

Not surprisingly, the company town's housing was stratified according to company position. The grandest homes are the freestanding duplexes built for executives on East 111th Street, behind the hotel. Foremen lived in the largest houses on South St. Lawrence Avenue between the hotel and the **Greenstone Church**, built as a nondenominational meetinghouse in a country-English Tudor style and named for the color of its serpentine rock. Housing for skilled craftsmen lined the street for a block south of the

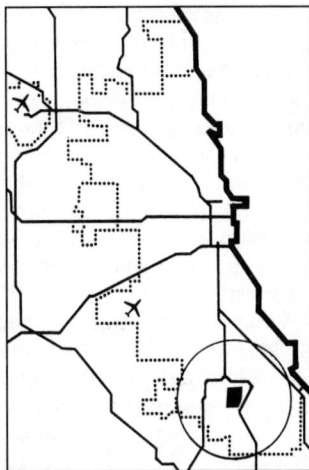

Pullman

Greenstone, which is now a Methodist church.

With the exception of the executives' houses, the differences between the homes of the select and of the humbler workers are less important than their similarities. They are all muted Queen Anne, two-story, attached row houses with little applied ornament, although the larger, better ones are faced with Indiana red pressed brick and the simpler ones with brown, common brick.

Farther from the amenities of the hotel and the long-gone shopping arcade building, the mass of workers lived in the smallest houses south of East 113th Street and along South Champlain Avenue. Only a few of the tenements that housed the lowest echelons and single men remain along South Langley Avenue, and several modern apartment buildings, which some misguided architect undoubtedly claimed were sympathetic to the streetscape, have been built here.

While most of Pullman's domestic architecture has a New England mill-town flavor, the **Market Hall** and surrounding Romanesque Colonnade Apartments evoke Savannah or New Orleans. Originally a one-story structure for food stalls with a central second story and tower meeting room, the building burned in 1882 and was rebuilt by

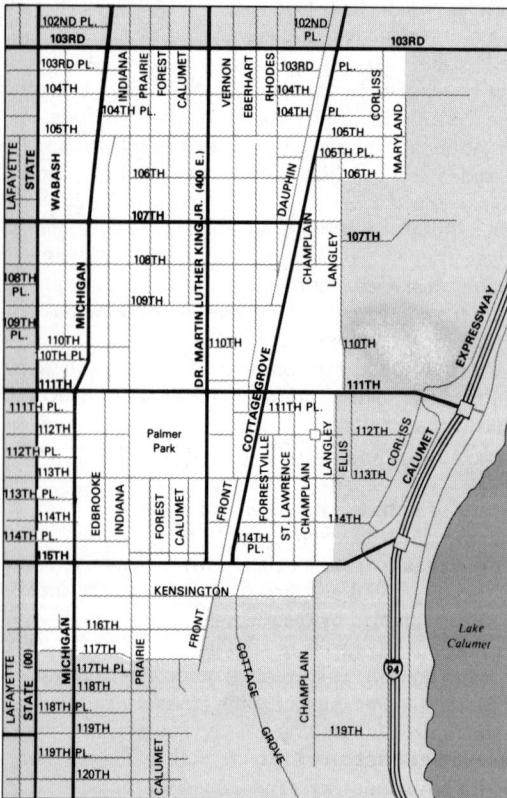

Solon Beman with an additional story. The four, curved-front Colonnade buildings were constructed at this time. Interrupted only by the intersecting streets, they circle the market, forming a handsome group. In 1932, another fire destroyed the upper floors of the market, but the deteriorating building remained in use until a final fire gutted it in 1973. The Historic Pullman Foundation now intends to adapt the Market Hall for condominiums and offices.

When Presbyterians rented the Greenstone Church, the only house of worship allowed in Pullman proper, Catholic and Swedish Lutherans petitioned Pullman for permission to build their own churches. The towers of **Holy Rosary Church**, a handsome, red-brick, 1890 Romanesque structure; **Reformation Lutheran Church**, built in 1888 as Elim Lutheran Church; and the **New**

Pullman

Pasadena Missionary Baptist Church, originally the 1892 Swedish Methodist Church, form a line along the south side of **Palmer Park**.

Like many other city parks, Palmer was landscaped by the Olmsted firm, and the 1904 field house was built by Daniel H. Burnham and Company. The auditorium sports three idealized, colorful murals done in 1934 by J. E. McBurney. They depict indigenous Indians, the explorer Père Marquette, and wooden-shoed farmers. The **George M. Pullman Branch Library**, a fine 1927 neoclassical building, nestles in one corner of the park. The collection of Pullman historical material is outstanding.

Mendel Catholic High School, north of the park, opened as the Pullman Free Trade School in 1917. The campus, which incorporated now-widely-accepted educational concepts, provided free technical training for the children of Pullman company workers until it closed in 1945. It was reopened in 1951 as an all-boys', Catholic college-prep school.

Joseph Schlitz built a beer mini-empire on a plot of land that escaped Pullman, just west of the Illinois Central tracks. The taverns did great business, as Pullman wouldn't allow workers' bars inside his town. Schlitz imitated Pullman's paternalism by building homes for his workers along South King Drive and a commercial block along East 111th Street. There are still a couple of bars on Front Avenue, between 114th and 115th streets, which have beautiful tile floors, tin ceilings, and colorful 1950s murals.

Interesting Places

▶ **Florence Hotel/Historic Pullman Foundation**
11111 S. Forrestville Ave.
785-8181

▶ **Greenstone Church (Pullman United Methodist Church)**
112th St. and St. Lawrence Ave.
785-1492

Historic Pullman Center
614 E. 113th St.
660-1276

▶ **Holy Rosary Church**
113th St. and King Dr. ´
568-4455

▶ **Market Hall**
112th St. and Champlain Ave.

▶ **Mendel Catholic High School**
250 E. 111th St.
995-3700

▶ **New Pasadena Missionary Baptist Church**
113th St. and Indiana Ave.
995-9774

▶ **Palmer Park**
201 E. 111th St.
785-4277

▶ **George M. Pullman Branch Library**
11001 S. Indiana Ave.
785-4277

▶ **Reformation Lutheran Church**
113th St. and Forest Ave.
785-4570

Beverly Hills/Morgan Park

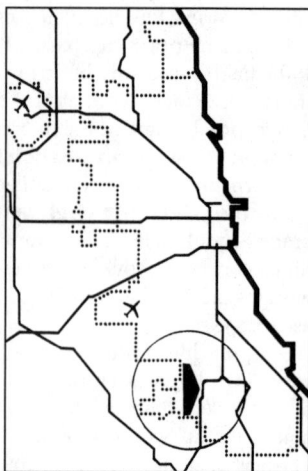

THE BEVERLY Area Planning Association, a pioneer community self-help organization, carries on a centuries-old tradition of internally motivated neighborhood improvement. Early settlers underwrote the cost of the first railway stations, built the many churches that are still local mainstays, and even started their own art group, named after local artist John H. Vanderpoel. The story of how this organization helped spawn a full-fledged community art center provides a good picture of the Beverly spirit.

Two years after the popular portraitist and longtime head of the Art Institute's instruction department died in 1911, a defunct North Side club offered one of Vanderpoel's paintings — *The Butter Makers* — to local residents. They raised the necessary $600 from one-dollar door-to-door solicitations, and the association was born. Additional purchases and contributions from the artist's friends and students augmented the collection. When the one-million-dollar holdings outgrew the Ridge Park field house, a local banker and his wife spearheaded a fund drive to build the **Beverly Art Center** on the grounds of the Morgan Park Academy in the late 1960s. Within three years the community had paid off the mortgage. In addition to housing most of the **Vanderpoel collection**, the Art Center offers a full range of art classes and hosts many cultural events, including an annual juried art fair, theater productions in the 445-seat theater, lectures, concerts, and gallery exhibits.

For a nice tour of the area (particularly by bicycle), start at the Art Center and note the small, wood-frame house across the street. Built in 1872 for the Rev. Justin A. Smith, one of the founders of the Chicago Baptist Theological Union, it was the scene of conferences between representatives of John D. Rockefeller, William Rainey Harper, Thomas Goodspeed, and others, leading to the founding of the University of Chicago.

Drive past the Norman-revival **Walker Branch Library**, turn left onto Longwood Drive — the area's most imposing homes are perched on its heights — and go north past the **Morgan Park United Methodist Church**, a rambling Prairie-school building with handsome stained-glass windows, designed in 1912 by Perkins, Fellows, and Hamilton. Howard L. Cheney designed the yellow-brick, neoclassical **Thirteenth Church of Christ, Scientist**. Nearby, the limestone hulk that now serves as the **Beverly Unitarian Church** is an 1886 replica of an Irish castle on the River Dee and perhaps the best-known landmark.

Continuing on Longwood Drive: Louis Sullivan designed the 20-room Horton House (10200) in 1887 for the founder of the Chicago Bridge and Iron Company — a fitting commission, given Sullivan's affection for decorative ironwork. Frank Lloyd Wright executed the Prairie-school Evans House (9914) in 1909, but seeing a style tailored for the flat prairie on some of the highest land for miles around can be disconcerting.

Travel west on 95th Street to Damen Avenue, then north to 92nd Street. Proceed east to Winchester Avenue, then north to 91st Street, and turn right. The boulder just before Pleasant Avenue marks the beginning of the old Vincennes Trail. The red-brick, Arts and Crafts Movement-inspired mansion designed by local architect John Hetherington is the parish house for the **Church of the Holy Nativity**.

Turn left at 95th Street and right onto Prospect Avenue and proceed to **Walter Burley Griffin Place**. Of the more than 30 Prairie-school houses in the area, 12 were designed by this Wright disciple. Off-center peaked roofs, pointed windows, and almost-Japanese wood-and-stucco façades make his work easily recognizable.

Return to Prospect Avenue on 105th Street and continue south past some of the community's oldest houses. The Tudor-revival Dickey House (10900) is on a four-acre lot — the largest in the district. The impressive Victorian Blackwelder House, built in 1886, was the home of the neighborhood's sixth resident.

As you head back toward the tour's starting point along 111th Street, detour south on Hoyne Avenue to the **Morgan Park Congregational Church**. The Prairie school-influenced building was constructed in 1915. The Masonic Hall across the street was the congregation's original building.

SHOPPING

South of Evergreen Plaza — a mall long-forgotten by most area

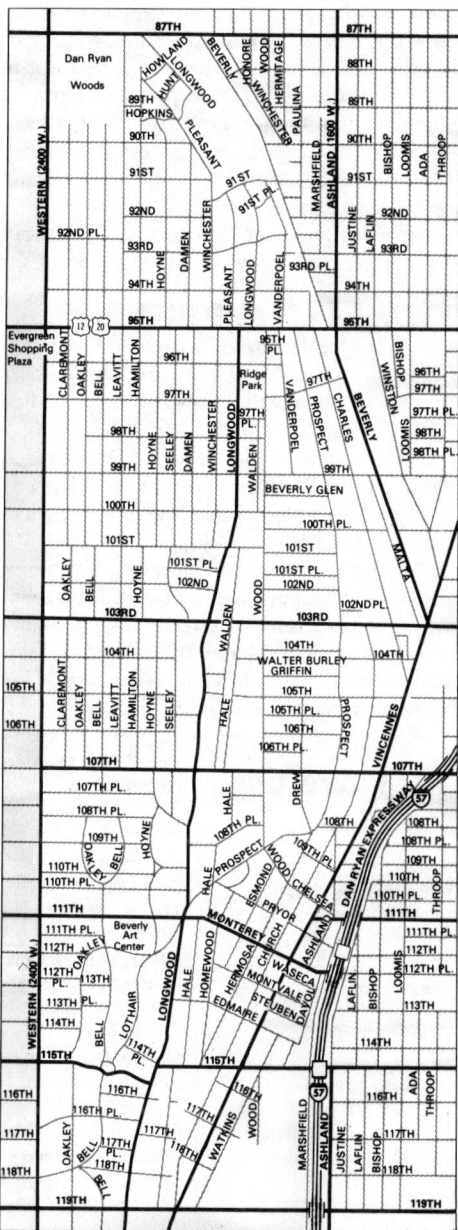

Beverly Hills/Morgan Park

residents, who prefer to shop at suburban centers — Western Avenue offers a discouraging mix of auto shops, nursery and garden centers, professional-office complexes, neighborhood service stores, and fast-food outlets. East of the mall on 95th Street, furniture stores, kitchen-remodeling places, tile shops, and carpet emporiums abound. With its fine array of Oriental carpets, the **Eastern Oriental Rug Company** is one of the few stores that attract shoppers from all over. Another is the **Guitar Center**, with its 15,000 square feet of guitars, basses, drums, keyboards, speakers, and amps.

Three generations of Himmels run **Himmel Furs**, one of the largest exclusive furriers in America. Custom-fitted furs of top-quality pelts are made on the premises.

RESTAURANTS AND NIGHTLIFE

Many of the locals dine at the area's three country clubs, which may explain the dearth of exciting restaurants. A cozy, tree-shaded beer garden with lawn chairs and a small play area for kids is the main attraction at the Cajun-Creole **Maple Tree Inn**. The place is crowded, and on weekends there's live jazz. Try the traditional Cajun "boats" of garlic bread filled with delicate fried frog legs, soft-shell crabs, catfish nuggets, oysters, or shrimp. For a trip down memory lane, don't miss **Top Notch Beefburgers**, where you can dig into those flat, juicy burgers with grilled onions that take you back to your high-school days.

Erik the Red is where Southwest Side singles go to dance to loud rock and disco. It used to be an auto repair place but now has lots of dark wood, antique lighting fixtures, mirrors, a movie screen showing slides of dancers and sometimes movies, and a Viking-boat-shaped bar with serpent eyes that pulsate to the music. Pianists play pop and jazz on a nine-foot Steinway at **The Keye's**, where on Fridays an entire band entertains dancers and listeners alike.

Interesting Places

► **Beverly Area Planning Association**
10233 S. Wood St.
233-3100

► **Beverly Art Center**
2153 W. 111th St.
445-3838

► **Beverly Unitarian Church**
103rd St. at Longwood Dr.
233-7080

► **Church of the Holy Nativity**
93rd St. and Pleasant Ave.
445-4427

► **Morgan Park Congregational Church**
112th St. and Hoyne Ave.
238-8020

► **Morgan Park United Methodist Church**
110th Pl. and Longwood Dr.
238-2600

► **Sacred Heart Church**
Church St. between 116th and 117th streets
233-3955

► **Thirteenth Church of Christ, Scientist**
103rd St. and Longwood Dr.
238-2378

► **Walker Branch Library**
11071 S. Hoyne Ave.
233-1920

Shopping

► **Eastern Oriental Rug Company**
1814 W. 95th St.
233-4295

► **Evergreen Plaza**
95th St. and Western Ave.
445-8900

► **Guitar Center**
2215 W. 95th St.
881-8800

▶ **Himmel Furs**
2201 W. 95th St.
779-7000

✕ Restaurants

▶ **Erik the Red**
11050 S. Spaulding Ave.
779-3033

▶ **The Keye's**
9936 S. Western Ave.
233-3211

▶ **Maple Tree Inn**
10730 S. Western Ave.
239-3688

▶ **Top Notch Beefburgers**
2116 W. 95th St.
445-7218

Boul Mich/River North

THE BOUL MICH AND RIVER NORTH areas are bounded by the Chicago River on the south and west, Oak Street on the north, and Lake Michigan on the east. Though a feeling of tradition remains, change comes quickly, too: Hotels seem to spring up overnight, new restaurants serving anything from the finest haute to the trendiest nouvelle cuisine open weekly, and the mélange of shops, boutiques, and galleries offers an ever-evolving array of clothes, books, works of art, housewares, and accessories.

Michigan Avenue: the Magnificent Mile, the Miracle Mile, Boul Mich. The names for it are many, but they all mean the same thing—elegance, opulence, and excitement. Many of the city's ritziest hotels, finest restaurants, and classiest shops are on the avenue or on the neighboring side streets (particularly on Oak Street, which is fast becoming Chicago's premier street for designer boutiques, so far including Gianni Versace, Sonia Rykiel, and Giorgio Armani). In addition to the myriad of fine specialty shops, Michigan Avenue is home to one of the highest concentrations of de luxe department stores in the world: Water Tower Place, a vertical mall with more than 125 stores, including Marshall Field's and Lord & Taylor; 900 North Michigan Avenue, with 80 shops, including Bloomingdale's; Saks Fifth Avenue; I. Magnin; Bonwit Teller; and Neiman-Marcus.

The area hosts the media (both daily newspapers' headquarters, two television networks' facilities, many radio stations, numerous magazines, plus a lot of advertising agencies) and is also the home of the huge Northwestern University educational-medical complex. In addition, fine high-rise residences, from pre-World War Two beauties to sleek Mies van der Rohe glass-and-metal boxes to more recently built marble-clad edifices, line both Michigan Avenue and its immediate side streets.

Michigan Avenue's present fame rests on a bedrock of peerless shops, but the area had been prime residential real estate for two hundred years. Jean Baptiste Point du Sable probably built the city's first house here around 1779, and John Kinzie, Chicago's first big-time trader, purchased it in 1803. The site is marked by **Pioneer Court**, in the Equitable Building plaza just north of the Michigan Avenue bridge. By 1840, homes of such luminaries as William B. Ogden, Chicago's first mayor, dotted the fashionable neighborhood.

The 1871 Chicago Fire wiped out 40 years' work. The old **Water Tower**, designed by W. W. Boyington and completed in 1869, was one of the few buildings to survive. Oscar Wilde may have called the Gothic limestone tower a "castellated monstrosity with pepper boxes stuck all over it," but Chicago's unofficial "first landmark" endures as a symbol of the city's strength and heritage.

River North, a relatively new moniker for the area west of Dearborn Street, is full of galleries (more than 50 at last count; for individual listings, see Galleries), antiques

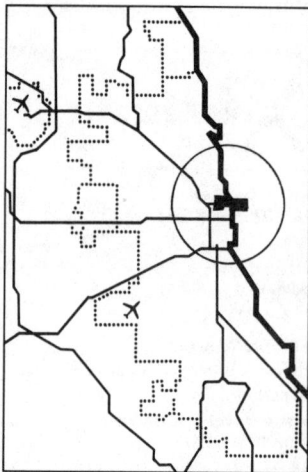

dealers, auction houses, graphic and architectural design studios, art-related services, clothing shops, and restaurants. Many of these are housed in renovated factories and afford unusually high ceilings, large unbroken expanses of floor space, and rich architectural detail. In addition to retail and wholesale concerns (Leaf Candy, maker of Milk Duds, Slow Pokes, and Tootsie Rolls, is located here and often permeates the neighborhood with the smell of chocolate), many buildings have been turned into residential lofts. Anchoring the area's southern edge is the giant Merchandise Mart and, attached by a Helmut Jahn-designed skywalk, the Apparel Center.

Interesting Places

Annunciation Greek Orthodox Cathedral
La Salle Dr. and Oak St.
664-5485
Erected in 1910, this lovely little church's mural-rich interior has been restored.

Assumption Church
Illinois and Orleans streets
644-0036
At the turn of the century, loft buildings, warehouses, and tenements filled River North. It was an Italian ghetto, and life centered around this, the city's first Italian parish. It was built by Servite fathers between 1884 and 1886 to resemble their mother church in Rome, but on a smaller scale.

John Carroll Sons Funeral Home
22 E. Erie St.
944-6060
Built in 1878 for Ransom Cable, it was designed by Henry Ives Cobb, the University of Chicago's first architect, and eventually occupied by a McCormick. It was typical of the grand mansions that blanketed the Michigan Avenue area (and one of three imposing Richardson Romanesque buildings — all still standing — in the immediate neighborhood) after the Great Fire.

Cathedral of St. James
Wabash Ave. and Huron St.
787-7360
After the fire of 1871, only the tower of the Edward Burling-designed St. James Episcopal Church, now the Cathedral of St. James, survived. In 1874 the church was rebuilt along its original lines. Bertram G. Goodhue's Chapel of St. Andrew was added in 1913. Modeled on an ancient Scottish abbey, it honors the place where the Brotherhood of St. Andrew was founded.

Cathedral of the Holy Name
State and Superior streets
787-8040
Holy Name Cathedral, another Edward Burling-designed fire casualty, was rebuilt in the same year as was St. James and remodeled by Henry J. Schlacks in 1915. Six masses are celebrated daily in the lovely, intricately arched cathedral, which, along with Catholic schools, a convent, and the rectory, takes up an entire city block.

CBS, Inc.
630 N. McClurg Ct.
944-6000
WBBM television and radio emanate from a former ice-skating rink and horse arena.

Church of the Ascension
Elm St. and La Salle Dr.
664-1271
Started from a schism in St. James Episcopal Church, this was a poor congregation until

the 1940s when a rector donated his personal fortune. Built in the 1880s, the limestone church, with nice stained glass and a 64-rank organ, has mostly 1950s decorations.

860-80 Lake Shore Drive Apartments
860-80 N. Lake Shore Dr.
Designed by Mies van der Rohe and built in 1952, these beautifully sleek, sensitively detailed buildings — for which Mies did the basic designs as far back as the 1920s — were the first apartment towers built that embraced the commercial glass-wall style.

Fourth Presbyterian Church
Michigan Ave. at Chestnut St.
787-4570
This gray limestone building is distinguished by larger-than-life muses of the Psalms mounted on massive pillars, an unusual patterned ceiling painted by Frederic C. Bartlett, and an Aeolian-Skinner organ. Designed by Ralph Adams Cram, a prominent ecclesiastical architect and Gothic revivalist, it was completed in 1914. The congregants included the cream of society, such as the McCormicks and Howard Van Doren Shaw, who designed the parish house and the fountain in the tranquil garden.

John Hancock Center
875 N. Michigan Ave.
751-3681 (observatory)
Designed by Skidmore,

Owings & Merrill and built in 1969, the Hancock is 1,105 feet tall. The building includes a shopping center, offices, a swimming pool on the 44th floor, and residences above. The observatory is on the 94th floor and, weather permitting, affords great views.

IBM Building
Wabash Ave. and Kinzie St.
This is the last building designed by Mies, and the tower typifies his life's work.

Lake Point Tower
505 N. Lake Shore Dr.
The tallest apartment building in the world is also one of the handsomest. The bronzed-glass-and-anodized-aluminum, three-lobed tower was adapted by Schipporeit-Heinrich Associates from a 1921 Mies proposal.

Lake Shore Dr. Bridge
Crossing the Chicago River
One of the world's biggest bascule bridges, this is where FDR gave a dedication speech in 1937, chastising "aggressor nations."

LaSalle Street Church
La Salle Dr. and Elm St.
944-2488
Built as an English Lutheran church in the early 1880s, now it's an independent nondenominational church.

MAP LEGEND

- Underground road system
- Passage to and from underground road system
- ▲ One-way passage from underground to street level
- ▼ One-way passage to underground from street level
- Ⓟ Underground parking access

SCOTT

DIVISION (1200 N.)

STATE

ELM

HILL

MAPLE

WENDELL

WELLS (200 W.)

CLARK (100 W.)

DEARBORN

ORLEANS

OAK (1000 N.)

WALTON

STATE (00)

LOCUST

LOCUST

DELAWARE

FRANKLIN

TOOKER

INSTITUTE

LA SALLE

CHICAGO (800 N.)

SUPERIOR

HURON

ERIE

ONTARIO

CLARK

To 90 94

OHIO (600 N.)

CAMPBELL

GRAND

FRANKLIN (300 W.)

WELLS

ILLINOIS

DEARBORN

STATE (00)

ORLEANS

HUBBARD

S17

KINZIE

MERCHANDISE MART
PLAZA

POST

LA SALLE

GARVEY

LAKE

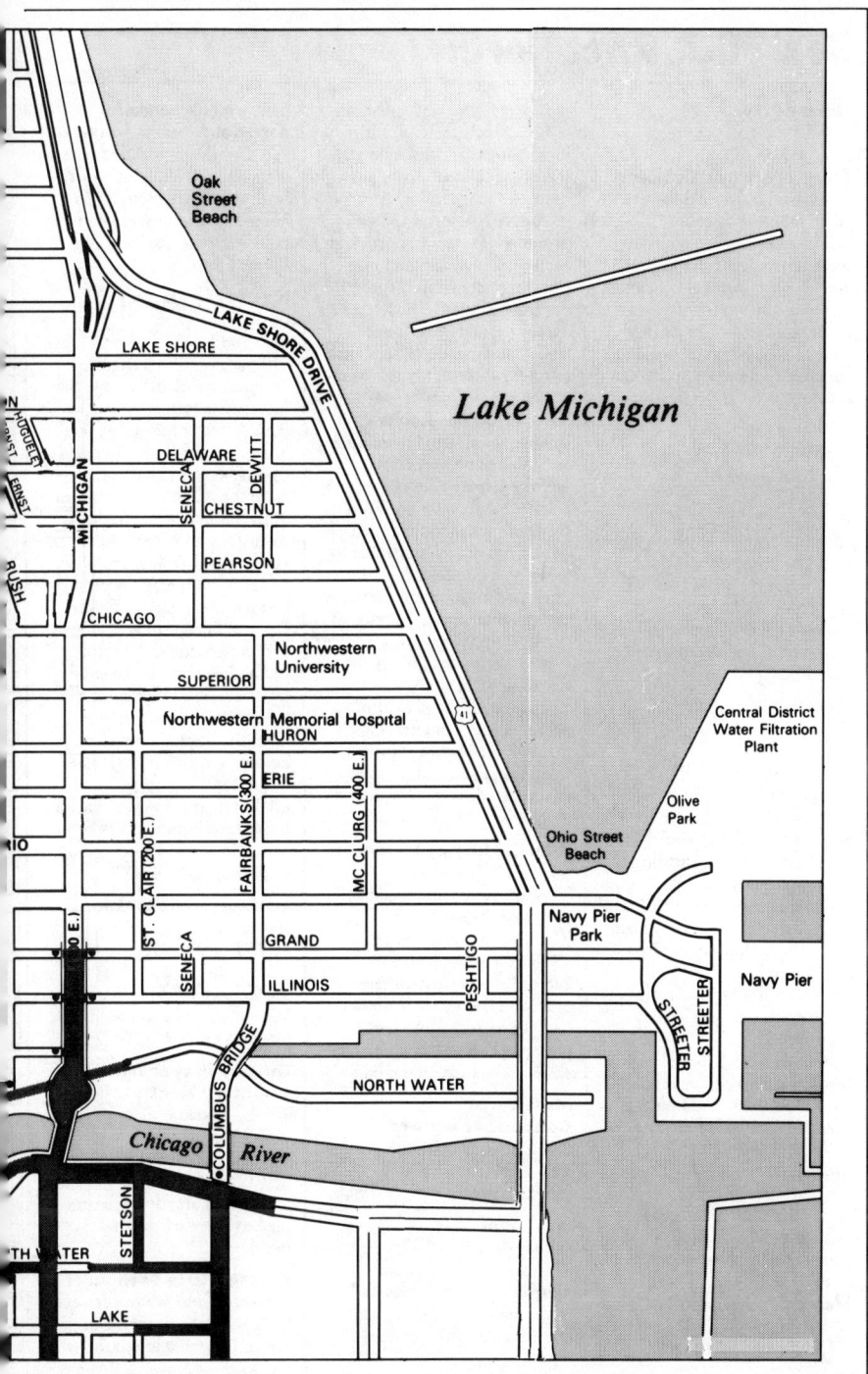

Oak Street Beach

LAKE SHORE DRIVE

LAKE SHORE

Lake Michigan

MICHIGAN

N HUGGETT

ERNST

SENECA

DELAWARE

DEWITT

CHESTNUT

PEARSON

RUSH

CHICAGO

Northwestern University

SUPERIOR

Northwestern Memorial Hospital
HURON

41

Central District Water Filtration Plant

FAIRBANKS (300 E.)

ERIE

MC CLURG (400 E.)

ST. CLAIR (200 E.)

RIO

Olive Park

Ohio Street Beach

0 E.)

SENECA

GRAND

ILLINOIS

PESHTIGO

Navy Pier Park

STREETER

STREETER

Navy Pier

COLUMBUS BRIDGE

NORTH WATER

Chicago River

STETSON

TH WATER

LAKE

Boul Mich/River North

Marina City
300 N. State St.
222-1111
Architect Bertrand Goldberg's
cylindrical balconied towers
(with pie-shaped rooms
inside) won raves when they
were constructed in the 1960s
and are an unofficial Chicago
symbol. The model of a
modern city has everything:
apartments, an office building,
garages, restaurants, a bank, a
bowling alley, and a health
club.

Medinah Temple
600 N. Wabash Ave.
266-5000
Hoehl and Schmid's 1912
Moorish temple was built for
the Shriners of Chicago and
has a central cupola flanked
by two smaller ones, small
arches with delicate floral
stained glass, and a dramatic
entrance.

Merchandise Mart
Wells and Kinzie streets
527-4141
With seven and a half miles of
corridors on 97 acres of floor
space (which would cover the
entire Loop, if spread out), the
Midwest's home-furnishings
foundation and once the
world's largest building occupies a square block. Designed
by Graham, Anderson, Probst,
and White in 1930, it stands
on Wolf Point at the conflu-
ence of the Chicago River's
branches.

Built as Marshall Field's
wholesale-division warehouse,
the debt-ridden building was
snapped up by Joseph P. Kennedy after World War Two
to create the country's first
mega-wholesale center. Eight
larger-than-life bronze busts
facing the Mart honor the
giants of American merchandising, including Chicagoans
Marshall Field and Julius
Rosenwald.

Devoted mainly to four
industries — home furnishings,
contract (commercial) furnishings, floor coverings, and gift-
wares — the Mart hosts more
than 20 "markets" a year to
introduce new products and
promote old ones to hordes of
accredited retailers and interior designers from throughout the Midwest. The Mart's
exhibitors sell only "to the
trade" and can be divided into
two very different types. Manufacturers — from broad-
based giants like Knoll to
smaller, specialized firms such
as Scalamandré — maintain
factory display rooms devoted
solely to their own products.
Designer show rooms, each
the exclusive area outlet for as
many as a hundred different
lines, and antiques and art specialists, take up the balance of
the 1,000-plus spaces.

An interior designer is the
key to unlocking the Mart's
treasures. Although nothing
prevents you from peering
through the show rooms'
windows, almost all require
a Mart card to consummate
a deal.

John B. Murphy Memorial
50 E. Erie St.
This fanciful, rococo auditorium was designed by
Marshall and Fox and built in
1926. It was dedicated to an
early 20th-century surgeon
and is owned by the American
College of Surgeons. The
panels in the massive doors
show the history of medicine.

Museum of Contemporary Art
237 E. Ontario St.
280-2660
(see Museums)

Navy Pier
Grand Ave. and the lake
Though built in 1916 for commercial shipping, it has had
many uses. In 1976, the east
end of the 3,000-foot-long
pier, with its wonderful
domed auditorium, was renovated by the city, and murals
were painted along the north
walkway. Since then, it has
hosted a variety of events from
ethnic fairs to the New Art
Forms Expo.

Newberry Library
60 W. Walton St.
943-9090
The stately 1893 building,
designed by Henry Ives Cobb,
faces Washington Square
Park — better known as Bug-
house Square. The collection
covers Western civilization
from the Middle Ages to the
20th century, with emphasis
on history and the humanities.
Four special-collection
research centers focus on the
history of cartography, American and European genealogy
and local history, American
Indian history, and Renaissance studies. Outstanding
exhibits are mostly drawn
from the library's own rich
holdings, which include five
million manuscripts and
60,000 maps. A new adjacent
bookstack building was completed in 1982. There's a fine
bookshop as well.

Samuel M. Nickerson House
40 E. Erie St.
Edward Burling was responsible for this 1883 residence,
known for years as the "marble palace."

Quigley Preparatory Seminary North
103 E. Chestnut St.
787-9343
Constructed between 1910
and 1920, the seminary
and chapel are modeled on
medieval French Gothic
buildings.

Scottish Rite Cathedral
Dearborn and Walton streets
Originally the Second Uni-
tarian Church and rebuilt as

such after the Chicago Fire, the building was bought by the Shriners in 1902 and used by them until the Medinah Temple was erected. Then it was sold to this Masonic order.

Sun-Times Building
401 N. Wabash Ave.
321-3000
Designed by Naess and Murphy and built in 1957 to house both the *Sun-Times* and the now-defunct *Daily News*, the plant has a pleasant riverfront plaza.

Terra Museum of American Art
664 N. Michigan Ave.
664-3939
(see Museums)

Tree Studios
6 E. Ohio St.
Judge Lambert Tree commissioned Brooklyn's Parfitt Brothers to re-create their studio complex in his back yard in 1894, hoping to keep some of the World's Columbian Exposition artists in town. Over the years, several architects were involved, and another generation of artists still works in the bright, high-ceilinged studios surrounding a hidden-from-the-street garden.

Tribune Tower
435 N. Michigan Ave.
222-3232
The tale of the *Chicago Tribune*'s competition that led to Hood and Howell's 1925 Gothic tower, studded with stones from renowned buildings around the world, is almost as famous as the building itself. The marble-clad lobby, inscribed with freedom-of-the-press quotations, is well worth a look; or take a tour.

Wrigley Building
400 N. Michigan Ave.
558-8080
The first Michigan Avenue

skyscraper, sparked by the new access to the south riverbank and the Loop, was this gleaming white, terra cotta-covered building, designed by Graham, Anderson, Probst, and White in a French Renaissance style. The clock-tower-topped building was completed in 1921, the Greek-temple-capped annex in 1924. Brightly illuminated at night, it is one of Chicago's grandest evening sights.

Major Institutions

American College of Surgeons
55 E. Erie St.
664-4050
This association serves surgeons from the United States, Canada, and some foreign countries.

American Dental Association
211 E. Chicago Ave.
440-2500

American Library Association
50 E. Huron St.
944-6780
This is the world's oldest and largest nonprofit organization dedicated to improving library services.

American Medical Association
535 N. Dearborn St.
645-5000

American Red Cross Mid-America Chapter
43 E. Ohio St.
440-2000
Services here include disaster relief, blood banks, community services, classes, and literature.

Dr. William M. Scholl College of Podiatric Medicine
1001 N. Dearborn St.
280-2880
Founded in 1912, this is a four-year postgraduate institution. There's also a nonprofit, inexpensive foot clinic open to the public.

Loyola University Water Tower Campus
820 N. Michigan Ave.
670-3000
This is the downtown branch of Loyola University.

Moody Bible Institute
820 N. La Salle Dr.
329-4000
Started by Dwight L. Moody in 1886 to train lay leaders in the church, this large complex offers three-year programs teaching general Christianity and the Bible in order to turn out Christian leaders.

Northwestern Memorial Hospital
Superior St. and Fairbanks Ct.
908-2000

Northwestern University Chicago Campus
339 E. Chicago Ave.
908-8649
This includes the Evanston university's medical, dental, and law schools, as well as some of the graduate division of the Medill School of Journalism and the extension classes.

Hotels

(Weekend packages are subject to availability and change.)

Allerton Hotel
701 N. Michigan Ave.
440-1500
This budget business hotel has weekend rates at a discount.

Boul Mich/River North

Barclay Chicago Hotel
166 E. Superior St.
787-6000
Luxury suites here are
at reduced prices on the
weekends.

Chicago Marriott Hotel
540 N. Michigan Ave.
836-0100
This 46-story hotel has
more than 1,100 rooms, a
shopping arcade, and numerous restaurants.

Drake Hotel
140 E. Walton St.
787-2200
Marshall and Fox's 1920 hotel
boasts grand public spaces,
including an English Great
Hall lobby and a shopping
concourse. The food at the
Cape Cod Room, long
a Chicago tradition, has
seen better days.

Hotel Nikko Chicago
320 N. Dearborn St.
744-1900
The newest addition to the
area's hotel scene, this hotel
has a tranquil Japanese ambiance, as well as several guest
rooms in the Japanese style,
complete with tatami mats.

Holiday Inn Mart Plaza
350 N. Orleans St.
836-5000
This hotel sits atop the
Apparel Center.

**Knickerbocker-Chicago
Hotel**
163 E. Walton St.
751-8100
There are reduced weekend
rates on luxury rooms.

Mayfair Regent Hotel
181 E. Lake Shore Dr.
787-8500
This hotel offers luxury
accommodations to elite business travelers, as well as
reduced rates on weekends.

**Park Hyatt on Water
Tower Square**
800 N. Michigan Ave.
280-2222
This hotel recently underwent
a $10-million renovation and
includes a penthouse suite
with a music room, library,
dining room, kitchen,
and valet.

Raphael Hotel
201 E. Delaware Pl.
943-5000
Already less expensive than
the other little luxury hotels in
the city, it still offers discounts
on weekends.

Richmont Hotel
162 E. Ontario St.
787-3580
This budget operation cuts
rates and tosses in a few frills
on rooms and suites on the
weekends.

Ritz-Carlton Hotel
160 E. Pearson St.
266-1000
Attached to Water Tower
Place, this hotel is one of the
city's most luxurious.

Sheraton Plaza Hotel
160 E. Huron St.
787-2900
This busy convention hotel
offers discounted weekend
rates.

Tremont Hotel
100 E. Chestnut St.
751-1900
This small but luxurious hotel
offers big savings on the
weekends and such perks as
room service from Cricket's,
its fine restaurant.

Westin Hotel Chicago
909 N. Michigan Ave.
943-7200
This bustling convention hotel
offers a variety of weekend
packages.

Whitehall Hotel
105 E. Delaware Pl.
944-6300
This is another small luxury
hotel that offers attractive
weekend rates.

Shopping

VERTICAL SHOPPING AND DEPARTMENT STORES

Bonwit Teller
875 N. Michigan Ave.
751-1800
Located in the Hancock Center, this three-level store offers
high-quality men's and
women's clothes and accessories to a decidedly upscale
clientele. Space near the elegant cosmetics and perfume
department is leased to
Hermès, saddler to royalty for
centuries (and more recently
maker of that ubiquitous
power tie), which also manufactures superb leather bags
and accessories.

Lord & Taylor
Water Tower Place
835 N. Michigan Ave.
787-7400
This is the flagship of a seven-
store Chicago-area group and
offers menswear, housewares,
linens, and all the other usual
department-store fare in a
very gracious setting. As with
Lord & Taylors in general, the
Water Tower store concen-
trates on high-quality
women's clothes, with a strong
emphasis on an American-
spirit town-and-country look.

Neiman-Marcus
737 N. Michigan Ave.
642-5900
A three-story barrel-vaulted
arch greets shoppers at the
Chicago outlet of this Dallas-
based institution. The marble-

clad building, designed by Skidmore, Owings & Merrill, is enlivened by an interior escalator court set off with a 74-foot wooden sculpture called *Dryad* ("wood nymph" in Greek). More than any other big store on Michigan Avenue, the flashy and moneyed ambiance created by the glass-brass-and-marble interior, as well as that of the army of great-looking salespeople, can be intimidating at first. But if you're "doing the avenue," a stop at Neiman's is essential.

Neiman's doesn't consider itself a department store, really, but a specialty store. Among its offerings, there's Chicago's only Turnbull & Asser men's boutique and the city's only Petrossian shop (in Neiman's wonderful Epicure Shop). In addition, there's a Chanel *prêt à porter* boutique, a fur salon carrying the wares of top designers (with a special Galanos boutique), an extensive salon of women's shoes, a couture department representing all the most important American and European designers, and a precious-jewels section. There are also a beauty salon and two restaurants, Zodiac and the more casual Fresh Market.

900 North Michigan
900 N. Michigan Ave.
Brand spanking new, this Perkins and Will-designed building contains 125 condominiums, 20 floors of office space, a 346-room Four Seasons hotel, a parking garage, and the six-story vertical shopping mall called Avenue Atrium.

Anchored by Bloomingdale's (see below) and a two-story Gucci, Avenue Atrium has 85 luxury stores, including such Chicago mainstays as Bigsby & Kruthers and

Joseph's. In addition, at least five international retailers' first Chicago outlets are here: Cactus, a women's store from Canada; Fogal, a Swiss legwear boutique; Mondi, which offers women casual clothes from Europe; Neuchatel Chocolate; and Ports International, another women's clothing store. Other retailers in the Atrium include Coach Leatherware; Laura Todd Cookies; Bailey, Banks & Biddle; and Atlas Galleries.

Other highlights of the mall include various restaurants, some with spectacular views of the lake and of Michigan Avenue, and two movie theaters.

Saks Fifth Avenue
669 N. Michigan Ave.
944-6500
All the big designers are on hand here, but there's still a comfortable, calming air about Saks, and praise for the sales help is frequently extravagant. The peerless children's department, traditional men's clothing, jewelry selection, and beauty parlor are much touted.

Water Tower Place
845 N. Michigan Ave.
Water Tower Place opened in 1976 to accolades mitigated only by some controversy over its architecture. Michigan Avenue's $200-million marble-clad monolith houses not only the 22-story Ritz-Carlton Hotel but also luxury condominiums, indoor parking, offices, theaters, restaurants, and the seven-level Atrium Shopping Mall.

Faced in Italian travertine marble, with *Ficus benjamina* trees flanking the Michigan Avenue entrance waterfall and with dramatic, glass-walled elevators, the Atrium Shopping Mall is jammed almost every day, and on weekends and at

Christmastime it can be near-impossible to get around comfortably. Lacking places to sit down and people-watch, the mall can be hard-edged and austere. Many shops are on corridors off the central area, which means you have to seek them out.

Nonetheless, there are 125 stores, which account for almost half of the Magnificent Mile's business and are among Chicago's main attractions. They range from Hemisphere, a division of the Gap, which sells upscale casual wear and sportswear, to Laura Ashley to Hoffritz for Cutlery to Charles Jourdan. The mall also includes a seven-story Lord & Taylor and an eight-story Marshall Field's, as well as such institutions as Kroch's & Brentano's, Louis Vuitton, Rizzoli International Bookstore and Gallery, and a Pappagallo shop, among many others. The mall includes four children's stores, 20 men's clothing stores, twice that number of women's clothiers, 11 jewelers, 11 shoe stores, two tobacconists, and three toy shops.

Water Tower Place offers 15 restaurants, ranging from the mall's Chestnut Street Grill to the Dining Room at the Ritz-Carlton to a McDonald's to Dos Hermanos Restaurant. In addition, there are six movie theaters on two levels.

CLOTHING AND ACCESSORIES

ACA JOE
622 N. Michigan Ave.
337-0280
A youthful spirit pervades this glass-fronted men's and women's sportswear store. Best bets here include heavy cotton sweats, khakis, shorts, and shirts.

Giorgio Armani
113 E. Oak St.
751-2244
Enter underneath a cream-
colored awning and through
glass doors, and step into Oak
Street's latest designer boutique, the only Armani outlet
between New York and Los
Angeles. Here you'll find
Armani's top two lines,
including his entire couture
collection for both men and
women.

Avenue Five-Forty
540 N. Michigan Ave.
321-9540
Verne Castress carries unique
and almost-unique clothes by
up-and-coming designers.
Wearable art, cotton dresses,
patchwork suede jackets, and
unusual handbags are a few of
the things you may find here,
even if the shop doesn't look
like much at first.

Bally of Switzerland
919 N. Michigan Ave.
787-8110
Known for fine, handmade
leather footwear for men, this
firm also carries men's suede
and leather jackets, attaché
cases, women's shoes and
handbags, and small accessories for men and women.

Bottega Veneta
106 E. Oak St.
664-3220
High-quality, buttery-soft,
and often brightly colored
woven leather goods are the
norm here.

Brittany, Ltd.
999 N. Michigan Ave.
642-6550
This store carries traditionally
styled, reasonably priced
men's and women's clothes in
a clubby, rarefied atmosphere.

Burberrys Limited
633 N. Michigan Ave.
787-2500
Stylish versions of the famous

coat Thomas Burberry
designed for trench warfare
are available here in all their
permutations for men and
women, along with outer
wear, tailored slacks and
skirts, sports jackets and
blazers, Shetland and cashmere sweaters, shirts, and
sundries.

Burdi
68 E. Walton St.
642-9166
This sleek men's boutique
sells high-fashion European
designs.

Cashmere, Cashmere
104 E. Oak St.
337-6558
You get exactly what you
expect at this fine store selling
all-cashmere clothes, including dresses, sweaters, scarves,
hats, gloves, and more.

Chanel Boutique
940 N. Michigan Ave.
787-5500
Coco Chanel's legacy is alive
at this plush shop, which
offers the the city's widest
selection of Chanel clothes, as
well as shoes, jewelry, handbags, and other accessories.

Jean Charles
1003 N. Rush St.
787-3535
From one-of-a-kind sweaters
to sexy dresses to flashy
evening wear, the women's
clothes here are mostly French
and lean toward the avant-
garde. Not everyone is ready
for such sophistication,
though, so Jean and Nancy
Kevorkian also buy more traditional, highly wearable
clothing like soft suedes and
Italian-style men's suits.
There's also a good selection
of high-fashion shoes.

Cole-Haan Foot Ware
645 N. Michigan Ave.
642-8995
A sprightly green awning wel-

comes shoppers into this boutique offering Cole-Haan's
fine line of men's, women's,
and boys' shoes, belts, and
some socks.

Evans
744 N. Michigan Ave.
855-0333
Though more elegant than the
Loop store, this Evans carries
many of the same fashionable
women's clothes and furs.

Sidney Garber Jewelers
840 N. Michigan Ave.
944-5225
Jewelry here is designed by
Garber himself, as well
as others.

Intrinsic
440 N. Wells St.
644-6212
Men's and women's sports-
wear is available at this store,
located in a renovated loft
building near the Merchandise
Mart. The emphasis is on
European designers like Mario
Valentino and S'fera, but the
range includes hot Americans
like Stephen Sprouse as well.

Janis
200 W. Superior St.
280-5357
In addition to representing an
international array of
designers, highlights at this
women's store include one-of-
a-kind artist-made clothing.

Jeraz
51 E. Oak St.
266-7300
Sleek European men's clothes
are available here at prices to
match. Suits and casual wear
come mainly from Italy; such
handmade items as one-of-a-
kind sweaters are gorgeous,
and so are leather coats and
jackets.

Joseph
679 N. Michigan Ave.
944-1111
Shoes and boots by Anne
Klein, Joan and David,

Charles Jourdan, and many others are available, as well as designer fashions, Susan Gail handbags, jewelry, and other accessories.

Stanley Korshak
940 N. Michigan Ave.
280-0520
Once staid, Stanley Korshak has shed a dour image and has flowered into one of Chicago's premier fashion sources. Visually diverting, the clothes offered here reflect the fast-paced and moneyed lives led by the shop's many clients.

Optica
129 E. Oak St.
642-2550
Fashionable frames for prescription glasses, as well as ready-to-wear sunglasses by top designers, are available here.

Orvis
142 E. Ontario St.
440-0662
The outdoorsy atmosphere here puts shoppers looking to buy fishing and hunting gear in the appropriate mood. Also available are gifts, Clothing, shoes, and camping accouterments.

Polo Ralph Lauren
960 N. Michigan Ave.
280-1655
Located in the One Magnificent Mile building, this shop offers much of Ralph Lauren's line of men's and women's traditionally styled clothes, as well as shoes, belts, glasses, and home furnishings accessories.

Pompian
57 E. Oak St.
337-6604
Here you'll find wonderful sweaters from England and Italy, loads of silk blouses, exquisite quilted silk jackets, and lots of European sportswear, as well as dresses, suits,

and coats from designers around the world.

Poseyfisher
501 N. Wells St.
644-1749
Designer shoes and Italian imports for women priced from 20 to 60 percent below retail are the specialty at this attractive shop.

Ringolevio
301 W. Superior St.
751-1850
Trendy men's and women's clothes from American and European designers and brands, such as Hugo Boss and Axis, are available here. In addition, there are jewelry, cosmetics, greeting cards, and a small gifts and housewares section.

N. H. Rosenthal Furs
940 N. Michigan Ave.
943-1365
This is one of the first and best furriers on Michigan Avenue. Family-run, it has a reputation for good service and a high-quality selection of designer furs.

Sonia Rykiel
106 E. Oak St.
951-0800
The buyer here chooses from Rykiel's complete line those items she thinks will appeal to Chicago women. In addition, there may soon be children's clothes.

Schwartz's Intimate Apparel
945 N. Rush St.
787-2976
Everything in lingerie from cotton flannel gowns to slinky polyester is here. Some silk swimwear and a large selection of bras, including many in hard-to-find sizes, are also on hand.

Season's Best
645 N. Michigan Ave.
943-6161

Brightly lit and decorated with wood trellises, the store is aptly named. Though there are far more shoes available than clothes, there is a smattering of trendy sportswear as well.

Mark Shale
919 N. Michigan Ave.
440-0720
The main floor here has scads of traditionally styled men's suits, casual wear, accessories, and shoes, while the upper level is devoted to a similar display of women's clothes.

Spaulding & Company
959 N. Michigan Ave.
337-4800
Founded in 1855, this firm has taken and continues to take a conservative approach to the carriage trade, although it had a hand in popularizing gold as an alternative to platinum precious-jewel settings in the 1930s. Unheralded craftsmen produce the traditional jewelry in house and out. Sterling is from the "guild" manufacturers — Gorham, Reed & Barton, Towle, Kirk, and so forth — while tableware is made by such fine old houses as Spode, Wedgwood, and Waterford. Spaulding also sells an exclusive line of stationery and maintains a bridal registry.

Stuart/Chicago
102 E. Oak St.
266-9881
High-style Italian men's clothes — suits, sport coats, slacks, sweaters, and a great selection of ties — are available in this boutique. Though the place sells high style, the sales personnel are helpful and not at all off-putting.

Sugar Magnolia
110 E. Oak St.
944-0885
Stylish, fun clothes and accessories — lots and lots of denim — are sold here.

Boul Mich/River North

Ann Taylor
103 E. Oak St.
943-5411
This two-story shop is one of the more affordable retailers on Oak Street and offers an appealing mix of casual and business wear, ranging from sporty khakis and silk blouses to various designers' clothes.

Tiffany & Company
715 N. Michigan Ave.
944-7500
Founded in New York in 1837, Tiffany's offers exquisite jewels from designers like Paloma Picasso and Elsa Peretti. The walls are lined with representative patterns of crystal and hand-painted china, and Tiffany's own sterling hollowware and flatware. Mixed in with it all are surprisingly affordable gifts.

Ultimo
114 E. Oak St.
787-0906
If you can get past the sometimes haughty salespersons, the clothes here are some of the most sophisticated and special in the city. First to ride the crest of Italian designers — Ferre, Ungaro, Gautier — found in department stores, Ultimo boasts men's and women's sportswear and evening clothes designed by both the stars and the soon-to-be stars of American and European fashion. The accessories — hats, belts, scarves, bags, jewelry — are equally distinctive, and the bilevel boutique is itself a visual treat.

Gianni Versace
101 E. Oak St.
337-1111
There are women's clothes on the first floor here and men's on the second. The selection is from the Italian designer's full line and includes both the far-out and the tame, though, whatever you choose, it's sure to be beautifully designed, expertly tailored, and fine to the touch.

BOOKS

B. Dalton Bookseller
645 N. Michigan Ave.
944-3702
This great big general bookstore has a wide selection of fiction and nonfiction best sellers, as well as a pretty good back-list choice and software.

Book Market
6 E. Cedar St.
944-3358
This is a good place to find the latest paperback fiction, some hardbacks, and nonfiction. There are many magazines as well.

Stuart Brent Books
670 N. Michigan Ave.
337-6357
Modeled on Oxford's Blackwell's, this carpeted shop looks like a library and has a stock tailored to serious readers; the owner has a reputation for loving books more than people, but he must like kids because he writes children's books, and the lower-level kids' books and toys section is charming.

Kroch's & Brentano's
Water Tower Place
835 N. Michigan Ave.
943-2452
This is a big store, oriented toward a general audience, though it's pretty strong in the arts. The bargain-books tables draw large crowds and are often filled with slightly damaged but pretty-new books.

Abraham Lincoln Book Shop
18 E. Chestnut St.
944-3085
You've guessed it: This store specializes in United States history, with an emphasis on Abraham Lincoln and the Civil War, Chicago and Illinois material, rare books, imprints, autograph letters, and documents.

Oak Street Bookshop
54 E. Oak St.
642-3070
Shop here a few times and *voilà!* you're a regular. This Oak Street fixture's proprietress has turned the shop into a real neighborhood place, with a great selection of hardcovers and paperbacks, particularly in the arts. The back room may have one of the city's best theater and film collections.

Rizzoli International Bookstore and Gallery
Water Tower Place
835 N. Michigan Ave.
642-3500
Classical music, classical décor, and contemporary art exhibits in the upstairs gallery space make this one of the city's most pleasant bookstores for browsing. It's particularly strong in art, architecture, design, fashion, and photography, though its fiction and nonfiction selection holds its own as well. Foreign-language magazines and newspapers are available, and there's a small but well-chosen record, tape, and CD section.

GENERAL

Alaska Shop
104 E. Oak St.
943-3393
Here you'll find Eskimo handicrafts in a gallerylike setting: soapstone carvings, a bit of scrimshaw, and naive lithos.

Anti-Cruelty Society
510 N. La Salle Dr.
644-8338
Get your cat or dog from the Ritz of animal shelters. Stanley

Tigerman's playful building allows pets-to-be to see the world and passersby to see them.

Aquariums by Design
730 N. Franklin St.
944-5566
This is unlike any retail aquarium store you've ever visited — it calls itself a gallery of living art. Huge tanks hold a vast international array of spectacularly colorful fresh-water and salt-water fish, corals, and invertebrates. In addition, the store will custom-design aquariums for your home or business, and even maintain them for you once they're installed. Fish range in price from six dollars to more than $400.

Elizabeth Arden
717 N. Michigan Ave.
266-5750
Enter the red door a mess and depart a new woman: Massages, facials, haircuts, shampoos, sets, manicures, the famous cosmetics, high-fashion clothes, and accessories are available.

Bathwares
740 N. Wells St.
642-9420
Here the specialty is highly stylized Italian fixtures and other bathroom paraphernalia.

Chiasso
13 E. Chestnut St.
642-2808
Here you'll find modern — and mostly Italian — designs for the home and office. The store itself won a national design award from Interiors magazine.

City
361 W. Chestnut St.
664-9581
Newly relocated, City has expanded over the years and now offers — in addition to

High Tech furniture, furnishings, and accessories — a wide selection of mostly black-and-white clothes for men and women by top designers, many of them Japanese. Not surprisingly, much of the clothing is minimally designed.

Clearwater Hot Tubs, Inc.
15 W. Hubbard St.
527-1311
This place sells and installs hot tubs, fiber-glass spas, and whirlpool baths, to both the retail and the wholesale trade. You can sample the wares by renting a hot tub in a private room (reservations essential).

Coach Horse Livery, Ltd.
Pearson St. and Michigan Ave.
266-7878
Rent a horse and carriage for a romantic moonlit ride up and down Michigan Avenue.

Cose
750 N. Franklin St.
787-0304
This little shop offers contemporary and modern European objects, with a heavy Italian emphasis. Included are jewelry, crystal, clocks, marble, and table-top furnishings.

Crate & Barrel
850 N. Michigan Ave.
787-5900
Like the chain's other Chicago-area locations, this bright, woody store is a colorful riot of kitchen chic. Much of the sleek glassware and tableware is Scandinavian, and Crate & Barrel stocks tons of heavy, enamel-clad cookware. Bins of kitchen gadgets, food processors and other appliances, High Tech storage units, and other well-designed household delights compete for attention, while the impulse to buy a yard or two of bright Marimekko fabric (even if you don't know

what to do with it) is irresistible.

Mark Cross
909 N. Michigan Ave.
440-1072
This store stocks the elegant, classic leatherware made by the firm.

D & L Office Furniture
30 W. Hubbard St.
527-3636
Five stories of office furniture and furnishings are, for the most part, available for immediate delivery from here or from the huge warehouse.

Deutsch Luggage
111 E. Oak St.
337-2937
Quality luggage and accessories, as well as repairs, are available here.

Elements
738 N. Wells St.
642-6574
This spectacular store carries tableware, lamps, jewelry, and other one-of-a-kind artist-commissioned items. In addition, there are a bridal registry (for avant-garde brides only!) and Chicago's only water bar.

Flight Luggage and Repair
309 W. Chicago Ave.
664-2142
Here there's a large selection of better name-brand business cases, luggage, and some accessories at significant discounts.

Gamma Photo Labs, Inc.
314 W. Superior St.
337-0022
This very big lab offers complete services and enjoys a good reputation with the pros.

Hendricks Music Company
755 N. Wells St.
664-5522
This store was started by Lyon & Healy employees after that store closed down. It carries

Steinway and other pianos.

Herman's World of Sporting Goods
111 E. Chicago Ave.
951-8282
There's a good selection for all sports at reasonable prices in this multilevel store.

Hoffritz Cutlery
634 N. Michigan Ave.
664-4473
This New York-based firm carries fine knives as well as hip flasks, German beer mugs, bar sets, and other paraphernalia.

Jazz Record Mart
11 W. Grand Ave.
222-1467
This store stocks the largest and finest selection of used and new jazz and blues discs — everything from rare old collectors' items to hard-to-find little labels. The cutout bins sometimes yield real finds and always bargains.

Littman Brothers
734 N. Wells St.
943-2660
Old-style, heavy-duty ceiling fans in several finishes are available here.

Manifesto
200 W. Superior St.
664-0733
Perfect reproductions of architect-designed furniture and furnishings — Frank Lloyd Wright and Mies van der Rohe, for example — are available here.

Marilyn Miglin
112 E. Oak St.
943-1120
Located in an elegant little beaux-arts building dwarfed by the modernist monstrosity next door, this is a good place to go for make-up help. The cosmetics are manufactured in a spotless upstairs laboratory (ask to see it) and sold along with brushes and applicators

of all sorts.

Morrie Mages Sports
620 N. La Salle Dr.
337-6151
There's an absolutely huge selection of sportswear here.

North Pier
Lake Shore Drive between the Ogden Slip and Illinois St.
A new renovation of the 82-year-old pier provides a mix of shopping, restaurants, and offices (opens summer, 1988).

Nostalgia Shop
534 N. Clark St.
527-0079
This is a motherlode for magazines and old comics and a bewildering jungle of other stuff, such as advertising premiums, movie stills, and model trains.

Ronsley
363 W. Ontario St.
427-1948
Ronsley bills itself as a "total design center and probably the finest florist in the world." There's a bright, white, High Tech display floor full of flowers, plants, and decorative accessories.

Roman Marble Company
120 W. Kinzie St.
337-2217
This old firm sells antique mantels, alabaster tables, and marble slabs and fabrications, both at retail and to the trade.

Scandia Down Shop
607 N. Wells St.
787-6720
Goosedown quilts, covers, sheet sets, and pillows are available in this little shop accented by illuminated geese.

Scandinavian Design
875 N. Michigan Ave.
664-9232
The giftware department here is highlighted by Svend Jensen crystal, Rosenthal china, and Royal Copenhagen porcelain.

It leads to a block-long concourse-level labyrinth of room settings with that natural, Danish-modern look. This multiunit chain imports some of the finest teak and rosewood chairs, wall units, and dining- and living-room sets from Scandinavian manufacturers.

Shaxted, Inc.
940 N. Michigan Ave.
337-0855
Stylish table linens, bedding, and bathwares are available here. The store stocks a very good selection of the best brands of innovative accessories and will special-order extravagant silk sheets and Swiss-embroidered tablecloths. It will also make up towels, place mats, napkins, tablecloths, and more to match your wallpaper or décor.

Spencer's Marina City Bowl
300 N. State St.
527-0747
This is the only bowling alley in the area open to the public.

Standard Photo Supply
43 E. Chicago Ave.
440-4920
This is one of the country's oldest and largest photographic suppliers.

Table of Contents
448 N. Wells St.
644-9004
This beautiful shop carries distinctive tableware and silverware from around the world. Some of it's very formal, though much of it is casual and even fun.

Tiffany Stained Glass Ltd.
216 W. Ohio St.
642-0680
In addition to stained-glass restorations, offerings here include supplies, classes, books, and a studio, which

makes most of the panels, lamps, and windows on sale.

Tuscany Studios
601 N. Wells St.
664-7680
This outdoor statuary stand — simulated Pompeiian stone, pagodas, cherubs, owls, urns, fountains, all seven dwarfs, and more — is a local landmark.

Williams-Sonoma
17 E. Chestnut St.
642-1593
This is Chicago's only outlet of the famous San Francisco-based kitchenware shop. In addition to the sophisticated and unusual choice of kitchen gadgets and small appliances, there's a nice selection of cookbooks and table-top furnishings.

Write Impressions
42 E. Chicago Ave.
943-3306
Carried here is one of the city's widest selections of customized stationery and desk accessories, plus lots of fun casual notes, cards, and other paraphernalia.

Dining

Ananda
941 N. State St.
944-7440
This chic, high-ceilinged room can be either charming or oppressively noisy, but the Thai food quality seems consistently high. The surprisingly large wine list has many options by the glass.

Avanzare
161 E. Huron St.
337-8056
A buoyant, noisy, sophisticated clientele gives this chic spot an air of sociability, despite the massive granite

walls. Appealing first courses include marinated raw tuna with avocado and sweet onions, lightly grilled scallops with mint vinaigrette, and delicate grilled polenta with Italian sausage and goat cheese. Pastas, available in half portions, are beautifully cooked. Grilled seafood is another highlight.

Benkay
Hotel Nikko Chicago
320 N. Dearborn St.
744-1900
Four styles of Japanese dining, all in beautiful surroundings, are available. A spectacular river view, lovely table settings, exceptional food, and personalized service make zashiki-room dining here the most elegant in town. Menus change daily at the whim of the chef.

Bistro 110
110 E. Pearson St.
266-3110
The setting is bright and cosmopolitan, the customers relaxed and animated, and the servers lively and friendly. The menu is top-heavy with dishes flavored with garlic, rosemary, and thyme — a combination that can become boring. Meals begin with a crisp baguette and luscious roasted garlic to spread on it. The chicken may be the best of the roasted entrées, while the best dessert is a fresh fruit assortment.

Bombay Palace
50 E. Walton St.
664-9323
Exotic aromas, a chic room, and waiters in formal attire set the tone for generally satisfying meals. Some winning choices here include saag paneer (homemade cheese with spinach), nicely cooked fish in a rich cream sauce enlivened by almonds, and

tomato-scented butter chicken. Breads here, especially the puri and chewy nan, are a must.

Cafe Spiaggia
One Magnificent Mile
980 N. Michigan Ave.
280-2764
The setting is chic, the service savvy, and the food stylish. Cracker-thin pizzas and adventurous antipasti can be mixed and matched for a full meal; or focus on a novel pasta (such as earthy parchment-baked spaghettini with fresh tomatoes, garlic, and seafood) and a classic main course, perhaps fish or grilled veal. Don't skip dessert, either. It tastes as lovely as it looks.

Carson's—The Place for Ribs
612 N. Wells St.
280-9200
Carson's offers ample portions of very good food at reasonable prices.

Chestnut Street Grill
Water Tower Place
845 N. Michigan Ave.
280-2720
Distinctive ornamentation in the styles of Frank Lloyd Wright and Louis Sullivan provides visual attraction in this bustling room, but grilled seafood stars. Most grilled fish can be prepared in flavorful reduced-calorie-and-sodium versions by eliminating butter and substituting a nicely seasoned tomato purée for Chicago's best tartar sauce.

Ciel Bleu
Mayfair Regent Hotel
181 E. Lake Shore Dr.
951-2864
This glass-walled room overlooks Oak Street Beach and the north lakeshore. Main courses include starch, vegetable accompaniments, and nicely turned sorbet.

Boul Mich/River North

Club Lago
331 W. Superior St.
337-9444
This place is right out of a
1940s movie set. It's an old
neighborhood spot untouched
by the area's new sophistication, and the food prices are
just like at Taylor Street restaurants.

Convito Italiano
11 E. Chestnut St.
943-2984
The pan-Italian fare in this
graceful dining room occasionally succumbs to international trends, but the high-
quality ingredients — fine olive
oils, fresh herbs, good
cheeses — shine through.
Modern updates of classics are
the best bets: Both paper-thin
tuna carpaccio and saffron-
sauced linguine are delights,
and veal in creamy Gorgon-
zola sauce is delicious.

Cricket's
Tremont Hotel
100 E. Chestnut St.
280-2100
This comfortable room-cum-
corporate toyland is a refuge
for those who want to relax.
The menu offers two dozen
openers and about as many
entrées, plus a handful of daily
specials. The traditional dishes
tend to outshine the trendy ones.

Ed Debevic's
640 N. Wells St.
664-1707
The zany, fifties motif includes
sassy servers, wisecracking
signage, and relentless rock
and roll that are as close as
you'll come to experiencing
time travel. This is still the
only place where you can look
forward to meat loaf; the pot
roast, chicken pot pie, and
chicken-fried steak are also
rewarding. There are several
varieties of hamburgers on
freshly baked rolls, good chili,
a delicious barbecued-pork

sandwich, homemade potato
chips, great mashed potatoes
and gravy, and decent french
fries, too. For dessert: first-
class cream pies.

Foley's
211 E. Ohio St.
645-1261
This is a tastefully decorated,
sophisticated spot with
openers ranging from varia-
tions on the familiar — home-
cured salmon, a fish tartare —
to such Asian-inspired
creations as Szechwan-style
calamari, mussels steamed
with green curry and cream,
and perfectly simmered veal
sweetbreads accented by chive
and lemongrass. Of the seafood entrées, the stars are
grilled fish and such steamed
specials as beautifully moist
salmon with leeks and shii-
takes in a light cream sauce.
Chocolate desserts stand out,
especially the mousse-filled
torte or the ultrarich terrine
with a central nugget of
papaya.

Frontera Grill
445 N. Clark St.
661-1434
Though run by Anglos for
Anglos, this fashionable restaurant has the best and most
interesting Mexican cuisine in
town, despite timid seasoning.
The small menu hints at the
range and breadth of regional
fare, with special emphasis on
less exotic wares such as tacos
al carbón — hardwood grilled
meats served with flour torti-
llas, roasted peppers, guaca-
mole, and black beans. Grilled
game hen seasoned with garlic
and "sweet spices" is a delicious main course, as is the
marinated fresh fish baked in
banana leaves with tomato,
onion, and mild pepper.

Gordon
500 N. Clark St.
467-9780

The whimsical décor here enhances one of the most innovative, enjoyable, and
sophisticated restaurants in
town. The menu features New
American mainstays such as
free-range veal, baby vegetables, and fresh herbs. Bright
beginnings include the Gordon classic: artichoke fritters
with béarnaise sauce. The
desserts continue to shine,
with an archetypal coconut
bavarian cream, orange ice
cream with candied orange
slices, and superb maple custard topped with spiced
pecans.

Hard Rock Cafe
63 W. Ontario St.
943-2252
The walls of this noisy, manic
place are covered with rock
music artifacts and declara-
tions of world peace and universal love. The chili, grilled
burgers, and thick, smooth
milk shakes are very good.

Hat Dance
325 W. Huron St.
649-0066
This is a stagy, stylish, extravagant fantasy complete with
huge palms, etched glass,
mosaics, and a multitude of
captivating details. It also
serves very good food, though
the menu is still evolving and
the house gimmick — juxta-
posing Mexican and Japanese
cookery — doesn't add much.
Generous entrées include pork
chops adobado with creamy
corn pudding, tender carne
asada, grilled shrimp, nicely
cooked chile relleno, and half
a large, delicious wood-
roasted chicken with grilled
vegetables or an admirable
mole sauce.

Hatsuhana
160 E. Ontario St.
280-8287
This bright and attractive restaurant enjoys well-deserved

popularity. The sushi bar is one of the city's biggest and best, with a vast array and cute conceits, such as little racks to hold hand-rolls, among them cones of buttery yellowtail and fatty tuna chopped with scallions.

House of Hunan
535 N. Michigan Ave.
329-9494
At its best it may be the city's top Chinese restaurant. It has the glitter of Hong Kong and a broad menu that includes seldom-seen starters, among them chicken soong, a peppery mixture of diced white meat and minced vegetables rolled in lettuce, and five-color scallop roll, a deep-fried combination of minced scallops, seaweed, ham, and omelet. From the noodle selection, a winner is soft, flat noodles with watercress in hot-and-sour brown sauce. For special occasions there are sizzling-platter dishes; order a day ahead for spectacularly presented Peking duck, a seven-course moo-shu banquet, or special appetizer trays.

Lawry's — The Prime Rib
100 E. Ontario St.
787-5000
Housed in the elegant former McCormick mansion, this restaurant offers only one entrée on its dinner menu: succulent, dry-aged prime ribs of beef. It's worth coming here for that alone.

N.E.W. Cuisine
360 W. Erie St.
642-8885
This stylishly spare second-story spot is forging a new cuisine — nouvelle natural — without using meat or poultry, white flour, or refined sugar. Try a sophisticated cashew terrine in a fiery red-orange sauce or an equally good sun-walnut terrine on velvety cashew sauce. Salads range from simple dinner-variety to picture-pretty entrées, such as tricolor rotini spilling out of an avocado shell. The daily line-up usually includes a few hot pastas, with tarts and fish rounding out the choices.

The 95th
John Hancock Center
875 N. Michigan Ave.
787-9596
This aerie is a unique setting in which to enjoy seasonal native cuisine prepared with more imagination and style than one might expect, given the room's tourist appeal.

The Palm
Mayfair Regent Hotel
181 E. Lake Shore Dr.
944-0135
Fans slowly revolve on the tin ceiling, caricatures age on the walls, sawdust is strewn on the floors; the menu sticks to huge steaks, bigger lobsters, and standard Italo-American items. The food is best savored in elemental forms, so forgo the Italian items for the plain stuff. Quality justifies the steaks' high prices, and the prime ribs are as nice as you'll find.

Le Perroquet
70 E. Walton St.
944-7990
This remains a place of unflagging civility, subdued refinement, and reassuring predictability in menu, service, and cost. The presentations are handsome, and the cooking is careful and unstuffy. Desserts include a superb floating island with a nut glaze and strawberry sauce; homemade sorbets and ice creams are good, and soufflés are spectacularly airy.

Pizzerias Uno and Due
29 E. Ohio St.
321-1000
619 N. Wabash Ave.
943-2400
In simple surroundings, these busy, popular spots serve up some of the best deep-dish pizza in town. The pies start with a dense, yeasty crust topped with a thick layer of mozzarella followed by a choice from a limited number of ingredients, and are finished with a spread of zingy, chunky tomato sauce.

Randall's Ribhouse
41 E. Superior St.
280-2790
This noisy, upscale place with civilized cloth bibs and Turkish finger bowls could be the swankiest rib joint in town. Besides applewood-smoked ribs — good baby backs, bland veal, hearty beef — there are barbecued brisket, chicken, and shrimp; grilled seafood and burgers; salads; Cajun-style dishes; steaks; and prime ribs.

Restaurant Suntory
13 E. Huron St.
664-3344
Here there are three attractive restaurants in one building. The three-star sushi bar is one of the city's best, with uncommon treats such as sweet shako shrimp and pressed Osaka-style sushi. An expansive teppanyaki room griddles much of its very large selection of well-cooked foods with butter; swordfish and juicy sea scallops are good choices. The beautifully appointed dining room has a large, authentic, and interesting menu.

Ritz-Carlton / The Café
Water Tower Place
160 E. Pearson St.
266-1000
The amenities here are impressive: fresh flowers on the tables, many wines by the glass, and lots of china and silver. The menu is varied and tempting, and includes low-cal, low-sodium alternatives.

Boul Mich/River North

Ritz-Carlton/
The Dining Room
Water Tower Place
160 E. Pearson St.
266-1000
Genteel and gracious, this elegant room serves fresh, up-to-date cuisine without yuppie trendiness. A perfect room for special occasions, it has one of the country's best serving staffs, comfortable seating, and straightforward cooking from a seasonal menu.

Rue St. Clair
640 N. St. Clair St.
848-4250
This charming bistro has many assets: romantic lighting, antique posters, soft music, French-style doors opening onto a sidewalk café. The menu balances tradition and innovation, offering appetizers ranging from a daily pâté and gravlax to roasted goat cheese with heavily herbed ratatouille. French bellwethers are among more than a dozen entrées and specials, as are sautéed or baked fish; grilled meats; and a pasta or two.

Scoozi!
410 W. Huron St.
943-5900
This 320-seat house exudes the ebullience of real Italian restaurants. With about 50 dishes in small portions, and an affordable wine list, its only real drawbacks are the jammed bar, fairly high noise level, and very long waits for tables. Despite its comic name, though, Scoozi! is serious about its food. Good specials include spit-roasted leg of lamb with lamb sausage and chop, and a veal chop milanese with zippy pepper relish.

Shaw's Crab House and
Blue Crab Lounge
21 E. Hubbard St.
527-2722

The Crab House is a mammoth, faux-prewar seafood house with comfortable seating, attractive décor, and a vast menu. Next door, the Blue Crab has painted cement-and-brick walls, mostly stool-high oyster-bar accommodations, and a smaller menu. But both have brio, good cooking, and decent value. A long list of specials changes daily, and in their season you'll find stone or soft-shell crabs. Whole Dungeness crabs and blue-crab fingers are always available. Garlicked chicken and frog legs are carefully seasoned and worth a try, as are the many shrimp dishes, crab cakes, and grilled fish.

Spiaggia
One Magnificent Mile
980 N. Michigan Ave.
280-2750
This is the city's costliest Italian restaurant and one of its most innovative of the genre. Appetizer pizzas are thin, crisp, and sparked by toppings such as duck sausage, fresh sage, and goat cheese. In general, the food is often appealing and the servers are particularly good, but the visual beauty of the surroundings can be blemished by occasionally careless cooking that's difficult to overlook. Still, simple and reliable main courses include grilled fish bedded on escarole and drizzled with olive oil, and garlic sirloin with rosemary, pepper, olive oil, and lemon.

Szechwan House
600 N. Michigan Ave.
642-3900
The huge selection, upscale surroundings, and good food make this a reliable choice. Assets here include ginger duck, many beef and chicken dishes, a nice selection of vegetables, and several noodle options.

La Tour
Park Hyatt on
Water Tower Square
800 N. Michigan Ave.
280-2230
The surroundings, augmented with spectacular flowers, are among the fairest in Chicago, and the menu tempts so well that it's difficult to make choices. One solution: the nightly specials for a prix fixe. The chef produces seasonally changing menus that yield a beautifully presented range from commonplace to challenging dishes. Appetizers can run from smoked salmon to sea urchins with fresh noodles and Beluga caviar, and main courses from filet mignon with three sauces to chicken and foie gras in a brioche with a mille-feuille of potatoes and morels. For romantic occasions, try to book a cozy booth or a table near the windows.

Gold Coast & Old Town

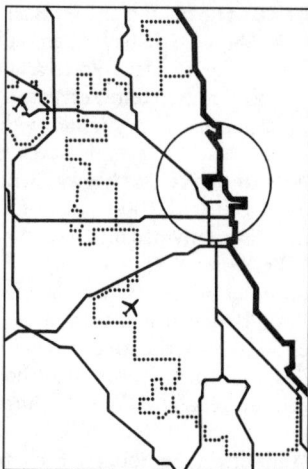

PART OF CHICAGO when the city was incorporated, the Gold Coast lies within the greater Old Town area and has always suggested wealth; it's one of Chicago's most desirable residential neighborhoods, stretching along the lakefront between the Magnificent Mile's glitter and Lincoln Park's greenery. The area is aptly named, too — it's expensive to live here, and the lifestyle has a special, rarefied air. High-rises shoulder one another along Lake Shore Drive, giving some Chicagoans superb lake and beach views. Behind them, more luxury apartments and elegant town houses in a rich variety of styles grace charming, tree-lined streets.

"Astor's Addition" — named for John Jacob Astor — was an area between Division and Schiller streets. The "Catholic Bishop of Chicago's Lake Shore Drive Addition" stretched to North Boulevard. The Queen Anne-style **Archbishop's Residence**, designed by Alfred F. Pashley, set the tone for the first wave of mansions built here in the 1880s.

By 1890, the upper crust flocking to the Gold Coast turned from flamboyance in its architecture toward the massive Romanesque style popularized by Boston architect H. H. Richardson. Of the many examples on Astor Street, perhaps the best are houses at 1316-22 designed by Charles Palmer (no relation) for Potter Palmer. Howard Van Doren Shaw, on the other hand, used English Tudor inspirations for the restrained residence at 1451.

When *Chicago Tribune* publisher Joseph Medill commissioned Stanford White to design a wedding present for his daughter Nellie and son-in-law Robert Patterson, they got a replica of a Renaissance palace. In 1927, architect David Adler expanded the already-huge house for Cyrus McCormick II and created the **Patterson-McCormick Mansion**. Today it's broken up into condos.

Charnley House was built for lumber merchant James Charnley in 1892 by the prestigious firm of Adler and Sullivan; Frank Lloyd Wright was the firm's chief designer at the time. A decade later, Hugh Garden, working in the offices of Richard E. Schmidt, gave a Chicago twist to **Madlener House**. The emphasis here is on the horizontal — a harbinger of the emerging Prairie-school style. Today it's the headquarters of the **Graham Foundation for Advanced Studies in the Fine Arts**.

The **Astor Street District** includes all the old houses on Astor and guarantees their protection, but don't limit your stroll just to this street. The **Frank Fisher Apartments** on North State Parkway, the work of Andrew Rebori, is a small, curved-front, white-brick-and-glass-block art moderne building wrapped around a court. Check out the **Playboy Mansion**, too, where Hef and his harem made their home. Nearby, the **Three Arts Club**, in a fine Holabird and Root building, provides a slightly different environment for young women studying at Chicago's art schools and conservatories.

Gold Coast & Old Town

With several exceptions, such as those that now house the **International College of Surgeons** and the **Polish Consulate General**, the mansions that once lined Lake Shore Drive have been replaced by lavish towers, in which old Chicago families, such as the Wrigleys, Potters, and Insulls, later lived in co-op apartments of 20 or more rooms, with separate servants' quarters on lower floors. Some have 20-foot-high ceilings, parquet floors inlaid with pewter, and organ lofts. Overlooking Lincoln Park rather than the lake, however, is one of the most elegant of these buildings at **1550 North State Parkway**. Benjamin Marshall, architect of the Blackstone and Drake hotels, created 9,000-square-foot residences on each of ten floors. Today, each apartment is subdivided into four.

By World War One, many of the mansions along La Salle Drive were converted to rooming houses. When the city widened the street in the 1930s, making it a major Loop-bound artery, decay accelerated as transient hotels multiplied. Over the past decade, however, the street has enjoyed a renaissance, with town houses converted to condos, and shabby apartment houses restored to their former luster. The delightfully eclectic rehabilitations of Burton Place's town houses are tangible symbols of the revival that was recognized by the city when the block was turned into a cul-de-sac at Wells Street. So, too, are Richard Haas's trompe l'oeil façades on 1211 North La Salle Drive, which give a fin de siècle rebirth to a 1920s high-rise. Image-conscious neighborhood residents even got their stretch of La Salle redesignated a Drive rather than a Street in the 1980s.

In the 1960s, Old Town's main drags between North Avenue and Division Street were jammed with visitors drawn to eat, drink, and shop at places like the College of Complexes, Big John's, Piper's Alley, the Quiet Knight, and Mother Blues. People came from the city and suburbs to rub elbows with the artists and hippies who were reputed to populate the neighborhood.

Developers competed frantically for the chance to build on a multiacre site stretching from North to Division between Clark Street and La Salle Drive. When the dust settled, Arthur Rubloff's mixed high- and low-rise scheme prevailed, and the first phase was completed in 1965. Planned as a middle-income, integrated "city within a city," **Carl Sandburg Village** has instead evolved into an in-town, high-rise suburb of condo owners.

The crowds who gave the neighborhood its sparkle waned in the 1970s, and much of the area took on a seedy, depressed feel. With the dawn of the eighties, however, and the beneficent fallout from the Near North Side residential renaissance, Old Town began an upswing.

Although commercial glitter draws most visitors, the neighborhood has another, quieter side: the **Old Town Triangle District**, bounded by North Avenue, Wells Street, and the imaginary extension of Ogden Avenue to Lincoln Park.

The earliest settlers could afford only the classic balloon-frame Chicago cottage, and these sprang up on cramped lots along the narrow, meandering streets. **St. Michael's Church**, erected in 1852 for $750 on land donated by brewer Michael Diversey, was the community's pride. To accommodate the parish's increased size and overall wealth, in 1866 a new church was built at Eugenie Street and Cleveland Avenue.

The Great Fire of 1871 left only three walls of St. Michael's standing. Residents immediately began rebuilding, and, while shoveling ashes into the basement, they dis-

Gold Coast & Old Town

covered, undamaged, a picture of Our Lady of Perpetual Help, entrusted to the church in 1865 by Pope Pius IX. The picture occupies a special place at one of the altars. In 1902, five altars, including the 56-foot-tall main one, were installed, as were 16 stained-glass windows from Munich. Stations of the Cross, carved in Austria, were added in 1920, and a year later frescoes were painted on the interior walls.

The same energy that went into the reconstruction of St. Michael's after the Fire went into rebuilding the surrounding area. Wooden cottages, cheap and easy to construct, emerged from the rubble. Many still exist. At the same time, with the creation of Lincoln Park on the site of the old municipal cemetery, the area became an attractive place to live. More elaborate, substantial masonry buildings in Italianate or Queen Anne style lined many streets. By the end of the 19th century, the area was completely built up.

With the onset of the Depression, the area began to decay. But some saw this as an opportunity. Many were artists, eking out a living on WPA stipends, attracted by the Old World feeling of the neighborhood. They stabilized the community and gave it the bohemian reputation it retains to this day. Old Town's arty ambiance flourished in the 1940s and 1950s, with its name coming from the Old Town Holiday, now the Old Town Art Fair and still a highlight of the city's outdoor summer events.

Try a walk that begins at St. Michael's. Walk northeast past Willow Street and Fern Court to the **Midwest Buddhist Temple**, built in 1972 to the design of Hideaki Arao.

A short distance east, on Sedgwick Street between Menomonee and Wisconsin streets, ten modern town houses by nine of Chicago's major architects (south from the southeast corner of Wisconsin and Sedgwick: Stanley Tigerman; Booth/Hansen & Architects; Will Ruer; Joseph Boggs/Studio of Dewberry, Nealon & Davis; James E. Economos and Joseph L. Anselmo for Urban Six Associates, Inc.; Booth/Hansen again; Mits Otsuji; Wayne Hanson; Robert Erdmann and Keith Youngquist for Jerome Cerny Associates, Inc.; Thomas E. Greene) stretch out like a life-size museum exhibit.

Continuing northeast, past the new **Church of the Three Crosses**, you'll come to the beginning of Lincoln Park.

Another pleasant walk begins at Lincoln Avenue and Lincoln Park West. Head south on Lincoln Park West to the **Louis Sullivan Town Houses**, designed in 1885 and in splendid condition. The **Tonk House** was designed by an unknown French architect and is now noted for its carved doors — advertisements for woodcutter Max Tonk, son of the first owner.

You might concur with architect John Holabird, Jr., who said: "The houses in Old Town look well by themselves and they look well in groups; they produce neighborhood and street façades. In absolute fact, they make a city — and in half a hundred years we have not done so well."

SHOPPING

Neighborhood amenities on the Gold Coast are few but first-class. Nannies hover over kids playing in the Goudy Square Tot Lot (at Astor and Goethe streets), and many of the neighborhood kids attend the **Latin School of Chicago**, housed in a Harry Weese-designed building. A branch of **Stop & Shop** caters to grocery needs in style. The very fashion-conscious will be appeased at **Parachute**, the Chicago branch of the Canadian-based store selling Japanese-inspired clothing and accessories. Its minimalist décor is the perfect backdrop for the equally minimalist clothes. Don't, however, expect minimalist prices.

At **Chicago Blooms**, baskets filled with the latest seasonal flowers overflow onto the sidewalk outside. Offering a wide selection of both cut flowers and potted plants, Chicago Blooms is also known for its imaginative holiday floral creations.

Old Town itself has many more shops and restaurants, particularly along Wells Street. In a charming courtyard, the **Old Print Store** carries a varied collection of 18th- and 19th-century, old and rare prints and specializes in Currier and Ives, Winslow Homer, and early American lithographs and engravings. **Barbara's Bookstore** is attractive and fertile ground for browsers, with a fine selection of periodicals, paperbacks, and hardcovers, including books from small presses. The literature, cookbook, and children's sections are particularly good.

One of Chicago's merchandising success stories began on Wells Street at **Crate & Barrel**. After launching a sleek fleet of kitchen-and-housewares stores, the original has become the chain's outlet store. Discontinued patterns, overstocks, and seconds of great tableware and cookware at bargain prices fill the brick-and-wood main floor. Linens and fabrics are in the loft.

Bigsby & Kruthers on the Park epitomizes the area's prosperity. It caters to well-heeled men seeking British and Italian suits, conservative business attire, and stylish sportswear, as well as accessories such as leather suspenders and cashmere socks. There's also a special section of clothes for short men, as well as a hair salon and a florist. Across the arcade from the main store, Bigsby's opened Bigsbysport, which carries casual jeans, cords, shirts, and jackets. The building houses an Ann Taylor for women, as well.

With its curious façade, the **Treasure Island** grocery is one of Old Town's best-known stores. T.I.'s collection of esoteric and imported foodstuffs, produce, and gourmet cheeses may be unsurpassed in Chicago. To round out a picnic in the park, head to the **House of Glunz**, where Louis Glunz's family has sold wine and beer since the 1880s, surviving Prohibition by selling sacramental and medicinal libations. A collection of memorabilia dates

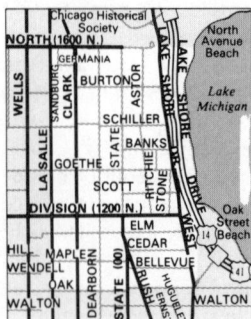

Gold Coast (top) and Old Town

back to the days when it was a tavern catering to neighbors Oscar Mayer and Dr. Scholl.

The **Chicago Clock Co.** is housed where the now-defunct Ripley's Believe It or Not Museum had been. With over 1,000 clocks on display, from alarm clocks to huge grandfather clocks, this could be the largest selection you'll find outside Switzerland. Just up the block is the Feline Inn, which will board your cat and sell you luxurious cat accouterments.

RESTAURANTS AND NIGHTLIFE

In the days when stage and screen stars paused in Chicago on their journeys between New York and Hollywood, they spent time between the Twentieth Century Limited and the Super Chief at the **Pump Room**. Perhaps the city's most famous, flashiest restaurant, its Booth Number One was always reserved for the most celebrated celebrities. Under Lettuce Entertain You Enterprises' ownership, waiters in knee breeches and tights have given way to more subdued finery, but the American cuisine often promises more than it can deliver. Nevertheless, the Pump Room remains a place to see and be seen.

Biggs is housed in a stately Dearborn Street mansion, but that's as far as tradition goes, for the food, though de luxe and pricey, is fresh and contemporary. A relaxing refuge for a romantic tête-à-tête, **Toulouse** is an intimate, dimly lit supper club so old-fashioned that it's back in style.

Trattoria Pizzeria Roma is a chummy, cramped closet of a spot that favors regulars, but the lusty, homey cooking and the authentic atmosphere are likely to make you one. There are only 14 tables here, but the wait for crisp calamari, thin-crusted minipizzas, and big bowls of pasta is surely worth it.

Byfield's at the Omni Ambassador East hotel is a small, jewellike cabaret showcasing live classical piano six nights a week. Another chic spot is **F/X 1100**, where during the summertime you can while away the evening hours watching the street life of the rich and near-rich of the Gold Coast. The convivial atmosphere and a large crowd of young urban professionals make **P. J. Clarke's** a fun and always interesting place to spend the evening with friends.

One of Chicago's oldest and still busiest nightclubs is **Carol's Speakeasy**, which caters to a mostly gay crowd but is open to everyone. Friday night is the hottest of the week. **Zanies** hosts standup and improvisational comedians and full-blown satirical shows for an always-packed and enthusiastic audience. It's one of Old Town's most popular spots.

For people-watching and just plain drinking, Old Town has two near-legendary taverns. The **Old Town Ale House** attracts interesting crowds, as it did when Eric Van Gelder first drew a beer here in 1958. Though many of its customers can no longer afford to live nearby, they return to play the eclectic juke box, converse in a sort of near-shout, and watch other people watching them. **O'Rourke's Public House** is plastered with photos of Irish writers, IRA graffiti, and Chicago journalists who wander in after late-night beats.

Gold Coast & Old Town

For a completely different atmosphere, try the **Hunt Club Bar and Grill**, owned by Chicago Bears safety and local heartthrob Gary Fencik. The place is preppy to the max, jammed nightly, and serves up surprisingly good food. There's live music six nights a week as well.

Interesting Places

▶ **Archbishop's Residence**
1555 N. State Pkwy.

▶ **Astor Street District**
Astor St. from North Blvd. to Division St.

▶ **Charnley House**
1365 N. Astor St.

Church of the Three Crosses
Wisconsin and Orleans streets
951-7916

▶ **Frank Fisher Apartments**
1207 N. State Pkwy.

▶ **Graham Foundation for Advanced Studies in the Fine Arts**
4 W. Burton Pl.
787-4071

▶ **International College of Surgeons**
1516 N. Lake Shore Dr.
642-3555

International College of Surgeons Hall of Fame and Museum of Surgical Science
1524 N. Lake Shore Dr.

▶ **Latin School of Chicago**
59 W. North Blvd.
787-0820

▶ **Louis Sullivan Town Houses**
1826-34 N. Lincoln Park West

▶ **Midwest Buddhist Temple**
Menomonee St. and Hudson Ave.
943-7801

Moody Memorial Church
La Salle Dr. and North Ave.
943-0466

▶ **Patterson-McCormick Mansion**
20 E. Burton Pl.
664-5058

▶ **Playboy Mansion**
1340 N. State Pkwy.

▶ **Polish Consulate General**
1530 N. Lake Shore Dr.
337-8166

▶ **St. Michael's Church**
Eugenie St. and Cleveland Ave.
642-2498

▶ **Three Arts Club**
1300 N. Dearborn St.
944-6250

▶ **Tonk House**
1817 N. Lincoln Park West

▶ **Wacker House**
1838 N. Lincoln Park West

 ## Shopping

A New Leaf
1645 N. Wells St.
642-1576

Ambassador West Hotel
1300 N. State Pkwy.
787-7900

▶ **Ann Taylor**
1750 N. Clark St.
337-4462

▶ **Barbara's Bookstore**
1434 N. Wells St.
642-5044

▶ **Bigsby & Kruthers on the Park**
1750 N. Clark St.
440-1750

Blockbuster Video
1201 N. Clark St.
664-1225

▶ **Chicago Blooms**
1149 N. State St.
951-1688

▶ **Chicago Clock Co.**
1502 N. Wells St.
751-1980

▶ **Crate & Barrel Warehouse Store**
1510 N. Wells St.
787-4775

▶ **Feline Inn**
1445 N. Wells St.
943-2230

▶ **House of Glunz**
1206 N. Wells St.
642-3000

▶ **Old Print Store**
1407 N. Wells St.
266-8631

Omni Ambassador East Hotel
1301 N. State Pkwy.
787-7200

▶ **Parachute**
22 W. Maple St.
943-9292

Racquet Club of Chicago
1365 N. Dearborn St.
787-3200

Rose Records
1122 N. State St.
943-8530

▶ **Stop & Shop**
1313 N. Ritchie Ct.
853-2150

▶ **Treasure Island**
1639 N. Wells St.
642-1105

Up Down Tobacco Shop
1550 N. Wells St.
337-8025

Gold Coast & Old Town

Wild Goose Chase Quilt Gallery
1248 N. Wells St.
787-9778

Restaurants

Bagel Nosh
1135 N. State St.
266-6369

▶ **Biggs** — eclectic
1150 N. Dearborn St.
787-0900

Café Azteca — Mexican
215 W. North Ave.
944-9854

Ciao — Italian
1516 N. Wells St.
266-0048

Elm Street Cafe — eclectic
1141 N. State St.
944-0098

Jeff's Laugh Inn — coffee shop
1800 N. Lincoln Ave.
751-0434

Kamehachi of Tokyo — Japanese
1617 N. Wells St.
664-3663

Mangia Italiana Ristorante — Italian
1560 N. Wells St.
951-8707

Martha's Vineyard — fish
1160 N. Dearborn St.
337-6617

▶ **Pump Room** — Continental
Omni Ambassador East Hotel
1301 N. State Pkwy.
266-0360

Ristorante Zio — Italian
1148 N. State St.
337-2474

Royal Thai Orchid — Thai
1123 N. State St.
943-4966

▶ **Toulouse** — French
51 W. Division St.
944-2606

Third Coast — coffee house
1260 N. Dearborn St.
649-0730

▶ **Trattoria Pizzeria Roma** — Italian
1557 N. Wells St.
664-7907

Nightlife

▶ **Byfield's**
Omni Ambassador East Hotel
1301 N. State Pkwy.
787-6433

▶ **Carol's Speakeasy**
1355 N. Wells St.
944-4226

▶ **F/X 1100**
1100 N. State St.
280-2282

▶ **Hunt Club Bar and Grill**
1983 N. Clybourn Ave.
549-3020

▶ **Old Town Ale House**
219 W. North Ave.
944-7020

▶ **O'Rourke's Public House**
319 W. North Ave.
944-1030

▶ **P.J. Clarke's Restaurant and Bar**
1204 N. State Pkwy.
664-1650

Second City
1616 N. Wells St.
337-3992

▶ **Zanies**
1548 N. Wells St.
337-4027

Lincoln Park/DePaul

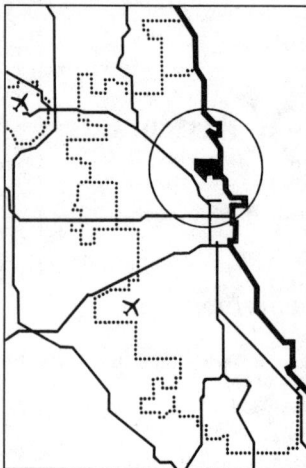

LINCOLN PARK AND DEPAUL represent the good life — Chicago style.

The neighborhood is a sampler of the city's best: fashionable boutiques, restaurants, charming streetscapes, and fine architecture. Yet, with all its 24-hour-a-day glamour, the Lincoln Park/DePaul area retains a human scale. The side streets are tranquil, tree-shaded wonders of urban revitalization; the mass of high-rises on and east of Clark Street is softened by the neighborhood's front yard — the stretch of Lincoln Park with the zoo, conservatory, and boating lagoon.

The pattern for Lincoln Park fashionability was set a century ago. Middle-class merchants and skilled craftsmen built their homes amid the early farms that edged Clark Street's forerunner — Green Bay Road, an old Indian trail and pioneer route to Wisconsin. As Chicago grew, travelers on the road skirted the swamplands to the east, known as the Ten-Mile Ditch, on their way to the picnic groves and resorts of Lake View. By the end of the Civil War, the area, especially Lincoln Park, was heavy with balloon-frame cottages — perfect fuel for the Fire of 1871, which devastated it.

Today, FOR SALE signs beckon from scores of dilapidated buildings west of Halsted Street, in the DePaul area. Old frame cottages are suddenly sporting angled cedar siding, solariums, or skylights. New town houses are popping up everywhere. DePaul, it seems, is the model neighborhood-on-the-make, with a solid core of newly renovated, fancifully fronted, turn-of-the-century brick two- and three-flats, and newfound activity on streets that seemed lost only a decade ago. Halsted Street and Armitage Avenue house almost as many real estate brokers as trendy shops and bars. The area is a low-key sort of place with lots of old-timers sticking it out in carefully maintained, ungentrified homes next to those rehabbed by young families.

INTERESTING SITES

Three handsome churches on Fullerton Parkway attest to the neighborhood's relative affluence. Prominent hotel architect Clinton J. Warren designed the Norman-Romanesque **Church of Our Saviour** in the late 1880s. The limestone-faced, red-brick Episcopal church is graced with Victorian decoration, including striking oak woodwork, beautiful stained glass (especially the Tiffany altar window), and exquisite terra-cotta tile. At the **Lincoln Park Presbyterian Church**, the Michigan sandstone dates from the same period. Red-oak pews radiate from the communion table in semicircular rows, and the sanctuary windows are outstanding; the Johnson & Son tracker organ is the only one of its kind still heard in Chicago. **St. Pauls United Church of Christ**, one of the city's oldest congregations, has twice succumbed to fire: in 1871 during the Great Fire and again on Christmas Day, 1955. Benjamin Franklin Olsen, who had designed the 1950 chapel and parish house, harmonized the replacement church with his earlier efforts. The 1957 building houses one of Chicago's few Aeolian-Skinner organs.

A strong institutional base — **Children's Memorial**, **Grant**, **Columbus**, and **Augustana** hospitals; **DePaul University**; **Francis Parker School** — added stability, and the neighborhood prospered, with some ups and downs, through World War Two. DePaul University began as St. Vincent's College and grew around the lovely **St. Vincent de Paul Church**. Lush stained glass, including a deep-blue rose window, pierces the gray stone walls of the 1895 Romanesque church, which has a striking coffered ceiling and marble altars. Campus and community are strongly linked, with locals attending lectures, concerts, and theater performances. Although the university is currently known for its basketball team, a less transitory reputation stems in large part from its Loop-campus law school. The alma mater of many judges, lawyers, and politicians, it's considered something of a prep school for Chicago power brokers.

The doldrums that affected Lincoln Park-DePaul after the war were broken in the 1960s as an influx of newcomers, eager to restore and renovate, moved to the area. So successful was the effort that in 1977 the Commission on Chicago Historical and Architectural Landmarks designated much of the neighborhood the **Mid-North District**, asserting that it "vividly portrays the character of the typical Chicago residential neighborhood at the end of the 19th century."

This is a neighborhood for strolling. Not only are narrow streets a congested maze of frustrating one-ways, but parking borders on the impossible. In any case, you'll want to let the area's subtly shifting moods envelop you. On warm summer evenings the side streets evoke Paris's Left Bank. On weekend afternoons, Clark and Halsted streets' sidewalks are jammed with shoppers and browsers. In spring, summer, and fall, joggers and picnickers stream to park and beach.

Almost every street is a visual treat. Start on Cleveland Avenue, from Fullerton Parkway to Dickens Avenue, a street that includes a pastiche of styles. The two-story houses (2239 and 2243) that survived the Fire are said to mark the blaze's northern limits. The beautifully maintained Italianate town house (2234-36) splendidly plays off the row of shared-wall masonry town houses across the street. A Greek Revival cottage (2208) stands next to a new concrete home designed by Lawrence Booth in 1980; Bruce Graham, who designed the John Hancock Center, is responsible for 2215. The façade of the older building at 2150 was replaced with striking art deco, diamond-shaped leaded glass in the 1930s; across the street the unusual brick cottage with a triangular bay (2147) is sometimes attributed to Louis Sullivan. A mansard-roofed, Queen Anne-influenced chateau (2114-16) provides a graceful contrast to Booth and Nagle's modern 1970 house of brick, glass, steel, and wood on the corner. Turn here onto Lincoln Avenue and see a delightful red-brick Victorian mansion that withstood the blandishments of the urban-renewal project that cleared the rest of the block for modern, modified A-frame town houses.

Other rewarding walks include Hudson Avenue, Belden Avenue, Cambridge Avenue's cul-de-sac (the little mewslike court's buildings were carriage houses for the homes on Belden), and Fullerton Parkway, which is lined with some of the city's grandest town houses. Don't overlook the side streets north of Fullerton, either.

The lakefront attracted the wealthy, and some of their residences fortunately remain. Two of particular interest are the **Theuer-Wrigley House** and the **Francis J. Dewes House**. Built in 1896 for German brewers, both are official city landmarks.

Lincoln Park/DePaul

The Theuer mansion was the work of Richard E. Schmidt. Splendid details, such as terra-cotta ornamentation and the copper cornice, add distinction to this Italian Renaissance gem. At the Dewes house, European architects Adolph Cudell and Arthur Hercz created a baroque fantasy, complete with caryatids supporting the wrought-iron balcony.

A spate of high-rise building in the teens left a legacy of a gracious bygone age. Peer through the windows at 451 West Wrightwood Avenue and see a medieval cloister in pink marble. The **Belden-Stratford Hotel** has a magnificent two-story, marble-clad lobby and a photo gallery of luminaries who made the hotel their name.

SHOPPING

Lincoln Park-DePaul is a shopper's haven, with scores of new- and-antique-clothing stores, art and antiques galleries, and bookstores that cater to both those who live in the neighborhood and those who just come to play in it.

Lill Street Studios, an old horsecar stable where the Robbins Clay Company produces clay for both students and ceramists, houses 17 potters whose work is on display. Bold paintings by such artists as Fritz Scholder and Len Agrella cover the walls of **American West**. Devoted to contemporary art of the Southwest, this gallery also carries posters from major exhibitions of Western art, ceremonial artifacts, pottery, and some jewelry.

Maya Imports ranges farther south with high-quality arts and crafts from Latin America, including a collection of Amazonian Indian objects such as masks and tapa wall hangings. There are handwoven Peruvian rugs, primitive bark paintings, replicas of Mayan statues, and other decorative items, plus clothes that range from embroidered Mexican shirts and dresses to handknit Peruvian sweaters. Lacy Mexican wedding gowns, Guatemalan shirts and blouses, embroidered dresses, and colorful ponchos are a few of the attractions at **Mexican Folk Arts**, an airy shop that looks as south-of-the-border as its stock. Both inexpensive trinkets and pricey masks of Mexican and Latin American descent line the walls.

Fearsome masks from Papua New Guinea are among the art objects at **Les Primitifs**, a fascinating store that specializes in African and Oceanian "ethnographic art." Working with African specialists, the owners handpick all the items for the shop. **Old World Antiques** features post-Civil War American

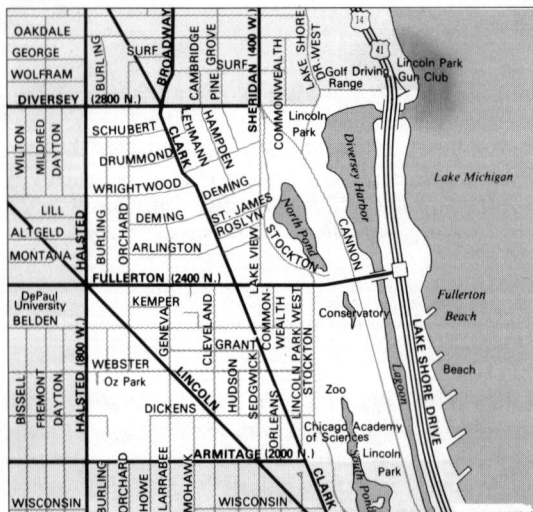

Lincoln Park

and European furniture, art nouveau bronzes, and wonderful French advertising broadsheets by Mucha and other artists. **Quercus Antiques** sells expensive, refinished oak and walnut furniture in an airy show room. A beautiful store carved out of an old stable, the **Antiquery Warehouse** is rich with American and European period furniture and some fine dinnerware. Restored lighting fixtures and hardware are available at **Brass Works**.

The stretch of Armitage Avenue from Halsted Street to Sheffield Avenue is a delightful stroll past renovated cottages and steep-stooped brick row houses with shops on the high first floors. The antiques shops fit right in. In a ramshackle old building, **Adam Monroe's Antiques** offers two floors of mostly as-is jumble, as well as a backyard of architectural antiques. Look especially for old advertising paraphernalia, fixtures, and accessories. The whitewashed **Turtle Creek Antiques** is a perfect setting for wicker furniture and patchwork antique quilts, as well as various other textiles. Pricey, nicely refinished, turn-of-the-century oak and other furniture can be found at the crowded **Collectibles Antiques**, the spare **Elf Shoppe**, and **Century Clocks**, along with a few nice case clocks and pocketwatches at the last-named store.

Late 19th-century and early 20th-century oak dressers, hall stands, and buffets are sold at **Paul James Antiques**. In addition to wood pieces, the store has marble-topped tables, brass beds, dictionary stands, candlesticks, and other accessories. A forest of brass chandeliers with fancy frosted and etched-glass globes cast a warm glow in **Stanley Galleries Antiques**. Ken Stanley specializes in American lighting fixtures from 1850 to 1925. All the brass lamps and chandeliers have been disassembled, buffed with a succession of polishes, washed in solvent, sprayed with lacquer, baked to fuse the lacquer so it won't need to be polished for years, and reassembled. The prices reflect the gleam of the results. Some stained-glass and terra-cotta ornaments are also on hand.

There are two locations of **Something Different**, the former of which at 837 West Armitage Avenue carries crystal, silk, dried and cut flowers, and other plants. At 816, a charming add-on behind an old house, rag rugs, ceramics, and other items that lean toward the kitschy proliferate. The

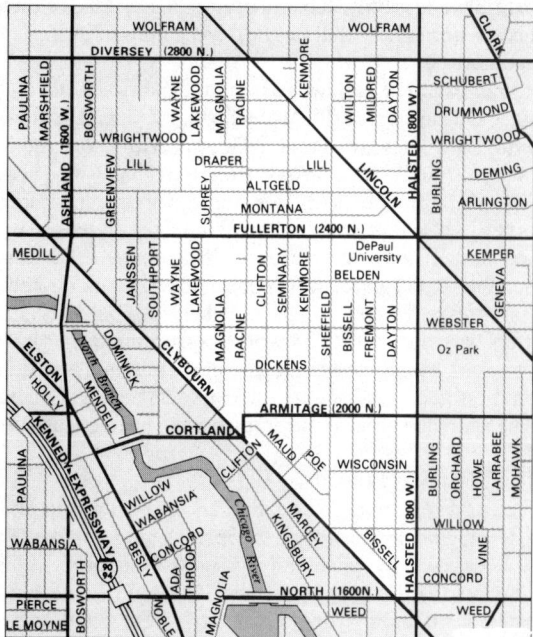

DePaul

Lincoln Park/DePaul

small, hidden **Greenhouse Unlimited** is another of the numerous plant shops satisfying the plants-and-antiques interior-decorating treatment the neighborhood's Victorian buildings seem to cry for.

The decidedly upscale Lincoln Park neighborhood and the university probably contribute to the wealth of bookstores in the area. **Women and Children First** is devoted to feminist issues, families, and children. All of the fiction and poetry is by women; some of the kids' books aim specifically at debunking cultural stereotypes. **Aspidistra Bookshop** is a jammed-to-the-rafters store with more than 40 sections. There's a constant influx of new arrivals, and prices are fair, though few under priced treasures last long.

Lincoln Avenue, just north of Fullerton, is a bookbuyers' paradise, with numerous used- and new-book stores lining both sides of the street. At **Guild Books**, loads of politically oriented books and periodicals on social issues, the social sciences, history, politics, and the like are featured, as well as books from little presses, general literature, and works on the arts. Special programs and autographing parties draw big, interesting crowds. Another bookstore of note is **Booksellers Row**.

Nonpareil is wonderfully eclectic, with everything from unique folk art to a selection of handcrafted items that includes Peruvian textiles, colorful soft sculptures, woodcarvings, jewelry, and ceramics. There's also a good selection of contemporary and offbeat clothes and scarves.

Clothing stores in Lincoln Park-DePaul come and go as fast as many fads do, but that only adds to the fun and ever-changing face of the neighborhood. Still, there are success stories here that provide everything from the latest fashions to classics to vintage clothes.

Aran sweaters, handwoven scarves, and tweed jackets are among the fine woolens at Mary Dugan's **Erinisle**. Women's coats, suits, and dresses tend to be wool in winter, cotton and linen in summer. This cheerful shop, redolent of potpourri and scented soaps, also sells rustic thrown stoneware, handsome heavy glassware, and handicrafts, all to the strains of Irish folk music. City sophistication is the message at **Port of Entry**, a chic shop in an old row house, which sells trendy separates by Francesca Sterlacci and Richard Dayhoff, and handwoven silks. Equally sophisticated clothing is available at **Dégagé**, which specializes in mixing and matching clothes (mostly by American designers) in unexpected ways to outfit its enthusiastic clientele. **Presence** offers bargains aplenty on women's clothing from places like India and China. All of it's casual, trendy, and fun: colorful overalls and jumpsuits, simple jumpers, gauzy cotton dresses, outlandish socks, Chinese rayon jackets, cotton and pure silk blouses, tons of lighthearted jewelry and accessories. The frequent sales are legendary.

RESTAURANTS

There is a restaurant in Lincoln Park-DePaul to suit almost every culinary and ethnic taste imaginable, from a yen for Spanish tapas at **Cafe Ba-Ba-Reeba!** to a hankering for Lebanese baba ghannouj at **Uncle Tannous**.

Located off the lobby of the once-grand Belden-Stratford Hotel, art nouveau-inspired **Ambria** is one of the city's best restaurants. Nouvelle cuisine here means sophisticated entrées, unusual combinations of ingredients, ethereal sauces, beautiful presentations, and great style, matched only by the prices and difficulty in getting reservations. Across the lobby is another of the city's most glamorous, though less formal, bistros, **Un Grand Café.**

Geja's Cafe is a cramped but fun and romantic spot mostly serving fondues — from a rich, kirsch-spiked cheese to seafood, beef, or chicken. Afterward, try fresh fruit dipped in a flaming chocolate dessert fondue. The service is smooth and practiced; a classical-flamenco guitarist helps create the mood.

Other ethnic choices abound in the neighborhood as well, including **Salvatore's**, a chic but expensive spot serving northern Italian food in a traditional, old-world setting. **Carlucci** serves both stylish Italian food and stylish diners in an austere, striking room enlivened with modern Italian paintings.

Cafe Royal is a tastefully appointed multilevel collection of bars, salons, and dining rooms offering pleasant, better-than-average British cuisine. For a romantic evening, request one of the one-table rooms. A few steps up the street is **Blue Mesa**, where the stunning décor is highlighted by a rustic fireplace, Indian art, and lots of bleached wood. There are stuffed sopaipillas, blue-corn enchiladas, and shrimp and steak fajitas, as well as an array of novelty drinks. For a different approach to south-of-the-border dining, try **El Criollo**, which dishes up food from Mexico, Argentina, and Puerto Rico. **Rinconcito Sudamericano**, decorated with llama rugs and enlivened by Latin music, serves exciting and sometimes quite exotic Peruvian food.

There's usually a wait at **Itto Sushi**, but it's worth it. The sushi is topnotch, but don't hesitate to order the cooked selections; chicken and beef teriyaki are fine, and there's a tantalizing selection of small tidbits, such as shitashi (dried fish), kushikatsu (deep-fried pork), and goma-ae (spinach with sesame sauce). Another fine spot for sushi is **Sai Cafe**, where superior taste and presentation are given equal consideration.

R. J. Grunts was the first fun-food restaurant in the neighborhood, and remains one of the best. A top-of-the-line salad bar, great burgers, and an informal atmosphere keep bringing people back for more. Laid-back and relaxing, **John Barleycorn Memorial Pub** is not exactly a singles bar but has long attracted hip, intellectual sorts with classical music, free silent movies, and one of the best bar burgers in town.

One of Chicago's most lovely, intimate settings for nouvelle cuisine is at **Jackie's**, where fresh fish dishes often have Asian overtones. Everything from appetizers to desserts on the small but varied menu is expertly prepared and exquisitely served. Don't miss the chocolate "bag" stuffed with white chocolate mousse and fruit, in a pool of raspberry sauce. The newest addition to the neighborhood's nouvelle scene is **Charlie Trotter's**. This elegant little place has a new menu daily and serves chic pre-entrée sorbets in flavors like herbal lemon and ginger-orange.

Finally, for a late-night bite, go directly to the **Belden Deli**, where matzoh ball soup, pastrami, corned beef, and Boston cream pie are served up, straight through the morning. The later the hour, the weirder the crowd.

NIGHTLIFE

Park West is a large, glitzy nightclub with a stupendous sound system. It brings in top jazz, rock, and comedy acts. Decorated with 1950s and '60s paraphernalia, **Juke Box Saturday Night** offers a live disc jockey, a large dance floor, and malt-shop munchies. **Neo** is a New Wave dance club catering to what's left of the New Wave crowd in Lincoln Park. There's good music, though, so old-wavers will enjoy it, too.

Lincoln Park/DePaul

At the **Ultimate Sports Bar and Grill**, memorabilia covers the walls, some of the tables are in a boxing ring, and there's a basketball hoop at the bar. **Kelly's Pub** is a DePaul tradition. Part old-time Irish saloon, part college hangout, it's always noisy, always crowded — except during finals week — and always fun, except when DePaul loses a basketball game. In fact, most of the bars around the university share a congenial, unhassled feeling you won't find on Rush Street.

More than a quarter century old, the **Old Town School of Folk Music** is a neighborhood institution. Step inside and you'll hear the echoes of Win Stracke, Fleming Brown, Jo Mapes, Ella Jenkins, and Bob Gibson. Classes, workshops, concerts, kids' programs, and several all-night folk-music parties per year keep the flame burning. Another hangout for folk music lovers is **Earl's Pub**.

Some of the city's best blues clubs are right in this neighborhood, as well. **B.L.U.E.S.** is Hollywood-set perfect: crowded, noisy, smoky, and dumpy-looking. It's also a great place to hear hard-driving, Chicago-style blues. There's music nightly, and even the juke box keeps the faith. Many of the same performers hold forth across the street at **Kingston Mines**. The music is continual, and the place really hops "after-hours," when musicians wander in from other gigs for hot jam sessions.

Exciting programs of new films and retrospectives seven days a week have made **Facets Multimedia Center** nationally famous. Milos Stehlik and company put together events ranging from science-fiction and rock-and-roll film festivals to workshops with distinguished directors, such as Louis Malle, Werner Herzog, and Costa-Gavras. The screens are small and the seats less than luxurious, but that just adds to the arty camaraderie. In addition, a host of classic and foreign films on video is available for rental.

The **Biograph Theater** is the area's most famous landmark. Neighborhood residents still drag visitors to the spot where G-men gunned down John Dillinger, whether they're interested or not. (The film was *Manhattan Melodrama* and nobody knows if he enjoyed it.) The theater shows high-quality foreign and American films too chancy for general distribution.

Interesting Places

▶ **Belden-Stratford Hotel**
2300 N. Lincoln Park West
281-2900

Chicago Academy of Sciences
2001 N. Clark St.
549-0606

Chicago Historical Society
Clark St. at North Blvd.
642-4600

▶ **Church of Our Saviour**
Fullerton Pkwy. at Cambridge
549-3832

DePaul University
bounded by Fullerton Pkwy., Halsted St., Racine Ave., and Webster Ave.

Elks National Memorial Building
2750 N. Lake View Ave.
477-2750

▶ **Francis J. Dewes House**
503 W. Wrightwood Ave.

Lincoln Park Conservatory
Fullerton Dr. at Stockton Dr.
294-4770

▶ **Lincoln Park Presbyterian Church**
Fullerton Pkwy. at Geneva Terr.
248-8288

Lincoln Park Zoological Gardens
2200 N. Cannon Dr.
294-4660

▶ **Mid-North District**
bounded roughly by Clark St., Armitage Ave., Lincoln Ave., Fullerton Pkwy.

Policeman Bellinger's Cottage
2121 N. Hudson Ave.

St. Pauls United Church of Christ
Fullerton Pkwy. at Orchard St.
348-3829

Lincoln Park/DePaul

▶ **St. Vincent de Paul Church**
Webster and Sheffield avenues

▶ **Theuer-Wrigley House**
2466 N. Lake View Ave.

Shopping

Aca Joe
2740 N. Clark St.
248-8802

Act I Bookstore
2633 N. Halsted St.
348-6757

Aged Experience Antiques, Etc.
2034 N. Halsted St.
975-9790

All Our Children
2217 N. Halsted St.
327-1868

▶ **American West**
2110 N. Halsted St.
871-0400

And Feathers Bird Studio — bird store
1015 W. Webster Ave.
549-6944

Ann Taylor
1750 N. Clark St.
337-4462

AnnaBa Design — women's apparel
531 W. Drummond Pl.
327-4031

▶ **Antiquery Warehouse**
2050 N. Halsted St.
528-0545

▶ **Aspidistra Bookshop**
2630 N. Clark St.
549-3129

Australian Kangaroo Connection
1113 W. Webster Ave.
248-5499

Bathlines
2154 N. Halsted St.
472-0777

Bellini Juvenile Furniture
2001 N. Halsted St.
943-6696

▶ **Bigsby & Kruthers**
1750 N. Clark St.
440-1750

▶ **Booksellers Row**
2445 N. Lincoln Ave.
348-1170

Bountiful Board — gourmet food
2650 N. Clark St.
549-1999

▶ **Brass Works**
2142 N. Halsted St.
935-1800

▶ **Century Clocks**
844 W. Armitage Ave.
549-5727

Chewy's Nuts
845 W. Armitage Ave.
929-2439

Chia on Halsted
2202 N. Halsted St.
248-9595

Children's Bookstore
2465 N. Lincoln Ave.
248-2665

Cignal
2828 N. Clark St.
281-6635

J. L. Clark Bookstore
2463 N. Lincoln Ave.
929-5119

Dan Howard's Maternity
2413 N. Clark St.
528-9600

▶ **Dégagé**
2252 N. Clark St.
935-7737

▶ **Elf Shoppe**
846 W. Armitage Ave.

▶ **Erinisle**
2246 N. Clark St.
975-6616

Findables
2050 N. Halsted St.
348-0674

Foodworks
935 W. Armitage Ave.
935-6800

Granitza European Fashion
826 W. Armitage Ave.
525-5442

▶ **Greenhouse Unlimited**
849 W. Armitage Ave.
281-7484

▶ **Guild Books**
2456 N. Lincoln Ave.
525-3667

House Store
620 W. Schubert Ave.
525-7771

Kinko's — 24-hour copy service
2451 N. Lincoln Ave.
327-7770

Legacy Vintage
953 W. Armitage Ave.
935-0374

Limited
2828 N. Clark St.
549-2075

Mary's Pet Shop
951 W. Armitage Ave.
549-7110

▶ **Maya Imports**
2044 N. Halsted St.

▶ **Mexican Folk Arts**
2433 N. Clark St.
871-1511

Mike and Maud's — women's apparel
954 W. Webster Ave.
935-9111

My Own Two Feet
2148 N. Halsted St.
935-3338

New England Trader
2116 N. Halsted St.
935-6767

▶ **Nonpareil**
2300 N. Clark St.
477-2933

▶ **Old World Antiques**
2040 N. Halsted St.

Lincoln Park/DePaul

▶ **Paul James Antiques**
2727 N. Clark St.

▶ **Port of Entry**
2032 N. Halsted St.
348-4550

▶ **Presence**
2501 N. Clark St.
248-1761

▶ **Les Primitifs**
2038 N. Clark St.
528-5200

▶ **Quercus Antiques**
2148 N. Halsted St.

Ringolevio — men's and
women's apparel
2001 N. Halsted St.
642-4999

Robert Daniels Florist
1964 N. Halsted St.
525-7300

Saturday's Child
2146 N. Halsted St.
525-8697

Second Hand Tunes —
used records
2550 N. Clark St.
929-6325

SirReal — men's apparel
2204 N. Clark St.
929-8538

Socks Life
545 W. Diversey Pkwy.
871-7840

▶ **Something Different**
837 and 816 W. Armitage Ave.
871-6810

Spare Parts
2947 N. Broadway
525-4242

▶ **Stanley Gallery Antiques**
2118 N. Clark St.
281-1614

Sugar Magnolia —
men's and women's apparel
2130 N. Halsted St.
525-9188

That Girl Boutique
833 W. Armitage Ave.
477-3422

▶ **Turtle Creek Antiques**
850 W. Armitage Ave.
327-2630

Underthings
804 W. Webster Ave.
472-9291

Wax Trax Records
2449 N. Lincoln Ave.
929-0221

Wine Emporium
2540 N. Lincoln Ave.
883-0500

▶ **Women and Children First**
1967 N. Halsted St.
440-8824

✕ Restaurants

▶ **Ambria**
2300 N. Lincoln Park West
472-5959

▶ **Belden Deli**
2315 N. Clark St.
935-2752

▶ **Blue Mesa**
1729 N. Halsted St.
944-5990

▶ **Cafe Ba-Ba-Reeba!**
2024 N. Halsted St.
935-5000

Cafe Phoenicia — Middle
Eastern
2814 N. Halsted St.
549-7088

▶ **Cafe Royal**
1633 N. Halsted St.
266-3394

▶ **Carlucci**
2215 N. Halsted St.
281-1220

Casbah — Middle Eastern
514 W. Diversey Pkwy.
935-7570

Chardonnay — French
2635 N. Halsted St.
477-5130

▶ **Charlie Trotter's**
816 W. Armitage Ave.
248-6228

La Crêperie — crêpes
2845 N. Clark St.
528-9050

El Criollo
1706 W. Fullerton Ave.
549-3373

L'Escargot on Halsted —
French
2925 N. Halsted St.
525-5522

Fricano's — seafood
2512 N. Halsted St.
929-7550

▶ **Geja's Cafe**
340 W. Armitage Ave.
281-9101

▶ **Un Grand Café**
2300 N. Lincoln Park West
348-8886

▶ **Itto Sushi**
2616 N. Halsted St.
871-1800

▶ **Jackie's**
2478 N. Lincoln Ave.
880-0003

▶ **John Barleycorn
Memorial Pub**
658 W. Belden Ave.
348-8899

▶ **Lindo Mexico** — Mexican
2642 N. Lincoln Ave.
871-4832

Muskie's Hamburgers
2870 N. Lincoln Ave.
883-1633

OFamè — Italian
750 W. Webster Ave.
929-5111

La Paella — Spanish
2920 N. Clark St.
528-0757

Periwinkle — eclectic
2511 N. Lincoln Ave.
883-9797

Les Plumes — French
2044 N. Halsted St.
525-0121

Ranalli's Pizzeria
1925 N. Lincoln Ave.
642-4700

RD Clucker's — chicken
2350 N. Clark St.
929-5200

Redamak's — burgers
2263 N. Lincoln Ave.
787-9866

▶**Sai Cafe**
2010 N. Sheffield Ave.
472-8080

▶**Salvatore's**
525 W. Arlington Pl.
528-1200

▶**Uncle Tannous**
2626 N. Halsted St.
929-1333

☾ Nightlife

Batteries Not Included —
rock
2201 N. Clybourn Ave.
348-9529

▶**Biograph Theater**
2433 N. Lincoln Ave.
348-4123

▶**B.L.U.E.S.**
2519 N. Halsted St.
528-1012

The Bulls — jazz
1916 N. Lincoln Park West
337-3000

▶**Earl's Pub**
2470 N. Lincoln Ave.
929-0660

▶**Facets Multimedia Center**
1517 W. Fullerton Ave.
281-9075

Irish Eyes — Irish music
2519 N. Lincoln Ave.
348-9548

▶**Juke Box Saturday Night**
2215 N. Lincoln Ave.
525-5000

▶**Kelly's Pub**
949 W. Webster Ave.
281-0656

Kiku's — jazz
754 W. Wellington Ave.
281-7878

▶**Kingston Mines**
2548 N. Halsted St.
477-4646

Latin Village — salsa
2528 N. Lincoln Ave.
472-6166

Lilly's — blues
2513 N. Lincoln Ave.
525-2422

▶**Neo**
2350 N. Clark St.
528-2622

950-Lucky Number — rock
950 W. Wrightwood Ave.
929-8955

Octagon — New Wave
2483 N. Clark St.
549-1132

▶**Old Town School of Folk Music**
909 W. Armitage Ave.
525-7793

Oz — jazz
2917 N. Sheffield Ave.
975-8100

▶**Ultimate Sports Bar and Grill**
354 W. Armitage Ave.
477-4630

Wise Fools — blues
2270 N. Lincoln Ave.
929-1510

New Town/Lake View

THE LAKE VIEW-NEW TOWN NEIGH-
BORHOOD is a little like a flat San Francisco. Eclectic shops selling everything
from essentials to the completely
superfluous compete for space with a
United Nations' worth of fast-food joints and fine
restaurants; bars cater to every taste. Upscale newcomers and long-time Latin, Asian, and Hispanic
residents — as well as the city's largest concentration
of gay men and lesbians — share the streets in quiet
harmony. Artists and performance groups have
snapped up some bargain-priced spaces, and to the
west, astute antiques dealers have given new life to a
once-dying stretch of stores. Closer to the lake, rents
are high, and parking is impossible.

Ever since the Lake View Inn opened at what was
Byron Street and the lake in 1853, the shoreline has
been a magnet for development. After completion of a plank road — now Broadway —
stately houses belonging to the owners of greenhouses and clay pits to the west arose
along the lakefront. Construction of the Lake View town hall (currently the site of the
23rd, or Town Hall, District police station) at Halsted and Addison streets reflected
the importance of the township's eastern half.

Lincoln Avenue, one of the area's main drags, traces an old Indian trail to the Green
Bay and Fox River portages. The fields and greenhouses of the early Luxembourgish
and German settlers fed nearby Chicago. A bit later, local clay pits supplied many of
the bricks used to repair the ravages of the Chicago Fire. Because it was outside the
city's stringent, post-Fire building codes, the neighborhood west of Sheffield Avenue
boomed in the 1880s and 1890s. Large landowners (including Chicago's first mayor,
William B. Ogden; governor-to-be and labor supporter John P. Altgeld; and McCormick Theological Seminary benefactor Mike Diversey) subdivided their holdings or
sold them outright to developers.

When the Redemptorist fathers from St. Michael's Church in Old Town established
a mission in 1882 near Lincoln and Wellington avenues, it "lay in the midst of corn
fields, vegetable gardens, and clay-holes." By the time they laid the cornerstone for the
magnificent **St. Alphonsus Church** in 1889, the surrounding land had been filled
in with rows of narrow, wood-frame, peaked-roof houses, occasionally interrupted by
a brick one. Lake View was annexed to Chicago the same year, and Lincoln Avenue
became the Hauptstrasse of the city's German community.

Churches began to take root to serve the area's diverse influx of new residents, which
now included English, Irish, and Swedes. The foundation stone of **St. Peter's Episcopal Church** was laid in 1893. **Lake View Presbyterian Church's** charming
frame building was designed in 1897 by the famed John Wellborn Root; subsequent
alterations haven't diminished its simple dignity.

Jewish residents worshiped at **Temple Sholom's** old building (now **Anshe Emet
Synagogue**) when the North Side's oldest Reform congregation — established in

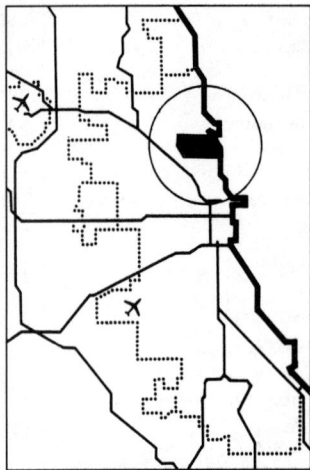

1873 — moved in 1911 from its Gold Coast location. The present Byzantine-inspired 1930 temple was the only synagogue built in Chicago between the Depression and World War Two.

Irish Catholics organized a Lake View parish as early as 1886, but it wasn't until 1913 that they laid the cornerstone of **Our Lady of Mt. Carmel Church**, a beautiful Tudor Gothic structure.

Spacious homes line both sides of Hawthorne Place between Broadway and Sheridan Road. And **Alta Vista Terrace** is a treasure: Hidden away on this London-mews-like street, facing rows of town houses will take you into another era. Built between 1900 and 1904 by Samuel Eberly Gross, self-proclaimed "World's Greatest Real Estate Promoter," the houses remain virtually unchanged; landmark protection will keep them that way. They offer a stunning streetscape and, close up, a parade of all the fashionable detail and decoration of their time.

Wrigley Field, one of the few remaining grass-field ballparks in America, stirs feelings of joy, even in the dead of winter. Since 1916, it's been the home of the Chicago Cubs, for whom some of baseball's greatest players have labored, mostly in vain. Because the late Philip Wrigley, long-time owner, looked at innovation with a jaundiced eye, it remained the only ballpark without lights for night games; had scoreboard numbers manipulated by hand; and required that gentlemen wear shirts in box seats. In 1981 the Tribune Company, which owns the *Chicago Tribune* newspaper, bought the Cubs and began to push for lights. The surrounding neighborhood balked, and to this day the controversy rages, though the first night games are scheduled for the summer of 1988.

Change, really, is what Lake View-New Town is all about. Thirty years ago there wasn't a duller neighborhood. Then Broadway, Halsted, and their side streets became a popular place for young people to live, and developers couldn't build studio and one-bedroom apartments fast enough. Tacky and depressing four-plus-ones (four stories atop a below-grade entrance level) replaced single-family houses on side streets, and high-rises the vintage lakefront low-rises. The churches, once withering as members died or moved to the suburbs, now actively serve growing congregations of the young; the gay; ethnic minorities; and pensioned seniors.

The **Brewster Apartments**, designed by E. Hill Turnock in 1893, exude Gay Nineties robustness and were lovingly restored by Mieki Hayano in 1970. The interior of the building proves that Hyatt Hotels' John Portman didn't invent central elevators and skylit atria.

SHOPPING

Lake View-New Town has such a variety of shopping experiences that you're sure to find one catering to your needs, whether it's for an ormolu-dripping antique bureau, a little silk black dress, or just a new coffeemaker. If it's made, chances are it's available here.

H. C. Struve opened the area's first dry-goods store in 1904 but, with remarkable prescience, sold out to Goldblatt's in 1929. The **Lincoln-Belmont** area's lower-priced department-store anchor is still there — though a little worse for wear — and dozens of other discount stores sprang up around it and continue to thrive. The clothing and shoe chain stores look the same from neighborhood to neighborhood, but

New Town/Lake View

Schreck Army Navy Surplus is one of a kind. This huge wholesale-and-retail warehouse is crammed to the rafters with enough battle-chic materiel to outfit a small army. It's a quartermaster's olive-drab dream come true. Prices aren't low, but there's nothing drab about the quality.

If "antique-ing" is your bag, start at Sheffield Avenue and head west on Belmont Avenue to find more than a dozen antiques stores selling everything from vintage American and European furniture, wicker, and accessories to Depression-era kitchen gadgets, knickknacks, and collectibles. Hours are unpredictable (at **Modern Art**, the sign says HOURS: WHENEVER/IF EVER), but most are open on weekends. Though most of the stores are clustered on Belmont, **Antique Palace** on Lincoln Avenue is a definite must-see. You have to be buzzed in through off-putting heavy wrought-iron gates, but it's worth it. The two cavernous floors are filled with high-quality furniture, and the store has 55,000 square feet of floor space.

There's also a run of antiques shops on Halsted Street between Belmont and Addison Street that's worth a stroll. At **3434**, the 20th-century designs for sale include jewelry, carpets, art, and furniture — from mission to art deco. **Indigo** also sells an interesting array of designs from this century. **Formerly Yours** is a multiroom shop with a fine selection of Victoriana, as well as English and French antiques. **Roan Galleries** has big-ticket elegant items, including some oil paintings and also lots of French and English antiques.

While on Halsted, don't miss **Antiques Intrigue, J. Russell Andrews Antiques, The Larc and the Hawk Antiques and Collectibles, Belinder Antiques, Aunt Edie's Glass**, the **Pumpkin Patch Antiques Gallery**, and the **Brokerage**.

If you've picked up a great stained-glass window with a cracked panel, consider taking it to **Drehobl Brothers Art Glass Co.** Frank Drehobl started the firm in 1919. His son and other family members custom-make stained- and beveled-glass windows for commercial customers and individuals, and they work magic on old stained glass, including pieces created decades ago by the company. Drehobl did the "interior sky-dome" of the now-defunct State Street Wieboldt's department store.

Many delicatessens, bakeries, and restaurants dotting the area around Lincoln and Belmont avenues recall its German heyday. Canny German-food lovers flock from afar to **Kuhn's Delicatessen**, a venerable *deutscher Supermarkt* with aisle upon aisle of luxurious sweets, liquor, beer, wine, and other imported delicacies, as well as breads from half a dozen bakeries. The women bustling behind the city's best-stocked Germanic deli counters unerringly greet English-speaking customers in English, German ones in German. Prices aren't low, but everything from sülzkotelett — pork chop and egg glistening in aspic — to chunks of unsalted butter hacked from a pale-yellow, farm-fresh mound is top-quality.

Kuhn's carries some pastries, but **Dinkel's Bakery** overflows with breads, rolls, outstanding butter cookies, tortes, great cheesecakes, and superb stollen and fruitcakes. Sweets can also be found at **Phillip's Butter Kist Bakery**. This 1950s-looking shop makes excellent Austrian pastries, melt-in-your-mouth butter cookies and pound cake, great breads, and the usual Danishes and cakes. The oak bread cabinets in the Ma-and-Pa **Reynen's Bakery** were probably antiques when the present owner's family opened the shop in 1936. Everything — the coarse pumpernickel, butter cookies, and sweet rolls — looks as if someone's grandmother baked it.

Closer to the lake, the stores cater to a more upscale crowd. The **Century** was once a jewel in the Balaban & Katz movie-house chain, but in the 1970s it was recycled as a shopping mall. Though the façade was supposed to be preserved, it wasn't, much to the community's chagrin. The marquee was ripped off, the façade pierced by windows, and the interior gutted. Millions were spent creating the glitzy, seven-story mall, but the results have been mixed. Of the 60-odd shops, only a few, such as the high-fashion men and women's store, **Cignal**, are worth going out of your way for. The rest (shoe stores, clothes stores, card shops, and others), though serviceable, cater mostly to neighborhood needs.

Natural-fiber separates and casual wear are among the attractions at **Apropos**, a whitewashed and track-lit store selling contemporary sportswear for women. **Elle** goes much further, offering high-style clothes and accouterments, many dramatic and many from Europe.

Bad Boys and **Traffick** are right next door to one another and offer a panoply of men's cotton chinos, sportswear, T-shirts, shorts, and accessories. The clothes tend to be on the trendy side. **Clean Socks and Underwear** is a neat little shop selling just that, though there are also shorts, swimsuits, and sunglasses.

Thousands of books all priced below a dollar are on sale every day at the **Brown Elephant**, a thrift shop run by the Howard Brown Memorial Clinic. Its four store-fronts carry a mishmash of things, including furniture, housewares, aisles of clothes,

small appliances, and a fabulous record selection. And to top it off, the money all goes to charity.

Another wonderful thrift shop up that way is **Flashy Trash**, which offers vintage clothing, beaded sweaters, urbane antique overcoats, pleated zoot-suit pants, and 1960s sunglasses and tuxedos. Flashy Trash says it has the largest selection of working antique watches in the city.

What may be the city's largest selection of books for gay men and lesbians is at **Unabridged Books**. In addition, there are little yellow signs with literary criticism stuck to the shelves, so you can see what the well-read staff recommends. Unabridged's selection of cookbooks, literature, and business, fitness, and children's books is outstanding as well. **Something Else Books** is an interesting little shop specializing in books from both small and university presses, though there's also a fine selection of hardback and paperback literature and nonfiction.

The **Occult Bookstore** specializes in witchcraft, astrology, cabala, and other spooky stuff and has an extensive line of new and used books on the occult, Oriental philosophy, yoga, magic, and mysticism, as well as candles, crystals, and incense to create the proper atmosphere.

Europa Books stocks a large selection of books in German, French, and Spanish, including general culture and history, reference and technical books, and kids' stuff. Browsing is a welcome sport at **Selected Works Used Books**, where the selection runs the gamut from religion and philosophy to fiction and art.

The **Greenhouse on Buckingham** recaptures an elegant past. Geo. Witbold Florists, "est. 1857," lost the location during the Depression. Witbold's legacy includes an enormous tropical greenhouse for plants and flowers, replete with pools and fountains at the back of the shop.

After shopping all day, stop off at one of the many fine food shops in the neighborhood. The **Bread Shop**, though nominally a health-food store, offers a small but wonderful selection of produce, bins of fresh grains, all-natural packaged goods and hygiene products, and a fine selection of carry-out prepared foods. The Bread Shop also offers bread-making lessons.

A more visible neighborhood institution looks like a Germanic castle left over from a movie set. Once a baronial restaurant, it's now part of the **Chalet Wine and Cheese** chain. The main floor is devoted to a huge assortment of wines, cheeses, and gourmet foods, while the catacombs serve as a wine cellar for the more prestigious vintages.

Many people don't know that **Kenessey Gourmets Internationale** has a downstairs; there you will find lots of imported wines, beers, cheeses, and gourmet foods. Part of the space is a wine-cellar-like dining area serving European open-faced sandwiches throughout the day and a Continental menu at night. Upstairs is the pastry shop with scores of Austro-Hungarian goodies to take out or eat there — espresso and cappuccino, too. **Martha's Candies** offers candy novelties — white-chocolate swans, custom bonbons — and uses dark chocolate, which is thought to be an East Coast taste.

RESTAURANTS

The Lake View-New Town area is checkered with restaurants serving up everything from the latest ethnic trend to haute cuisine.

At teeny but elegant **Yoshi's Café**, Japanese and American accents paired with classical French underpinnings create delightful — and at times, spectacular — results, such as veal medallions sauced with candied ginger and lemon zest. There's always boiled Maine lobster, too. Desserts may include Japanese pear with green-tea ice cream in a pastry cup. Another pleasant spot is **L'Escargot on Halsted**, which serves traditional French fare in a comfortable cream-and-celadon-colored room.

St. Tropez serves an eclectic menu in a glitzy new setting in the staid Belmont Hotel. There are always several seafood selections, such as grilled lobster, fillet of salmon, and sautéed soft-shell crab with three beurres blancs. An early-1970s sensibility thrives at **Wickline's**, a comfortable spot done in earth tones with warm wood, plants, and art. The menu is posted daily and includes topnotch soups, salads, signature mix-and-match quiches, and meat pies. All dinners begin with a delicious home-baked honey-whole-wheat bread.

The best choices for Italian include **Leona's**, a three-story restaurant featuring thick-crust pizzas, passable pastas, and reasonable prices. The crowds are often stifling, but the wait can be loads of fun: The place serves free pizza and wine to those in line. There's also **Not Just Pasta**, a storefront restaurant serving an entire menu, from veal to — you guessed it — pasta. Bring your own wine. **Da Nicola** is a charming old-line place that offers a more extensive menu, including fresh fish, game, and such unusual pastas as a poached and sliced "jelly roll" layered with ground meat, mozzarella, spinach, and prosciutto.

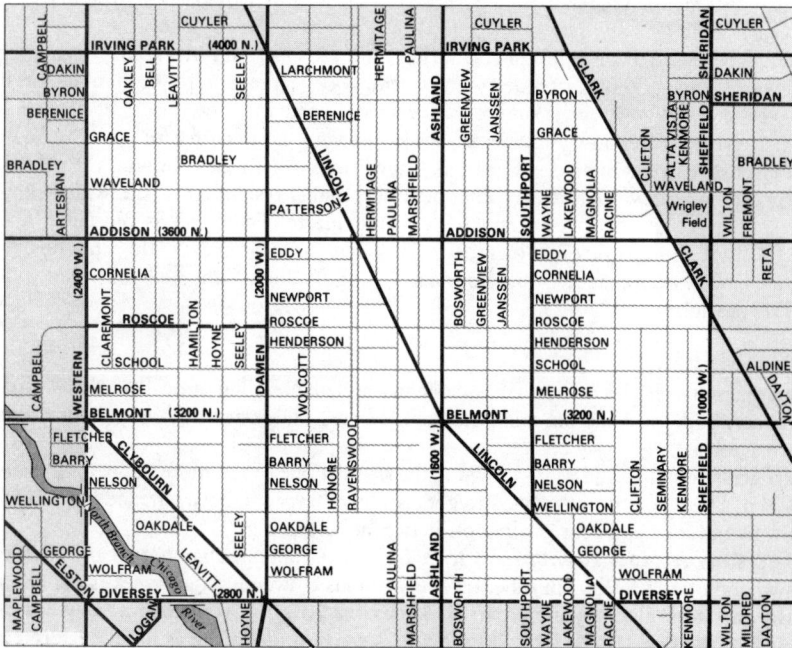

New Town/Lake View

At the **Helmand**, affordable yet exotic and elegant Afghan food is served in a plant-filled setting. Entrées include kabuli, tender lamb chunks atop baked rice strewn with lightly candied julienne carrot and raisins; koufta challow, meatballs in a spicy sauce; and various stews. Baked baby pumpkin is a must, and the baklava made with ground pistachios is a fine dessert.

Thai restaurants abound as well. Both **P.S. Bangkok** and **Thai Town** are good bets, the former serving particularly good satays and curries, the latter strong in the extensiveness of its menu — more than 100 items.

Armenian and Middle Eastern food is the specialty at **Casbah**, a small spot decorated with Oriental rugs, murals of hieroglyphs, and scenes of ancient Egypt. The cooking is uniformly good and includes a wide variety of couscous, kebabs, and chicken and veal dishes. Rose-water-scented custard is among the desserts offered.

Crisscross the world of ethnic food to **Schulien's Restaurant and Saloon**, a turn-of-the-century landmark that flaunts its German history and hearty cooking with pride. Dinners include schnitzel, crisp-skinned duckling, pork chops, and ribs. The **Yugo Inn** is a pleasant place to enjoy solid home-cooked Yugoslavian cuisine at moderate prices. Choices range from schnitzel to perfectly sautéed brains to skinned sausages to a boozy chocolate-rum torte.

La Paella presents the cuisine of Spain. Besides the rice-seafood-chicken mélange that is the restaurant's namesake, expect to find duck with mangoes and a variety of seafood specialties. **Boca del Río** serves some of the city's best Mexican-style seafood — cocktails, soups, snapper a la veracruzana, shrimp with garlic — in simple cantina surroundings.

Though housed in a former funeral parlor, the atmosphere at **Ann Sather** is homey and warm, and — no pun intended — the warm, gooey cinnamon rolls are to die for. It gets very crowded very early, but the wait is always worth it.

At **Scenes** coffeehouse cum theater-bookstore you can sip coffee for hours, read, or just discuss (patrons there don't just talk, they discuss). This Jack Kerouac throwback is a great place to waste time. Another dual-personality restaurant is **Joz**, which combines a burger-and-beer restaurant with a launderette. The music is Big Chill, and there's always a sporting event on the television screen. You can eat in the separate dining area while doing laundry and not miss a thing: Colored lights tell you when your clothes are done.

NIGHTLIFE

The area is plastered with bars and small clubs and one very big one called **ClubLand**. It attracts both local and big-name acts and features a large dance floor and numerous video screens.

Progressive music and a hip crowd make **Berlin** one of the more happening spots in town. The place attracts gays, straights, and whatever's in between, and has a summertime outdoor patio for cooling off between dances.

The **Ginger Man Tavern** and **Joel's** are after-hours hangouts for the theater crowd and offer a lively, fun time. Live reggae music seven nights a week is the order of the day at the always-jammed **Wild Hare and Singing Armadillo Frog Sanctuary**, while **B.L.U.E.S. Etcetera** features the best of Chicago's blues performers in a sleek, smoky setting. See if you can remember the samba or bossa nova at **Asi Es**

New Town/Lake View

Colombia, a dance club offering Latin jazz.

Pops for Champagne is a sophisticated jazz club that serves a wide array of Champagnes and wines by the glass. It can be expensive if you taste many kinds, but the experience — while heady — is worth it. If beer is more to your liking, head to **Resi's Bierstube**, where 48 imported beers, many of them German, are served in a genuine beer garden with real trees and grapevines or in a bar decorated in Bavarian style.

There's often an organ player in between films at the **Music Box** movie theater, which shows a different double bill almost every night of the week. The Music Box also annually hosts the Chicago Gay and Lesbian Film Festival and other specialties. The interior is a grand space — complete with stars twinkling on the ceiling and drifting clouds — and puts all other theaters to shame.

Besides its many antiques stores and cafés, Halsted Street is alive with gay bars and dance clubs; on sultry summer nights the throngs spill into the street.

At **Christopher Street**, the crowd is mostly young and mostly energetic enough to dance till the wee hours to popular disco and soul. There's also a separate, enclosed area with more than 20 video screens. There's one big screen (as well as a couple of small ones) at the **Sidetrack**, a narrow bar drawing a gay faux-preppy crowd. Monday nights are jammed with guys enjoying the all-Broadway and movie-musical selections. When was the last time you saw Ethel Merman sing "There's No Business Like Show Business"?

Roscoe's has picture windows overlooking the streetscape and a lovely patio with chaises and chairs for hanging out. Unlike Sidetrack, where the video screens seem omnipresent, Roscoe's keeps the video to a minimum. **Little Jim's** is one of the oldest gay bars in Chicago. Though all-male, X-rated videos play all night, the atmosphere really isn't at all seedy.

Club LaRay is a large disco attracting hip customers from all over the city, while the **Loading Dock** is a late-late-night place with a mostly young, neighborhood following. Dancing is the thing here — the music's too loud for talking.

The **Closet** is nice because it attracts a healthy mix of both gay men and lesbians. The atmosphere is friendly, a sports show is often on the television, and there's dancing later on. A very popular lesbian bar and disco is **Augie and CK's**.

Interesting Places

▶ **Alta Vista Terrace**
1054 West between Byron and Grace streets

▶ **Anshe Emet Synagogue**
Pine Grove Ave. and Grace St.
281-1423

▶ **Brewster Apartments**
2800 N. Pine Grove Ave.

Church of the Valley
Seminary and Barry avenues
525-4254

"Herstory," mural
Underpass, Addison St. and Lincoln Ave.

▶ **Lake View Presbyterian Church**
Addison St. and Broadway
281-2655

"A Mural for a New World"
West wall, Parish of the Holy Covenant
925 W. Diversey Pkwy.

▶ **Our Lady of Mount Carmel Church**
Belmont Ave. at Orchard St.
525-0453

▶ **St. Alphonsus Church**
Wellington and Southport avenues
525-0709

St. Benedict Church
2215 W. Irving Park Rd.
588-6484

▶ **St. Peter's Episcopal Church**
Belmont Ave. and Broadway
525-0844

GUIDE TO CHICAGO

163

New Town/Lake View

► **Temple Sholom**
Lake Shore Dr. and Stratford Pl.
525-4707

► **Wrigley Field**
Clark and Addison streets
281-5050

Shopping

Adam Monroe Antiques
1358 W. Belmont Ave.
525-1133

Ages Ago
2110 W. Belmont Ave.
281-2020

American Youth Hostels, Inc.
3712 N. Clark St.
327-8114

► **Antique Palace**
3020 N. Lincoln Ave.
477-6700

► **Apropos**
3315 N. Broadway
528-2130

Arise Futon
3157 N. Clark St.
348-7979

► **Aunt Edie's Glass**
3339 N. Halsted St.
528-1617

► **Bad Boys**
3311 N. Broadway
549-7701

Barbara's Bookstore
2907 N. Broadway
477-0411

Belmont Cycle
1444 W. Belmont Ave.
281-2623

Bon Ton Chicago —
men's clothing
2929 N. Broadway
935-0027

Bookman's Corner
2959 N. Clark St.
929-8298

Born Beautiful — children's
clothes
3206 N. Broadway
549-6770

► **Bread Shop**
3400 N. Halsted St.
528-8108

► **Brokerage**
3448 N. Halsted St.
248-1644

► **Brown Elephant Resale Shop**
3508 N. Broadway
549-3407

Buckingham Bike Shop, Ltd.
3126 N. Broadway
975-0050

Bygone Treasures
2155 W. Belmont Ave.
549-2388

► **Century Shopping Centre**
2828 N. Clark St.
929-8100

► **Chalet Wine and Cheese Shop**
3000 N. Clark St.
935-9400

Chicago School of Massage Therapy
2920 N. Lincoln Ave.
477-9444

Chicago Tattooing Co.
922 W. Belmont Ave.
528-6969

► **Cignal**
2828 N. Clark St.
281-6635

► **Clean Socks and Underwear**
3748 N. Broadway
348-6550

Cohen and Horowitz Kosher Meat and Poultry
3341 N. Broadway
528-6565

Cook's Cupboard —
kitchenware
3003 N. Clark St.
549-4651

Darkroom Aids
3449 N. Lincoln Ave.
248-4301

► **Dinkel's Bakery**
3329 N. Lincoln Ave.
281-7300

► **Drehobl Brothers Art Glass Co.**
2847 N. Lincoln Ave.
281-2022

Egghead Discount Software — computer
software
3019 N. Clark St.
929-8400

► **Elle**
3405 N. Broadway
327-2145

► **Europa Bookstore**
3229 N. Clark St.
929-1836

Fabrile Gallery — art glass
2945 N. Broadway
929-7471

Father Time Antiques
2108 W. Belmont Ave.
880-5599

► **Flashy Trash**
3524 N. Halsted St.
327-6900

► **Formerly Yours Antiques**
3443 N. Halsted St.
248-7766

Goldblatt's Department Store
3149 N. Lincoln Ave.
880-9200

Good Old Days Antiques
2138 W. Belmont Ave.
472-8837

Gracie's Antiques
1919 W. Belmont Ave.
472-2445

► **Greenhouse on Buckingham**
745 W. Buckingham Pl.
248-0044

Guitar Shack
3154 N. Clark St.
327-5565

He Who Eats Mud — cards and gifts
3247 N. Broadway
525-0616

Hep Cat Comics
3107 N. Lincoln Ave.
477-5033

Howard and Hyde Booksellers — used books
822 W. Belmont Ave.
525-2665

I.K. Don — men's clothes
3174 N. Clark St.
549-4449

▶**Indigo**
3450 N. Halsted St.
348-1418

International Antiques
2907 N. Clark St.
528-4602

▶**Kenessey Gourmets Internationale**
403 W. Belmont Ave.
929-7500

Kismet Vintage Clothing
2934 N. Lincoln Ave.

▶**Kuhn's Delicatessen**
3053 N. Lincoln Ave.
525-9019

▶**Larc and the Hawk**
3517 N. Halsted St.
528-5555

Male Hide Leathers
2816 N. Lincoln Ave.
929-0069

▶**Martha's Candies**
3257 N. Broadway
248-8733

Modern Art
2217 W. Belmont Ave.
975-4088

Mont Blanc Patisserie
1114 W. Belmont Ave.
525-7339

New Town Aquarium
925 W. Belmont Ave.
935-4200

Ninety-Ninth Floor — New Wave clothes
3400 N. Halsted St.

Nuts on Clark — nuts and dried fruit
3830 N. Clark St.
549-6622

▶**Occult Bookstore**
3230 N. Clark St.
281-0599

Ocean Scuba Center
1017 W. Diversey Pkwy.
929-0500

Offshore Marine — boating equipment
901 W. Irving Park Rd.
549-4446

Olde Chicago Antiques
2336 W. Belmont Ave.
935-1200

Les Parfums Shoppe
3017 N. Broadway
935-0543

Pastafina — fresh pastas and accouterments
921 W. Belmont Ave.
528-4499

Paul Rohe & Son Bookstore
3176 N. Clark St.
477-1999

Peerless Imported Rugs
3033 N. Lincoln Ave.
525-9034

▶**Phillip's Butter Kist Bakery**
1955 W. Belmont Ave.
281-4150

Pier I Imports
651 W. Diversey Pkwy.
871-1558

Poster Plus
2906 N. Broadway
549-2822

Powell's Bookstore — used books
2850 N. Lincoln Ave.
248-1444

Private Lives — bed and bath linens at discount
2725 N. Clark St.
525-6464
and 3011 N. Clark St.
348-4646

▶**Pumpkin Patch**
3250 N. Halsted St.
327-9166

▶**Rahmig's House of Fine Chocolates**
3109 N. Broadway
525-8338

▶**Roan Galleries**
3457 N. Halsted St.
935-9093
and 3268 N. Clark St.

▶**Schreck Army Navy Surplus**
3110 N. Lincoln Ave.
477-0112

▶**Something Else Books**
2805 N. Sheffield Ave.
549-0495

Sportmart
3134 N. Clark St.
871-8500

Star Japan Books and Records
3353 N. Clark St.
525-0394

▶**3434**
3434 N. Halsted St.
348-3988

Toys "R" Us
3330 N. Western Ave.
525-1690

▶**Traffick**
3313 N. Broadway
549-1502

▶**Unabridged Books**
3251 N. Broadway
883-9119

Victorian House Antiques
806 W. Belmont Ave.
348-8561

✕ Restaurants

▶**Ann Sather**
929 W. Belmont Ave.
348-2378

New Town/Lake View

▶ **Boca del Río**
3203 N. Clark St.
281-6698

**Caffè Pergolesi
Coffee House**
3404 N. Halsted St.
472-8602

▶ **Casbah**
514 W. Diversey Pkwy.
935-7570

Chicago Diner — vegetarian
3411 N. Halsted St.
935-6696

▶ **L'Escargot on Halsted**
2925 N. Halsted St.
525-5522

▶ **Helmand**
3201 N. Halsted St.
935-2447

▶ **Joz Launder Bar and Cafe**
3435 N. Southport Ave.
929-9274

▶ **Leona's**
3215 N. Sheffield Ave.
327-8861

La Llama — Peruvian
3811 N. Ashland Ave.
327-7756

Melrose Restaurant
3233 N. Broadway
327-2060

**Moti Mahal Indian
Restaurant**
1031 W. Belmont Ave.
348-4392

**Nakayoshi Sushi
Restaurant**
919 W. Belmont Ave.
929-9333

▶ **Da Nicola**
3114 N. Lincoln Ave.
935-8000

▶ **Not Just Pasta**
2965 N. Lincoln Ave.
348-2842

▶ **P.S. Bangkok**
3345 N. Clark St.
871-7777

▶ **La Paella**
2920 N. Clark St.
528-0757

▶ **St. Tropez**
3170 N. Sheridan Rd.
327-1100

▶ **Scenes**
3168 N. Clark St.
525-1007

▶ **Schulien's Restaurant
and Saloon**
2100 W. Irving Park Rd.
478-2100

Standard India Restaurant
917 W. Belmont Ave.
929-1123

▶ **Thai Town**
3201 N. Clark St.
528-2755

Vegetaria Fast Food
3182 N. Clark St.
549-0808

▶ **Wickline's**
3335 N. Halsted St.
525-4415

▶ **Yoshi's Café**
3257 N. Halsted St.
248-6160

▶ **Yugo Inn**
2824 N. Ashland Ave.
348-6444

☾ Nightlife

▶ **Asi Es Colombia**
3910 N. Lincoln Ave.
348-7444

▶ **Augie and CK's**
3726 N. Broadway
975-0449

▶ **B.L.U.E.S. Etcetera**
1122 W. Belmont Ave.
525-8989

▶ **Christopher Street**
3458 N. Halsted St.
975-9244

▶ **The Closet**
3325 N. Broadway
477-8533

▶ **ClubLand**
3145 N. Sheffield Ave.
248-7277

▶ **Club LaRay**
3150 N. Halsted St.
525-3150

▶ **Ginger Man Tavern**
3740 N. Clark St.
549-2050

▶ **Joel's**
3313 N. Clark St.
871-0896

▶ **Little Jim's**
3501 N. Halsted St.
871-6116

▶ **Loading Dock**
3702 N. Halsted St.
929-6108

▶ **Music Box Movie Theater**
3733 N. Southport
871-6604

▶ **Pops for Champagne**
2934 N. Sheffield Ave.
472-1000

▶ **Resi's Bierstube**
2034 W. Irving Park Rd.
472-1749

▶ **Roscoe's**
3356 N. Halsted St.
281-3355

▶ **Sidetrack**
3349 N. Halsted St.
477-9189

▶ **Wild Hare and Singing
Armadillo Frog Sanctuary**
3530 N. Clark St.
327-0800

Uptown/Edgewater

STUDS TERKEL, THE PROFESSIONAL "free spirit" of WFMT radio, calls Uptown "the United Nations of the have-nots." Uptown has more than its share of the poor and dispossessed, including one of Chicago's highest concentrations of the elderly. The people — Vietnamese, Laotians, Cambodians, blacks, Chinese — sometimes squabble and sometimes work together in their effort to make Uptown more livable.

Uptown also has its share of haves, particularly in its southern area (Buena Park) and its northern area (Edgewater). Elegant homes in Buena Park line Hutchinson Street and Castlewood Terrace; high-rise apartments in Edgewater line Marine Drive, and on North Sheridan Road, above Foster Avenue, buildings with names such as Malibu, Surfside Condominiums, and Hollywood Towers are heirs to the area's tradition of elegance.

In the 1920s, the flamboyant, pink, rococo (and unfortunately now-demolished) Edgewater Beach Hotel was a popular, de luxe resort, and the equally pink **Edgewater Beach Apartments** was one of Chicago's most sought-after co-ops. A string of Prairie-school-influenced mansions separated the co-ops from the Edgewater Golf Course. Edgewater epitomized the good life of the period.

And that's exactly what developer John L. Cochran had in mind when he began to subdivide lakefront marshes and farmlands north of Foster Avenue in the late 19th century. Cochran named the streets after stops along the Pennsylvania Railroad's main line out of Philadelphia — Bryn Mawr, Berwyn, Ardmore. After the extension of the el from Wilson Avenue to Evanston in 1907, the area east of Broadway blossomed with courtyard apartment buildings, fine single-family homes, and residential hotels. Lakefront land prices jumped from $200 a frontage foot in 1910 to $3,000 in 1929.

Buena Park, bounded by Irving Park Road, Montrose Avenue, Marine Drive, and Sheridan Road, was officially recognized by the city as a defined neighborhood in 1983. The houses along Hutchinson Street and Castlewood Terrace are among the finest in the area and recall a past many in the area would like to recapture.

Castlewood, conveniently near the old Essanay movie studios, attracted residents such as Mary Pickford, Wallace Beery, and Francis X. Bushman. Hutchinson Street, originally called Kenesaw Terrace, was developed by merchant John C. Scales in the 1890s. The first mansion, not surprisingly, was his own (840), a Queen Anne gem designed in 1894 by George W. Maher, one of America's great architects. Maher's growth is mirrored by the Lake House (826), which shows his vision of Prairie architecture, and the Seymour House (817), where the vision is combined with European influences. The houses at 750 and 839 are also attributed to him. The other houses on the street and in the immediate neighborhood, now protected by landmark designation, provide such rich examples of period design that they are a museum of Chicago's grand turn-of-the-century residential architecture.

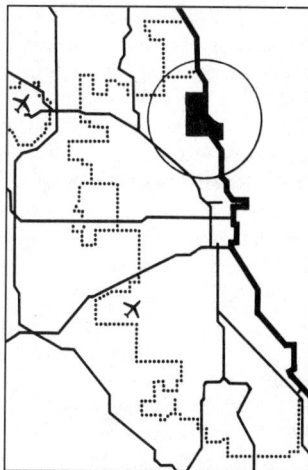

Uptown/Edgewater

Established in 1860, **Graceland Cemetery** took on much of its present character through careful planning by landscape architect Ossian Simonds, who also helped design Lincoln Park. The tombs were designed by distinguished architects as well, including the Getty Tomb, designed by Louis Sullivan. In fact, Sullivan is buried here, too, along with famous colleagues Daniel Burnham, Ludwig Mies van der Rohe, and Howard Van Doren Shaw. Potter Palmer, Joseph Medill, George Pullman, and Marshall Field are among the other Chicago luminaries who make their permanent homes there. **Rosehill Cemetery** isn't as famous as Graceland but still has a great deal of interest. The gates, designed by Water Tower architect W. W. Boyington, are an official Chicago landmark. Civil War burial plots and the memorial to onetime mayor "Long John" Wentworth are worth seeking out.

Though it's a little-known fact now, for about ten years Chicago reigned as the film capital of America, largely because of **Essanay Studios**, founded in 1907. Greats such as Gloria Swanson, Ben Turpin, and Charlie Chaplin starred in the movies cranked out at Essanay's 16-acre lot. The Little Tramp's image flickered across a mighty screen at the **Uptown Theater**. Covering an entire block and seating more than 4,000, this Balaban & Katz beauty brought a Spanish castle to Uptown. The furnishings were as florid as in any American theater, the mechanical facilities the most modern. Six feet of air space between the inner and outer walls shielded patrons from any hint of street noise.

In the 1970s, though, hard times hit and most of the fixtures were sold. After a stint with Spanish-language films and rock concerts, the Uptown closed in 1982. The

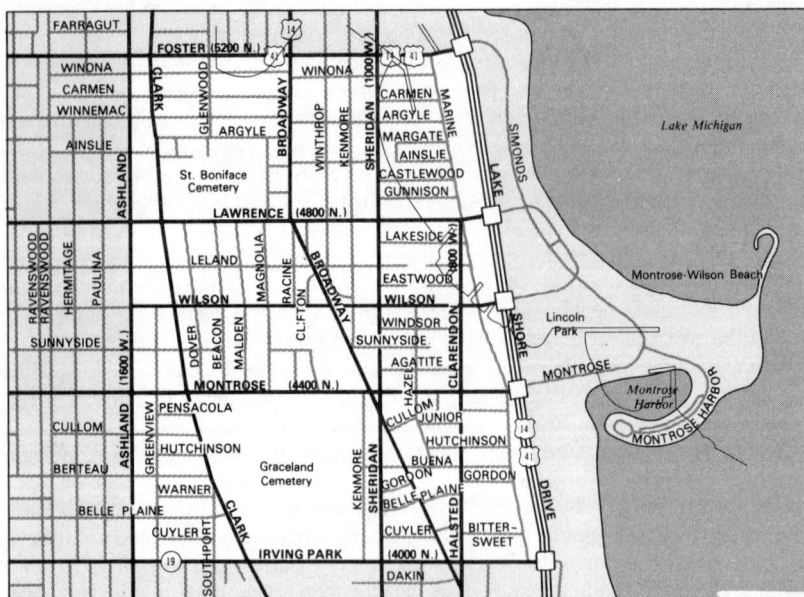

Uptown

Riviera Theater, another onetime Balaban & Katz house, is now a popular night-club complete with live music; the old Sheridan is now the **Teatro El Palacio**, show-ing Spanish-language features.

For many people, entertainment and dancing to some of the country's top bands meant the **Aragon Ballroom** in Uptown. Created in 1926 by Greek immigrants Andrew and William Karzas, the building's Moorish design owed more to Hollywood than to Iberia, but its lavish ornamentation fitted Uptown's flush feeling. Today it's only a rental ballroom.

To serve the burgeoning population, churches sprang up quickly. **Bethany Evangelical Lutheran Church** was in a small Prairie-style Tudor building that now houses the Rogers Park Montessori School; the present church building, a beautiful example of Prairie-style Gothic, was added in 1913. The expansion of the Episcopal **Church of the Atonement** incorporated part of the original 1888 building in a handsome Romanesque-Gothic structure with heavy stonework and fine stained glass.

The spirit of prosperity in the 1920s encouraged lavish adornments. The parish-ioners of the Italian Romanesque **Edgewater Presbyterian Church** hired one of the country's master woodcarvers, John O. Torell of Palatine, to create the interior decoration. Beautiful stained-glass windows from Munich enhance **St. Gertrude's Church**. At **St. Ita's Church**, architect Henry Schlacks drew heavily on the exam-ples of the church of Brou and Chartres Cathedral to design a masterpiece whose tower, with its delicate tracery, still dominates the neighborhood's skyline.

The 1920s glitter helped spawn today's grimy Uptown. Housing pressure in the trendy neighborhood led owners of less successful apartment houses to break up large flats, and single people replaced many families. As entertainment attracted larger crowds, honky-tonks sprang up, especially around the el station, giving the area an unsavory reputation. In the thirties, with new construction killed by the Depression, the area really began a downslide. The war years brought heavier demand for housing, and conversion accelerated.

Cheap rents and a glut of rooms after the war made Uptown a port of entry for immigrants coming to Chicago. Southern whites from Kentucky, Tennessee, and West Virginia moved to Uptown and, in the 1960s, were joined by blacks being displaced by urban renewal of their old neighborhoods, and American Indians, who were encour-aged by the Federal Government to leave their reservations.

Uptown is still considered a port of entry for Chicago's new immigrant population, the latest being those from Southeast Asia.

SHOPPING

The intersection of Argyle Street and Broadway and the surrounding blocks are Chica-go's center for Vietnamese life and commerce. Many restaurants (see below) and stores catering to both the immediate neighborhood and the rest of the North Side and sub-urbs have sprouted here over the past decade.

More conventional stores, such as **The Gap** and **Pier 1 Imports**, line the thor-oughfares, attesting to Uptown and Edgewater's growing revitalization.

The current generation of Native Americans has been around Uptown for a short time, even though it was their ancestors who held the original deed. Their presence can still be felt, as the neighborhood is home to the **American Indian Center**, the

Uptown/Edgewater

American Indian Kiva Gift Shop, the **American Indian Economic Development Association**, and the **American Indian Gift Store**, where beadwork, silver and turquoise jewelry, rugs, pottery, paintings, and Indian records are available.

If fishing is your hobby, stop by **Frank's Live Bait and Sports**, where both bait and fishing supplies, including smelt nets, make anglers' times at Montrose Harbor a bit easier.

Despite the opulent lakefront condominiums in the Edgewater area, most of the stores are quite ordinary. Convenience stores and fast-food joints cluster around el stops, particularly at Bryn Mawr and Granville avenues. Supermarkets, car dealerships, and auto repair shops dominate Broadway, and Clark Street, north of Ridge Avenue, is pretty desolate as far as shopping goes.

Still, there are a few exceptions, including **Beloian Rug Company**, which has been dealing in fine floor coverings since the area's first luxury housing was erected. It carries new and used Oriental carpets, as well as rare Persian rugs. **Smith's Clock Shop**, a local fixture for more than 40 years, repairs wall clocks and standing clocks and always has a fascinating assortment of timepieces on hand. **Admiral Music Company** (also known as the Piano Gallery) doesn't look like much from the outside, but at least two dozen restored instruments are always on the sales floor. The pianos are completely rebuilt from the soundboard up, and then carefully refinished by a couple of skilled craftsmen in the back room.

The area is also home to a Swedish enclave called Andersonville (when the king and queen of Sweden visited Chicago, this is where they went). The **Swedish Style Gift Shop** carries nice crystal, metalwork, the usual run of curios. If you want to assemble an authentic smörgåsbord, the cheerful **Wikstrom Scandinavian American Gourmet Foods** has lots of luncheon meats, hand-sliced smoked salmon, Scandinavian cheeses, homemade potato sausage, limpa bread, lingonberries and other jarred and tinned specialties, rye crackers, salads, herrings, and more. Across the street, **Erickson's Delicatessen** offers an equally wide selection of Swedish specialties, including herring prepared many ways, yellow-pea soup, and glögg mix. The **Swedish Bakery** carries excellent coffee cakes, cookies, sweet rolls,

Edgewater

170

miniature pastries, and Swedish-style napoleons to round out the meal.

RESTAURANTS

Though there are restaurants in the Uptown-Edgewater area to cater to every ethnic taste, perhaps those who like food from Southeast Asia are most in luck.

The lack of décor at **Mekong** is more than compensated by its low prices and broad menu of Vietnamese fare. First-rate choices include shrimp rice-paper rolls redolent of mint, spicy lemon-marinated beef salad, crisp egg rolls, and lemon-grass chicken. There are bananas in warm coconut milk for dessert. Another popular Vietnamese restaurant is **Pasteur**, a large, corner storefront that offers a good range of expertly prepared dishes at modest prices. There are eggy pancakes stuffed with shrimp and vegetables, outstanding grilled pork, and a few more unusual dishes, including gingery chicken cooked in a clay pot and frog legs in coconut-milk curry. Vietnamese versions of venison, poultry, and fish — as well as nearly a dozen vegetarian choices — are the strong points at **Song-Huong**, another popular storefront restaurant.

Korean cuisine is represented by **Seoul House**, one of the city's best bets for solidly prepared food at modest prices. Good bets include fried dumplings; a stew of pork ribs, potatoes, green peppers, and onions in spicy red sauce; and especially a concoction called "hot stew and rice" with hunks of fish, bean curd, and vegetables.

Siam Cafe serves Thai food and has the best fried greens with oyster sauce in the city, as well as good pork satay, charcoal chicken, succulent cuttlefish in heavy garlic sauce, and fiery chili chicken. The curries here are also topnotch. For Japanese food and sushi, try **Tokyo Marina**. Generously apportioned sushi comes in beautiful lacquer boxes, while soups and casseroles shine for those who aren't into raw fish. There's a 20-percent discount for seniors.

Ann Sather, a popular breakfast spot with a Swedish accent on Belmont Avenue, has opened in Andersonville as well. Though it offers hearty lunches and dinners, it truly shines at breakfast time with its justifiably famous cinnamon rolls.

Plenty of spices flavor the Spanish soups and casseroles at **Costa Brava**, a pleasant storefront with a menu and décor that speak of the sea.

NIGHTLIFE

Both a venue for top-name concert acts and a hot dance club, the **Riviera Night Club** is Uptown's chicest place to be. The laser and computer-controlled lighting creates the perfect ambiance for the mix of music, which includes everything from progressive pop to Latin. Middle Eastern music is on tap Tuesday and Wednesday nights at **Reza's**, a popular neighborhood Persian restaurant.

Started in 1910, the **Green Mill** used to attract greats like Sophie Tucker and Al Jolson. Today, top Chicago jazz acts play there every night but Sunday, when the Green Mill hosts the Uptown Poetry Slam. Amateur poets read their work at an open mike and then, once everyone is in the mood, the slam begins. The slam — it's like a boxing match with poems instead of gloves — comes complete with judges holding up scores à la a gymnastics meet.

The **New Bryn Mawr Theater**, just steps away from the el, isn't all that new really, but does show movies at a discount price; Tuesday is dollar night.

Uptown/Edgewater

🏢 Interesting Places

► **Bethany Evangelical Lutheran Church**
Thorndale and Magnolia avenues

► **Castlewood Terrace**
4862 North, between Sheridan Road and Marine Drive

► **Church of the Atonement**
Kenmore and Ardmore avenues
271-2727

► **Edgewater Beach Apartments**
5555 N. Sheridan Rd.

► **Edgewater Presbyterian Church**
Kenmore and Bryn Mawr avenues
561-4748

► **Essanay Studios**
1345 W. Argyle St.

► **Graceland Cemetery**
4001 N. Clark St.
525-1105

► **Hutchinson Street**
4232 North, between Marine Drive and Hazel Street

► **Riviera Theater (now the Riviera Night Club)**
4746 N. Racine Ave.
769-6300

► **Rosehill Cemetary**
5800 N. Ravenswood Ave.
561-5940

► **St. Gertrude's Church**
Glenwood and Granville avenues
764-3621

► **St. Ita's Church**
Broadway and Catalpa Ave.
561-5343

► **Uptown Theater**
4816 N. Broadway

🛍 Shopping

► **Admiral Music Co.**
5951 N. Clark St.
271-4400

► **American Indian Center and Kiva Gift Shop**
1630 W. Wilson Ave.
275-5871

► **American Indian Economic Development Association**
4753 N. Broadway
784-5505

► **American Indian Gift Store**
1756 W. Wilson Ave.
769-1170

► **Beloian Rug Co.**
6241 N. Broadway
743-1234

Channel 1 Caribbean and American Records
6221 N. Broadway
743-8795

► **Erickson's Delicatessen**
5250 N. Clark St.
561-5634

► **Frank's Live Bait and Sports**
1437 W. Montrose Ave.
549-0631

► **The Gap**
5300 N. Broadway
728-6866

Little Shop of Incense
6207 N. Broadway
973-0011

► **Pier 1 Imports**
5304 N. Broadway
271-7078

► **Smith's Clock Shop**
6217 N. Broadway
262-6151

► **Swedish Bakery**
5348 N. Clark St.
561-8919

► **Swedish Style Gift Shop**
5309 N. Clark St.

► **True Nature Health Foods**
6034 N. Broadway
465-6400

► **Wikstrom Scandinavian American Gourmet Foods**
5247 N. Clark St.
878-0601

🍴 Restaurants

► **Ann Sather**
5207 N. Clark St.
271-6677

Beirut Restaurant
5204 N. Clark St.
769-1250

Carson's—The Place for Ribs
5970 N. Ridge Ave.
271-4000

► **Costa Brava**
4006 N. Broadway
472-5322

► **Mekong**
4953 N. Broadway
271-0206

Moody's Pub
5910 N. Broadway
275-2696

► **Pasteur**
4759 N. Sheridan Rd.
271-6673

► **Seoul House**
5346 N. Clark St.
728-6756

► **Siam Cafe**
4712 N. Sheridan Rd.
769-6602

► **Song-Huong**
5424 N. Broadway
271-6702

▶ **Tokyo Marina**
5058 N. Clark St.
878-2900

☾ Nightlife

▶ **Aragon Entertainment Center**
1106 W. Lawrence Ave.
561-9500

▶ **Green Mill**
4802 N. Broadway
878-5552

▶ **New Bryn Mawr Theater**
1125 W. Bryn Mawr Ave.
728-0881

▶ **Reza's Restaurant**
1479 W. Berwyn Ave.
561-1898

▶ **Riviera Night Club**
4746 N. Racine Ave.
769-6300

Ravenswood/Lincoln Square

INCOLN SQUARE is best-known as Chicago's new Greektown, successor to the bulldozed Halsted Street original, but the blaze of Hellenic signs doesn't tell the whole story. Eastern European food stores and restaurants dot the streets; a varied Asian presence includes more than a smattering of Korean enterprises; and vestiges of a once-bold German influence still line Lincoln Avenue.

Reflections of Ravenswood (off Leland and Western avenues, near the el station), a bold, naive mural, catalogues the community's 125-year history in a splash of symbols: farmers and fruit stands, a brick works and a church, a tram and an omnibus, Riverview Amusement Park and the Louis Sullivan-designed Krause Music Store (now a funeral parlor), the 1956 Lincoln statue and the pylon marking the recent shopping-mall treatment of Lincoln Avenue between the mural and the statue.

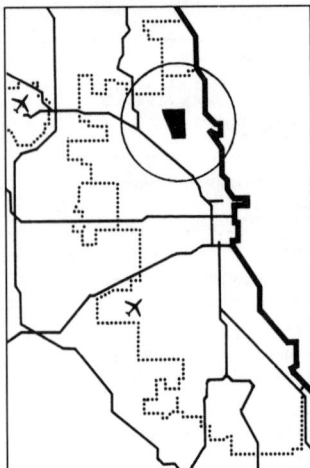

Immigration changed the farms, greenhouses, and brick works of an earlier era into a neighborhood of frame houses and cottages of modest scale compared to the grander homes of adjoining Ravenswood. When annexed to Chicago in 1893, the community was heavily residential. By the time streetcars began rumbling down Lincoln, Lawrence, and Damen avenues in 1900, these routes were commercial arteries. Completion of the Ravenswood elevated railway in 1907 solidly welded the area to 20th-century Chicago but, since then, the streetscape has changed slowly. Always overshadowed by the neighboring Lake View and Uptown shopping strips, the all-dressed-up-with-no-place-to-go commercial intersection of Lincoln and Western escaped booms and busts.

Though the neighborhood tends toward the nondescript — which many believe to be among its greatest assets — there are some notable sites. A branch of the German-American National Congress, **Dankhaus**, houses a hall, meeting rooms, library, and the offices of *Amerika-Woche* newspaper. Now the Arntzen-Coleman Funeral Home, Sullivan's **Krause Music Store** is lavished with so much ornamentation it's almost overwhelming.

The area's Greek community is anchored by **St. Demetrios Greek Orthodox Church**. A modest structure built in 1928, the church contains some interesting iconography, but its real strength lies in the community center, library, and 500-seat Solon Greek School. The complex is a magnet for immigrants, and even those who have left the neighborhood return every year for the parish festival. **St. Matthias Church** was established in 1887, though the present red-brick basilica was dedicated in 1916.

SHOPPING

The city's oldest pet shop, **Vahle's Bird Store**, started in New York City in 1866 and moved here in the 1890s. A colorful flurry of canaries, macaws, finches, and cockatoos chirps and squawks away in the aviary.

Set back from the street, the two-story **Griffins & Gargoyles** is easy to miss — but don't. The neighborhood's best antiques store is crowded with American and European furniture, including lots of case pieces, armoires, sideboards, and smaller items, too, priced to reflect the collection's quality. While much of the furniture at **Penn-Dutchman Antiques** is nothing special, every drawer in every dresser, sideboard, and highboy hides some collectible treasure. A flea market's worth of old photographs, dishes, glassware, kitchen gadgets, and other things lines the walls in all four rooms.

For embroidered table linens from China at reasonable prices, try **Chinese Linens**; and for high-quality dinnerware and cut crystal with which to set the table, head over to **European Import Center**. In the same vein, fresh flowers and plants — from bonsai to orchids — overflow at **Lincoln Flower and Gift**.

Since 1928, **Dr. Michael's Products** has been providing the area's residents with herbs, roots, and other medicinal plants, while **Magic, Inc.**, takes a more mystical approach. Chat with magicians who hang around this shop, or take some lessons so you can work the tricks that are sold here.

Howard Mundt learned cabinetmaking from his dad in the 1930s, and now, at a shop bearing his father's name, **Henry A. W. Mundt**, he repairs and restores old furniture, as well as making new pieces from scratch.

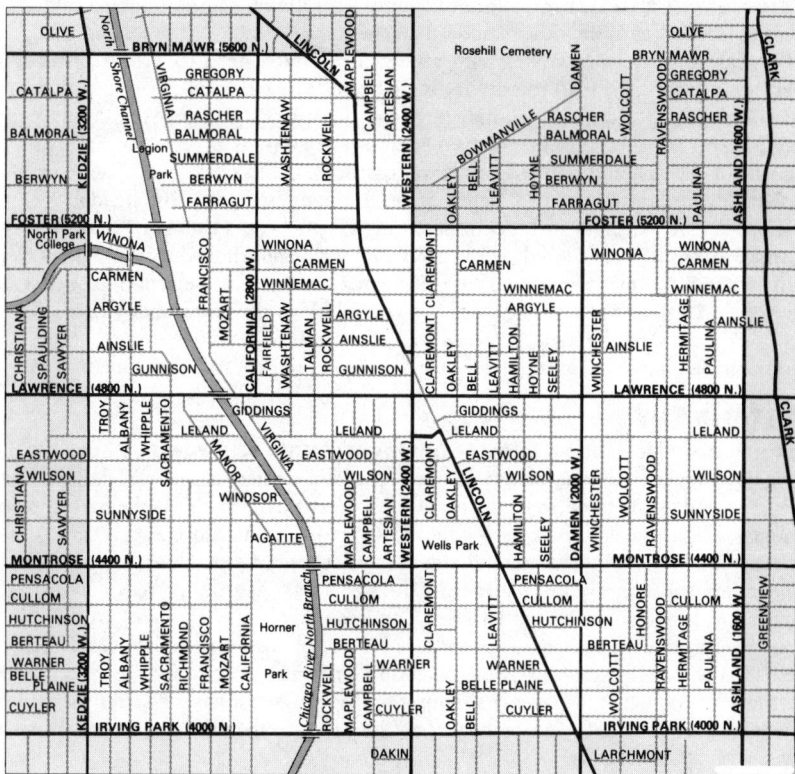

Ravenswood/Lincoln Square

Graceful imported robes from China are available at **Pacific Enterprises**, a Korean firm that also sells florid, embroidered synthetic fabrics and bed linens. For eatables and potables, head to **Delicatessen Meyer**. This crowded shop stocks more than 50 varieties of sausages, baked hams, pork and beef, homemade leberkäse (a smooth veal meat loaf), prepared seasonal salads such as herring and noodle, cheeses, and jams. **North Star Bakery** sells only bread — but what bread! The kommissbrot, bauernbrot, and pumpernickel are the real things, served by better German restaurants. Pastries laden with chocolate, buttercream torte slices, fruit-topped squares, beautiful cakes, and delicious butter cookies are all irresistible at the **European Pastry Shop**, an inviting bakery made all the cheerier by several tables where you can linger over a cup of coffee and a pastry or two or three.

All the ingredients for preparing a Greek meal at home are available at various shops on and just off Lawrence Avenue. In addition to a good selection of olives and cheeses, the **West Meat Market** sells almost every part of the lamb except the wool. Lambs' heads stare up from display cases, surrounded by chops, shanks, livers, breasts, kidneys, and brains. The little **Psaropoula Fish House** is the place to go for most of the fish used in Greek cooking, including sea bass, squid, octopus, and shrimp. **Tom's Delicatessen and Bakery** stocks some of everything: wines, liquors, cold cuts, cheeses, Greek bread, and other standard deli fare.

For Eastern European sweets with a homemade look, head to **Tomas Bakery**. Everything from the bread to cookies is first-rate. The whipped-cream creations are great, and the napoleons will remind you of the old country. Continue this culinary trip with Magyar delights from **European Sausage House**: debreceni sausages, disznó sagt (head cheese), and paprikás szalonna (garlicky, cured pork jaw). The store also carries Hungarian sweet and hot paprikas, prune or apricot lekvár, and strudel.

Shopping for sausages in Lincoln Square is a rare treat. **Michael Fless Homemade Sausage** produces a dazzling array of wursts and smoked meats, mostly German-style, but some Hungarian and Serbian. The Serbian selection is better at **George's Delicatessen**. The store is a ready link to the homeland with sausages, smoked meats, fresh kajmak (a spread that looks and tastes like a mix of butter and cream cheese), imported ajvar (a vinegary red-pepper relish), and Yugoslavian wines.

RESTAURANTS

A neighborhood institution, **Lutz's Continental Cafe and Pastry Shop**, has the city's best-stocked German bakery, as well as a trim dining room. Still, the real treat is the tranquil, plant-filled, walled patio. On summer evenings, this is the perfect place to enjoy a light meal, the tortes — rich and sweet in the Austro-German style — and *Kaffee mit Schlag*, all served on individual trays set with lovely china.

For more substantial fare, try **Heidelberger Fass**. Worthy entrées here include schnitzel à la Holstein, meaty kasseler rippchen (smoked pork chop), surprisingly moist beef rouladen, and sausages and are served by costumed waitresses. Much of the fish is outstanding, as well, and the crisp German fries, red cabbage, and spätzle are fine. Bavarian cream makes a soothing finish. **Hogen's** has a shorter menu, but this neighborhood spot can't be beat for values like a lunch-time bratwurst washed down with a German beer.

Prices are a bit high for basic Serbian dishes at **Miomir's Serbian Club**, but the entertainment makes up for them. Gypsy fiddlers, Cossack baritones, and an array of others are orchestrated by Miomir himself into a rollicking floor show.

Asians have made inroads into the restaurant scene here, and two of the best are **Manila-Manila**, a Filipino place, and **Poong Mee House**, which serves Korean food. Don't be put off by the plain exterior or not-too-clean interior at Manila-Manila, for the kitchen turns out such complicated delights as smoky stuffed eggplant; chicken stuffed with cinnamony ground meat, peas, and raisins; and fried, sautéed, stewed, or stuffed milkfish. Round out a meal of these or other well-prepared but more basic Filipino fare with a noodle dish, and save room for an intriguing pastry. Poong Mee House is plain-looking as well but is a solid source for hearty soups, noodles, seafood, and marinated grilled meats at rock-bottom prices.

Interesting Places

▶**Dankhaus**
4740 N. Western Ave.
561-9181

▶**Krause Music Store building**
4611 N. Lincoln Ave.

▶**St. Demetrios Greek Orthodox Church**
Winona St. and Washtenaw Ave.
561-5992

▶**St. Matthias Church**
Ainslie St. and Claremont Ave.
561-6020

Shopping

▶**Chinese Linens**
2607 W. Lawrence Ave.
334-6682

▶**Delicatessen Meyer**
4750 N. Lincoln Ave.
561-3377

▶**Dr. Michael's Products**
5109 N. Western Ave.
271-7738

▶**European Import Corner**
2316 W. Leland Ave.
271-7017

▶**European Pastry Shop**
4701 N. Lincoln Ave.
769-2220

▶**European Sausage House**
4361 N. Lincoln Ave.
472-9645

▶**Michael Fless Homemade Sausage**
4452 N. Western Ave.
478-5443

▶**Griffins & Gargoyles**
2140 W. Lawrence Ave.
769-1255

▶**Lincoln Flower and Gift**
4064 N. Lincoln Ave.
525-1640

▶**Magic, Inc.**
5082 N. Lincoln Ave.
334-2855

▶**Henry A. W. Mundt**
4143 N. Lincoln Ave.
935-5115

▶**North Star Bakery**
4545 N. Lincoln Ave.
561-9858

▶**Pacific Enterprises**
2554 W. Lawrence Ave.
334-3044

▶**Penn-Dutchman Antiques**
4912 N. Western Ave.
271-2208

▶**Psaropoula Fish House**
4755 N. Rockwell St.
728-5415

▶**Tomas Bakery**
4054 N. Lincoln Ave.
472-6401

▶**Tom's Delicatessen and Bakery**
2612 W. Lawrence Ave.
784-2431

▶**Vahle's Bird Store**
4710 N. Damen Ave.
271-1623

▶**West Meat Market**
2549 W. Lawrence Ave.
769-4956

Restaurants

▶**Heidelberger Fass**
4300 N. Lincoln Ave.
478-2486

▶**Hogen's**
4560 N. Lincoln Ave.
334-9406

▶**Lutz's Continental Cafe and Pastry Shop**
2458 W. Montrose Ave.
478-7785

▶**Manila-Manila**
3146 W. Montrose Ave.
478-7781

▶**Miomir's Serbian Club**
2255 W. Lawrence Ave.
784-2111

▶**Poong Mee House**
3752 W. Lawrence Ave.
478-0217

Rogers Park

ROGERS PARK has always been a staging area, a way station for those bound upward and elsewhere. Its earliest inhabitants were the Indians, who hunted here and roamed the natural trails formed after Lake Michigan rolled back to reveal a tall ridge—now Ridge Boulevard. They moved north of the Indian Boundary Line (today's Rogers Avenue) in 1816, ceding the land to the south and opening the way to future settlement.

Although the fields of West Rogers Park (originally called West Ridge) didn't begin to sprout suburban-like bungalows until well into the 20th century, the neighborhood east of Ridge exploded after the 1907 el expansion. The Irish, joining German landed gentry and tradesmen near the lakefront, built **St. Ignatius Church**, a 1917 Jesuit landmark designed by Henry J. Schlacks after the Gesù, the order's mother church in Rome. By the 1920s, area Jews had founded **Congregation B'nai Zion**—the city's first Conservative congregation—and **Temple Mizpah**, challenging the Germans as the neighborhood's largest ethnic group and, by mid-century, surpassing them.

Rogers Park's population quadrupled between 1910 and 1920, then doubled again in the next decade. The area was transformed by an apartment- and hotel-building boom. Many of the elegant, pre-World War Two three-flats and fine courtyard buildings remain; a sizable number are condos. The most desirable of the older buildings may be east of Sheridan Road by the lake, but the streetscape is much the same all the way to Ridge Boulevard. The beautifully maintained **Casa Bonita Apartments** are an exercise in Moorish splendor that stops just short of being garish.

Spacious apartments, convenient transportation to the Loop, and a string of beaches along Lake Michigan remain East Rogers Park's lures

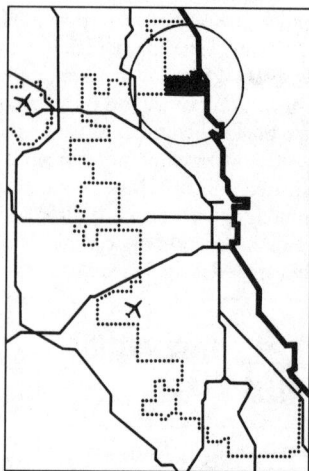

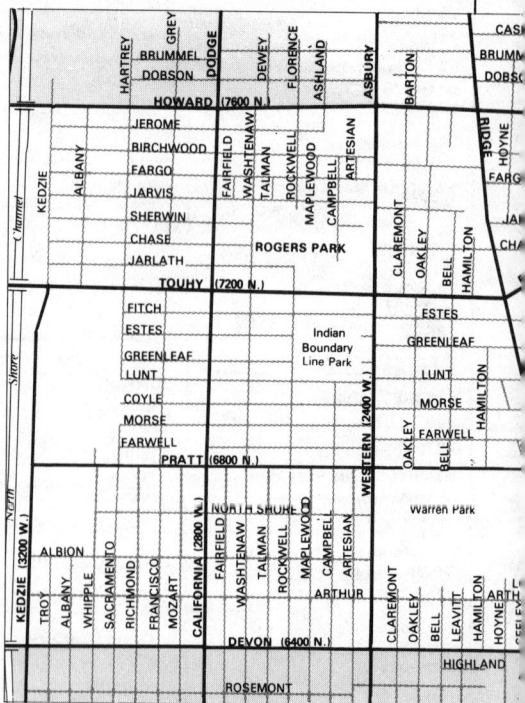

today, while the faces of the residents continue to change. There are still many Jews, a number of them recent arrivals from the Soviet Union, but current denizens include East Asians, East Indians, Chinese, Latinos, Koreans, and lots of college students.

Loyola University dominates the southern end of East Rogers Park. The campus buildings are a mixture of turn-of-the-century red brick and modern concrete and glass. Adjacent is **Mundelein College**, a Catholic women's school in a masonry skyscraper that is listed on the National Register of Historic Places. Construction began on the art moderne building with its art deco detailing in 1929, just three days after the stock-market crash that ended Rogers Park's building boom.

Among other interesting sites in Rogers Park is the **Cook County Federal Savings and Loan Association** building, a replica of Independence Hall. The commitment to patriotism is carried out by plaques inset on the façade and a statue of "the fighting Yank." **The Bernard Horwich Jewish Community Center** offers a panoply of cultural events and houses fine recreational facilities, including a gym and a swimming pool.

SHOPPING

For fine string instruments, musicians travel north to the Howard Street el stop and stroll east to **Fritz Reuter & Sons**. The original Fritz — he established the firm in 1921 to create fine violins, violas, and cellos — isn't around any more, but his two sons, Fritz, Jr., and Gunther, carry on the craft. In addition to selling instruments, the Reuters rent and repair all types of violins.

The makings for Mandarin fare — or for Cantonese, Korean, Japanese, Filipino, or any other Asian cuisine you favor — may be found at the **Oriental Food Market**. The store sells all the staples, from ginger and dried seaweed to sesame buns and rice sticks. At the triangular intersection of Clark Street with Rogers and Jarvis avenues is the **Rogers Park Fruit Market**. Enclosed and in the midst of the city, it still seems like an overstuffed roadside vegetable stand. **Affy Tapple**, the company that makes great taffy apples, sells seconds at a bargain price. Some are undersized, unevenly coated, or with broken sticks.

The area also has a few worthwhile antiques shops. **Kenneth**

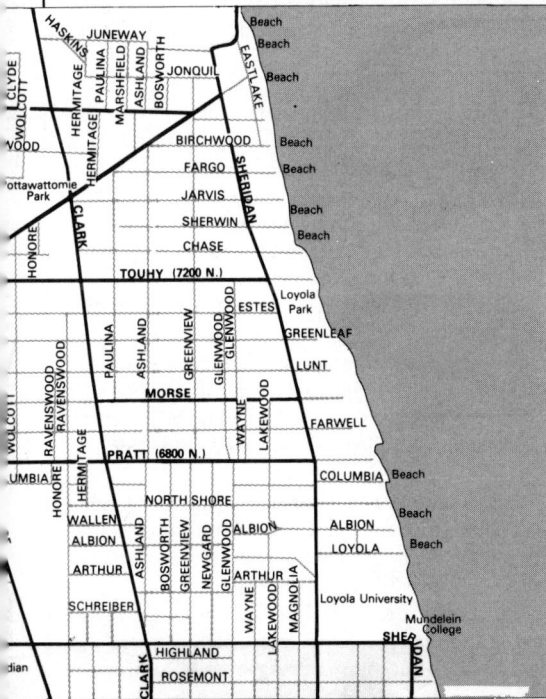

Rogers Park

L. Gustafson Antiques and Books has a sizable section devoted to Civil War history and Lincoln lore. Brass antique beds are featured at **Brown Beaver Antiques**, a multiroom store that claims it's the only establishment in the country specializing in such objects.

The shops of West Rogers Park exhibit eclecticism. Stroll down its main commercial street, Devon Avenue, and within a few blocks there are stores beckoning you to buy everything from topnotch gyros to a string of sari shops that probably rivals Calcutta.

The **Mid-West Fish Market** smokes its own whitefish and sable, and it will grind fish fillets for gefilte fish. Complete a brunch- buying trip by joining the number-clutching crowds at **Gitel's Bakery** for challah, almond rings, and, seasonally, hamantashen. Pass Damen Avenue and you're in East Indian country: Both sides of the street are lined with Indian and Pakistani restaurants, groceries, video rental and sales stores, and sari shops. There are **Suleiman's Brothers Farm City Meats**, **Bombay Fashions**, **Uma Sarees and Appliances**, **India Sari Palace**, **Royal Sari Palace**, and **Shard Sari Center**, just to name a few.

Western Avenue bisects the community, and between Peterson and Touhy avenues it's largely lined with car lots. Farther north, **Direct Auctioneers** is worth a visit for its celebrated Tuesday sales. Auctions of fine art and museum-quality antiques are seldom found at this gigantic former garage. But frequent sales offer enough run-of-the-mill 19th- and 20th-century furniture, tableware, and collectibles to stock a dozen antiques stores. There are no catalogues, but each lot is numbered, and bidders can get some real bargains. On the other hand, "estates and storage" auctions provide the best buys and most convivial gatherings.

RESTAURANTS AND NIGHTLIFE

As in many North Side neighborhoods, restaurants here cater to every taste and pocketbook. At the **Heartland Cafe**, salads with yogurt dressing and hearty soups with corn bread precede economically priced chicken, fish, and vegetarian dinners. Sandwiches, omelets, and more than 30 natural juices are also on the menu. Jazz, folk, or classical musicians hold forth on the makeshift stage on some evenings and during weekend brunches.

A stalwart of the neighborhood is **Capt'n Nemo's Submarine Sandwiches**, which slathers layers of meats, cheeses, eggs, and vegetables onto French bread and serves up a half-sandwich that will satiate any but the hungriest. Take-out soup is sold by the cup or the gallon. **The Bagel** dishes up unfussy Jewish fare just like Bubbe used to make. Standard dishes are bolstered by petcha (calf's-foot jelly) and tsimmes (carrot stew). Signature dishes: Polish-style whitefish and short ribs in sweet-and-sour cabbage borscht.

One of the oldest Thai places in town, **Bangkok House**, remains a good value, while **Dae Ho** serves good Korean and Chinese fare — the Korean stands out, though. There are good grilled meats, saucy chap chae, beef shish kebab, spicy octopus, chicken bokkim, and hot soups. Don't miss the excellent Chinese potato salad.

At **On the Tao**, moist crackling-skin hen is the best choice of appetizer before delving into the 20-or-so poultry, seafood, and vegetable entrées offered (there's no beef or pork here). A good, cheap Chinese take-out joint is **Yang-Tze River**, which makes a particularly tasty dish called Vegetarian Delight.

Jamaican food is the star at the **Caribbean Delight**, an attractive but simple place to sample island cooking. Almost everything is worth trying, including the ginger-spice chicken, thick sautéed red snapper, spicy-rich goat and mutton curries, and heavily cooked spice steak.

Devon Avenue, west of Damen, is lined with shops and restaurants catering to the area's East Indian population, as well as others in the city who enjoy Indian food and culture. Inexpensive yet exotic cooking is available at **Shalimar Garden**, a simple storefront serving Pakistani food. The lamb with spinach, karahi chicken, shrimps Karachi style, and karee are all good bets. The creamy rice pudding makes a good finale. Good Indian food is served at **Gandhi India**, which is surrounded on all sides by shops selling saris, Indian groceries, and gifts.

Just north of Howard Street, near Evanston, is the big, loud, and very popular Mexican restaurant, **La Choza**. During the summer months, dining alfresco is pleasant. And one more thing, bring your own beer or wine!

At **Kavkaz Restaurant and Club**, the generally excellent food is Georgian — a cuisine similar to Armenian or Middle Eastern and touted as the Soviet Union's best. Live music and dancing on the weekends make the atmosphere quite festive.

There are a few decent movie houses in Rogers Park, including the **North Shore Cinema** and the **400 Theater**. For music — the blues, some rockabilly, R & B, jazz, and soul — try **Biddy Mulligan's**. If pool is more your style, the **Campus Room** is a well-run place that also has video and pinball games.

The choice spot for entertainment, however, is the **No Exit Cafe and Gallery**, a relaxed, honest-to-goodness coffee house. Besides the coffees, teas, and pastries, performances by the best local and national folk musicians are the principal fare, although the stage is surrendered for jazz or classical on some evenings. There are occasional poetry readings, too.

Interesting Places

▶ **Bernard Horwich Jewish Community Center**
3003 W. Touhy Ave.
761-9100

▶ **Casa Bonita Apartments**
7340-50 N. Ridge Blvd.

Cobbler's Mall
1330 W. Morse Ave.
764-5906

▶ **Congregation B'nai Zion**
Pratt Blvd. and Greenview Ave.
465-2161

▶ **Cook County Federal Savings and Loan Association**
2720 W. Devon Ave.
761-2700

▶ **Loyola University**
6525 N. Sheridan Rd.
274-3000

▶ **Mundelein College**
6363 N. Sheridan Rd.
262-8100

▶ **St. Ignatius Church**
Glenwood and Loyola avenues
764-5936

▶ **Temple Mizpah**
(now the Korean United Presbyterian Church)
Morse and Ashland avenues
465-3377

Shopping

▶ **Affy Tapple**
7110 N. Clark St.
338-1100

Beck's Book Store
6590 N. Sheridan Rd.
743-2281

Bombay Fashions
2305 W. Devon Ave.
338-4037

Rogers Park

Bookleggers Used Books
6743 N. Sheridan Rd.
743-4195

▶ **Brown Beaver Antiques**
7006 N. Western Ave.
338-7372

Cheesecakes by JR
2841 W. Howard St.
465-6733

Chicago Hebrew Bookstore
2942 W. Devon Ave.
973-6636

Coren's Rod and Reel Service
6424 N. Western Ave.
743-2980

▶ **Direct Auctioneers**
7232 N. Western Ave.
465-3300

Elaine's Bakery
1412½ W. Morse Ave.
274-5444

Everybody's Bookstore
2120 W. Devon Ave.
764-0929

Frame Gallery
2925 W. Touhy Ave.
973-3888

Hobbymodels
2358 W. Devon Ave.
262-2136

▶ **Kenneth L. Gustafson Antiques and Books**
6962 N. Clark St.
761-0904

Kinko's Copies
6548 N. Sheridan Rd.
761-2777

▶ **Mid-West Fish Market**
2948 W. Devon Ave.
764-8115

Natural Rhythm Futon Co.
1947 W. Howard St.
338-3600

New York Kosher Sausage Corp.
2900 W. Devon Ave.
743-1664

▶ **Oriental Food Market and Cooking School**
2801 W. Howard St.
274-2826

▶ **Rogers Park Fruit Market**
7401 N. Clark St.
262-3663

Shaevitz Kosher Meat and Sausage
2907 W. Devon Ave.
743-9481

Suleiman Brothers Farm City Meats
2255 W. Devon Ave.
274-2255

Uma Sarees and Appliances
2535 W. Devon Ave.
338-6302

Restaurants and Nightlife

▶ **The Bagel**
3000 W. Devon Ave.
764-3377

▶ **Bangkok House**
2744 W. Pratt Ave.
338-5948

▶ **Biddy Mulligan's**
7644 N. Sheridan Rd.
761-6532

▶ **Capt'n Nemo's Submarine Sandwiches**
7367 N. Clark St.
973-0570

▶ **Campus Room**
6550 N. Sheridan Rd.
761-8960

▶ **Caribbean Delight**
7303 N. Damen Ave.
743-2900

▶ **La Choza**
7630 N. Paulina St.
465-9401

▶ **Dae Ho**
2741 W. Devon Ave.
274-8499

Edwardo's Pizza
1937 W. Howard St.
761-7040

Fluky's — hot dogs
6821 N. Western Ave.
274-3652

▶ **400 Theater**
6746 N. Sheridan Rd.
764-9100

▶ **Gandhi India**
2601 W. Devon Ave.
761-8714

▶ **Heartland Cafe**
7000 N. Glenwood Ave.
465-8005

▶ **Kavkaz Restaurant and Club**
6405 N. Claremont Ave.
338-1316

My Place For? — seafood
7545 N. Clark St.
262-5767

▶ **No Exit Cafe**
6970 N. Glenwod Ave.
743-3355

▶ **North Shore Theater**
7074 N. Clark St.
764-3656

▶ **On the Tao**
1218 W. Morse Ave.
743-5955

Poolgogi Steak House — Korean
1334 W. Morse Ave.
761-1366

▶ **Shalimar Gardens**
6418 N. Western Ave.
465-7777

▶ **Yang-Tze River**
1313 W. Morse Ave.
764-7517

Near Northwest Side

TERRA INCOGNITA to most tourists, suburbanites, and lakefront sophisticates, West Town, Wicker Park, and Logan Square — all wonderfully diverse neighborhoods — were once very much a part of the city's mainstream.

The tangled Division-Ashland-Milwaukee intersection, where the Polski kiosk stocks newspapers and periodicals from the old country, is the heart of West Town. Through World War Two, this was the Polish downtown — the commercial hub for the largest concentration of Poles outside Warsaw.

Blessed in 1881, **St. Stanislaus Kostka** is the oldest of the grand Polish churches. Patrick Charles Keely, who also designed Holy Name Cathedral, was the architect of this Italian Renaissance masterpiece. Inside, under the dome of the altar, Tadeusz Zukotynski's painting, *The Triumph of Christ*, looms large in the immense central nave. Keely may have designed the building, but Father Vincent Barzynski determined the course of the city's oldest Polish parish in the late 19th century. Under his leadership, St. Stanislaus became the world's largest parish. In 1893, its priests performed more than two thousand baptisms and officiated at a thousand funerals. Father Barzynski was also instrumental in founding schools, developing the Polish Roman Catholic Union, and starting a Polish daily newspaper.

In the mid-1870s, a group of dissidents formed Holy Trinity Parish, triggering a 20-year dispute ended only by the intercession of the Vatican's delegate to the United States. Completed in 1906, **Holy Trinity Church** rivals St. Stanislaus in grandeur. William Krieg finished the design by Washington architect Olszewski (known as Von Herbulis), which may account for the building's mixture of neoclassical and baroque elements. The church's open design was attained by using iron construction in the vaults, eliminating the need for internal supporting columns.

Perhaps most beautiful of all is **St. Mary of the Angels Church**. Begun in 1911 and completed nine years later, the two thousand-seat church was designed by Henry J. Schlacks and reminds some people of St. Peter's in Rome.

Churches are also the keystone of Ukrainian Village, another West Town ethnic community. Dedicated in 1915, **St. Nicholas Ukrainian Catholic Cathedral** was modeled on the Basilica of St. Sophia in Kiev, although only 13 of the original 32 copper-clad domes were incorporated into the Chicago version. When St. Nicholas switched to the Gregorian calendar, a rift between older congregants and more recent immigrants led to the formation of a new parish in 1973. At the conservative **SS. Volodymyr and Olha Ukrainian Catholic Church**, the old (Julian) calendar is maintained. The building's gilded Byzantine domes are set off by a colorful, two-story-high mural on the façade.

A city landmark, the neighborhood's most striking church is Louis Sullivan's 1901 **Holy Trinity Cathedral** of the Orthodox Church in America. It's a triumphant

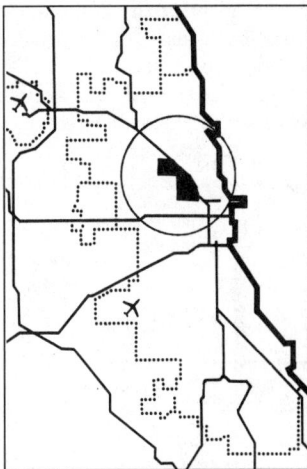

blend of functionalism and mysticism. The intimate, stucco-covered building is loosely based on wooden octagon-on-a-square churches familiar to original parishioners — rural Byelorussians, Carpathians, and Ukrainians. The lavishly stenciled polychrome interior contrasts dramatically with Sullivan's restrained, geometric ornamentation around the eaves, doors, and windows. As at other local Ukrainian churches, coffee and cake are served after the services.

Near Northwest Side

In the Wicker Park community, many of the homes date from the immediate post-Fire period, and here builders let their imaginations run rampant. Spurned by the lakefront Anglo-Saxon Protestant establishment as parvenus, German beer barons, packers, and merchants settled near the park, at that time a beautiful pleasure ground with a large swan pond. They were soon joined by their less wealthy countrymen and by Scandinavians who built more modest dwellings. Today, the area is some of the city's hottest real estate.

Elegant brick and stone mansions in a delightful range of styles stand lovingly restored in this National Historic District. Along Pierce Avenue, massive stone houses with classic columns and arches face Victorian Gothic ones highlighted by intricate gingerbread on porches and entranceways. The steamboat-Gothic, Swiss-chalet Runge House (2138) served as the Polish consulate in the 1930s.

A delicate wrought-iron fence surrounds two magnificent, early mansions on Hoyne Avenue. Set well back on a spacious lot, the John Raap House (1407) is a sprawling, three-story, brick, French Empire beauty with an adjoining coach house. Next door (1417), the Italianate home built in 1879 for furniture manufacturer Carl Warnecke boasts a lovely gazebo. The 1906 Romanesque **Wicker Park Lutheran Church** was built for a parish established in 1870, with stone salvaged from a local whorehouse. When asked about this seeming impropriety, the pastor is said to have replied, "It has served the Devil long enough. Let it now serve God." **St. Paul's Evangelical Lutheran Church** dates from 1892, although the parish is almost a decade older. The stained-glass windows and interior woodcarvings are worth a look.

Logan Square was conceived on a sweeping scale unknown to the rest of the North Side. Crisscrossed by grand residential streets, it is the northern terminus of Chicago's matchless park-linked boulevard system. Kedzie and Logan, the latter once dubbed "the boulevard of millionaires," along with Palmer and Humboldt boulevards, offer a picture of pre-Depression gentility. Although occasional homes, such as the John Maher-designed John Rath House, stand out, the streetscape depends not so much on individual mansions as in Wicker Park, but on the panoramas.

Strikingly set at the head of Logan Boulevard, one of the city's widest, the **Norwegian Lutheran Memorial Church** is a red-brick charmer. Built in 1912 as the Minnekirken, the church still has only one English service a month, even though the community hasn't been a Norwegian bastion for years.

SHOPPING

Shopping on the Near Northwest Side offers a multitude of ethnic specialty shops, as well as the usual array of service stores, discount outlets, and good, down-home bakeries and sausage makers.

Dyes, instruction books, and tips on how to make marvelous, Ukrainian Easter eggs can be found at the **Ukrainian-American**

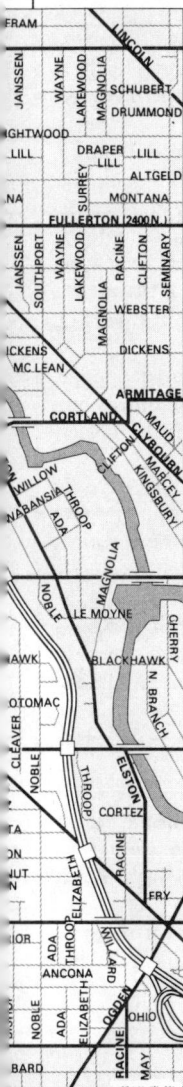

Near Northwest Side

Publishing Company, along with records, other gifts, and books. Stroll down the street to **Delta Import Company** for a nice selection of finished eggs, ceramics, jewelry, fabrics, linens, and Czechoslavak crystal. The shop also ships parcels to the Soviet Union and carries a large stock of blue jeans — much-sought-after status symbols in Eastern Europe.

The biggest and perhaps the best of all such stores, the **Amvets Thrift Store** has a broad, and often funky, selection of clothes and "whatnot."

If easy going browsing is your thing, try the **Polonia Book Store**, which carries an enormous selection of Polish-language books, records, cards, maps, and gifts. Religious, art, and other books, new and old, can be found at **Stauropegion Bookstore** as well.

The area abounds in fine bakeries. Among others, there's **La Baguette Bakery**, which stocks a full supply of its namesake, as well as very tasty Mexican cookylike pastries. **Las Villas Bakery**, on the other hand, specializes in fancy refrigerated pastries and cakes. Close by the vestiges of an old Italian neighborhood on Grand Avenue, the **Gonnella Baking Company**'s outlet store sells fresh bread until 10 p.m. six days a week and until midnight on Fridays. Another great Italian shop, **D'Amato's Bakery**, carries wonderful breads, cookies, and a few pastries. They'll also sell you uncooked pizza dough.

Margie's Candies, in the Poulos family for 70 years, dares dieters with fudge, heavenly hash, and other homemade ice creams and candies, in a genuinely old-fashioned shop crammed with stuffed animals and toys. The real treat is the 18-percent-butterfat ice cream.

RESTAURANTS AND NIGHTLIFE

Stylized folk murals in a cheery dining room behind the bar of **Sak's Ukrainian Village Restaurant** set the stage for a taste of the Old World. Borscht is always available, as are Ukrainian sausages, cabbage rolls, and chicken Kiev. Be sure to try the cheese-filled dessert crêpes topped with whipped cream or sour cream. Behind a chic, modern façade, **Galáns Ukrainian Cafe** brings together the old and the new. Besides Ukrainian specialties, the menu offers German, Rumanian, and American dishes.

One of the most popular area restaurants is the **Busy Bee**, an always-crowded place serving hearty and moderately priced Polish food.

The **Como Inn** is a Chicago institution serving OK food in a series of rooms ranging from the rococo to the High Tech. A large, clean spot is **La Lechonera**, which serves Cuban food from a menu 100 items long, ranging from blue-plate specials to paella. Like its sister restaurant on 18th Street in Pilsen, **Ostionería Playa Azul** serves good seafood dishes and shellfish cocktails.

The **Artful Dodger Pub** is a trendy neighborhood drinking spot for the new Wicker Park crowd. It's a good place to catch live folk, jazz, or blues on almost any night of the week.

Interesting Places

► **Holy Trinity Cathedral**
Leavitt St. and Haddon Ave.
486-6064

► **Holy Trinity Church**
Noble and Division streets
489-4140

► **Norwegian Lutheran Memorial Church**
Logan and Kedzie boulevards
252-7335

► **St. Mary of the Angels Church**
Hermitage Ave. and Cortland St.
278-2644

► **St. Nicholas Ukrainian Catholic Cathedral**
Oakley Blvd. and Rice St.
276-4537

► **St. Stanislaus Kostka Church**
1351 W. Evergreen Ave.
278-2470

► **SS. Volodymyr and Olha Ukrainian Catholic Church**
Oakley Blvd. and Superior St.
829-5209

► **Wicker Park Lutheran Church**
Hoyne Ave. and Le Moyne St.
276-0263

Shopping

► **Amvets Thrift Shop**
2032 N. Milwaukee Ave.

► **D'Amato's Bakery**
1124 W. Grand Ave.
733-5456

► **La Baguette Bakery**
1438 W. Chicago Ave.
421-2971

► **Delta Import Company**
2242 W. Chicago Ave.
235-7788

► **Gonnella Baking Co.**
2002 W. Erie St.
733-2020

► **Margie's Candies**
1960 N. Western Ave.
384-1035

► **Polonia Book Store**
2886 N. Milwaukee Ave.
489-2554

► **Stauropegion Bookstore**
2226 W. Chicago Ave.
276-0774

► **Ukrainian-American Publishing Company**
2315 W. Chicago Ave.
276-6373

Las Villas Bakery
1959 W. Division St.
278-3380

Restaurants

► **Artful Dodger Pub**
1734 W. Wabansia Ave.
227-6859

► **Busy Bee Restaurant**
1546 N. Damen Ave.
772-4433

► **Como Inn**
546 N. Milwaukee Ave.
421-5222

► **Galáns Ukrainian Cafe**
2210 W. Chicago Ave.
292-1000

► **La Lechonera**
2529 N. Milwaukee Ave.
772-6266

► **Ostionería Playa Azul**
821 N. Ashland Ave.
243-9244

► **Sak's Ukrainian Village Restaurant**
2301 W. Chicago Ave.
278-4445

SUBURBS

Evanston

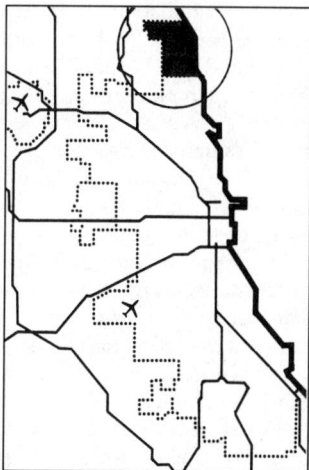

WHEN HE STEPPED ASHORE on Grosse Point's bluff in 1674, Père Marquette looked around and labeled the land worthless. Today it's one of our most cosmopolitan suburbs.

Although Evanston is just 30 minutes from the Loop and is linked to Chicago by history, commerce, and the CTA, it often seems worlds apart. Studded with stately homes and mansions, seat of a Big Ten university, and replete with shops worth a special trip, Evanston has a distinctive ambiance that's heightened by its small-town feel.

An expensive spraying program preserves a canopy of elms over many of the streets, and a spirited citizens' campaign saved Thomas Tallmadge's quaint 1920s street-lamp standards from the scrap heap. A pioneer desegregation program in the nationally respected school system continued a tradition of concern dating back to Underground Railroad days. And, though the city is no longer dry, it has been the headquarters of the Women's Christian Temperance Union for more than a century.

Ironically, the town's first structure was a tavern, constructed in 1836 near Chicago and Ridge avenues — then the Green Bay Trail. Within a few years, the area was a cluster of farmhouses, a few shops, and another couple of taverns. But the taverns were short-lived after **Northwestern University** purchased 379 acres of lakefront land and shaped the town's growth. A unique state charter that still sparks litigation gave the school unusual freedom from real-estate taxes and the right to exclude liquor sales within four miles of the campus. Northwestern platted much of the area; it donated land for churches, schools, and parks; it gave the town a *raison d'être*; and it bestowed John Evans upon the village as its founder and first president.

The three-story frame structure that opened its doors to ten scholars in 1855 has grown to a 162-building mix of architectural styles serving almost 10,000 students. Gothic stone towers blend with neoclassical colonnades, contrasting with the stark planes and bronze glass of modern and often ugly concrete halls. Because buildings buried deep within the campus bear Sheridan Road addresses, finding your way around can be difficult. Daily tours begin at the **Crown Center** Office of Admissions. You can pick up a map here or at the **Norris University Center**, which houses the university's main bookstore.

Several campus attractions include **Pick-Staiger Concert Hall**, a facility acclaimed for its acoustics and sight lines; the **Theater and Interpretation Center**, home of four stages; and the adjacent **Mary and Leigh Block Gallery**. Also, don't miss the **Shakespeare Garden**, just south of the Technological Institute.

The university owns many of the handsome old homes near the campus, but the grandest by far is the mansion left by Charles Gates Dawes, Vice President of the United States under Coolidge, to house a historical museum (see Museums). Buy

Evanston

Evanston Architecture: A Sampler of Self-guided Tours and use it to see some of the country's finest domestic architecture.

In general, the most spectacular homes are north of Main Street between the lakefront and Ridge Avenue. The earliest are Italianate, Queen Anne, and Victorian Gothic. A prime example of the last, the frame **Willard House** with carved bargeboard lining its eaves, was built in 1865 and, like the Dawes mansion, is a National Historic Landmark. Famous educator and temperance leader Frances Willard called her 17-room home a "rest cottage" and lived here until her death in 1898. Nine rooms are open to the public: Five are fitted out with her furniture and furnishings; four contain a temperance-history museum.

By the turn of the century, the genteel suburb attracted a wealthy clientele for many of the Midwest's finest architects, who worked in an imposing variety of styles. A short walk along Forest Avenue provides a delightful overview. Tallmadge and Watson designed the 1908 Prairie-school beauty at 1000; Ernest Mayo built the Tudor home at 1025 two years later. The massive brick mansion wrought for meat packer Oscar Mayer at 1030 contrasts with the work of popular local architect J. T. W. Jennings at 1043. Harvey L. Page created the neoclassical masterpiece at 1047 just a year later than Beer, Clay, and Dutton's 1896 French chateau at 1100 and 1101.

Stroll over to Judson Avenue to see Ernest Mayo's 1894 Tudor at 1110; a classic early Italianate at 1028, once a tannery and then home of pioneer settler John Clough; and Walter Burley Griffin's monumental Carter House at 1024. Hinman and Michigan avenues are also well worth touring, as are Sheridan Road and Lake Shore Boulevard.

Evanston's churches — there are more than 60 of them — also display touches of the masters. Tallmadge and Watson's **First Congregational Church** is one of the finest Georgian churches in the Midwest. They also worked with Ralph Adams Cram on the **First United Methodist Church** to create a striking English Gothic limestone building with superb carved oak and stained glass gracing the interior. Daniel Burnham not only built lakefront mansions in the community for himself and his children; he also designed the lovely, 1894 Romanesque **First Presbyterian Church** with fine woodcarvings in the sanctuary. **Emmanuel United Methodist Church** is one of John Root's last works. The low, red-sandstone building with a massive tower is reminiscent of Root's St. Gabriel in Canaryville. The marble altars in Evanstonian Holabird and Roche's **St. Mark's Episcopal Church**, with its castlelike tower, and in S. A. Jennings's rough-limestone **St. Mary's Church**, designed for Evanston's oldest Catholic parish, are alone sufficient reasons for a visit.

Thirty years of technical difficulties hindered translating Louis Bourgeois's bell-shaped, lacy-walled **Baha'i House of Worship** into concrete and steel. One of the area's most spectacular sites, the temple (which is actually just north of Evanston in Wilmette) is surrounded by lovely landscaping.

Concerts are regular features at several churches, but one of Evanston's major cultural focuses is in a building designed as a school by Burnham in 1892. The **Noyes Cultural Arts Center** sponsors arts, crafts, and dance classes and provides facilities for the **Lynda Martha Dance Company**, which gives dance classes and performances.

Kendall College, a small private school, houses a little-known resource: the **Mitchell Indian Museum** (see Museums). To experience bucolic charms, visit **Ladd**

Arboretum — 23 acres of grounds running alongside McCormick Boulevard, which also house the **Evanston Ecology Center** — or **Grosse Point Lighthouse Park**. Completed in 1873, the 113-foot-tall Grosse Point Lighthouse is a highlight of the park, which also includes a nature center and a maritime museum.

Other Evanston parks feature a variety of activities, among them indoor skating at the **Robert Crown Ice Center**, pedal boating at Lovelace Park, and winter skiing and tobogganing at James Park, where "Mount Trashmore" (built primarily of refuse) offers the area's tallest slopes. Almost half of the town's 4½-mile lakefront is park land, with an excellent blacktopped path for bikers and runners that winds through the entire green strip. Five public beaches dot the shore; to use them in summer, you need to buy a season token or pay a daily charge. Tokens are available at the **Evanston Civic Center**.

SHOPPING

Unlike bedroom suburbs, Evanston also has a real downtown; specialty shops spread out from the Davis Street stations of the CTA and Chicago & North Western Railway. For years, the area between the campus and church-bordered Raymond Park looked like an idealized movie set, right down to the ornate centennial casting in Fountain Square (which was eventually replaced with a modern, concrete one). The Marshall Field's store that anchored downtown Evanston since 1929 recently closed and has been turned into the Evanston Galleria, which will eventually be filled with shops and topped with residential lofts (a few stores, including clothing stores, a record and tape store, and a discount software store have already moved in).

Specialty shops are Evanston's big attraction, and each of the shopping strips along the el-stop streets has a special flavor. Main Street and the nearby Washington Street-Custer Avenue clump offer more antiques, trendy clothes, and handsome goods. West of the tracks, Davis Street combines a busy overflow from downtown with the neighborhood service shops that dot all the strips.

The ceramic, glass, wood, metal, and textile works that fill every nook at the large **Mindscape Gallery** transcend the rubric "crafts." A constant delight, the ever-expanding gallery represents hundreds of the country's most talented artists. Exhibits of paintings and sculptures change frequently at **Grove Street Galleries**; the **Botti Studio of Architectural Arts** excels at creating and restoring stained glass. Credits include work at the Chicago Public Library, Roosevelt University, and a Greek Orthodox church in New York; the firm also builds and restores architectural metalwork, sculptures, and mosaics.

Peggie Robinson Design is one of several shops specializing in original gold and silver jewelry. Smoothly sculptured, classy pieces often feature naturalistic patterns, such as necklaces of lithe leaves, or bracelets and pendants of picture agate and jasper. Precious-metal and stone jewelry is also available at **Calf & Dragon**.

Adornments at the **Mexican Shop** range from exotic, handcrafted African bracelets and heavy beadwork to funky jewelry and crazy glasses. A steady stream of customers committed to the natural look browses for peasant skirts and tapestry tops, as well as dresses made from handwoven Guatemalan fabrics; batik and embroidered Indonesian dresses and separates; Indian prints; kimonos; and antique embroidered Syrian dresses. There are also comfortable cotton pants and shirts for both men and

Evanston

women. For women looking for thoughtfully designed and selected business attire and accessories, **Mary Walter** is your answer.

A few guitars at **Hogeye Music** are antiques, but the store sells everything a folk musician needs. It also offers lessons, makes and repairs instruments, and has weekend miniconcerts and workshops of down-home music. At the **Saxophone Shop, Ltd.**, you can find the obvious, as well as getting the obvious repaired. The **Sound Post** is a general music store featuring guitars, keyboards, PA systems, and the like.

Gerry Morris displays his leather work at **Off the Hoof**, a spare, exposed-brick show room. Find the expected there — belts, purses, cases, wallets — plus unusual small boxes, all expertly handcrafted. Practical, durable, trendy casual wear for men and

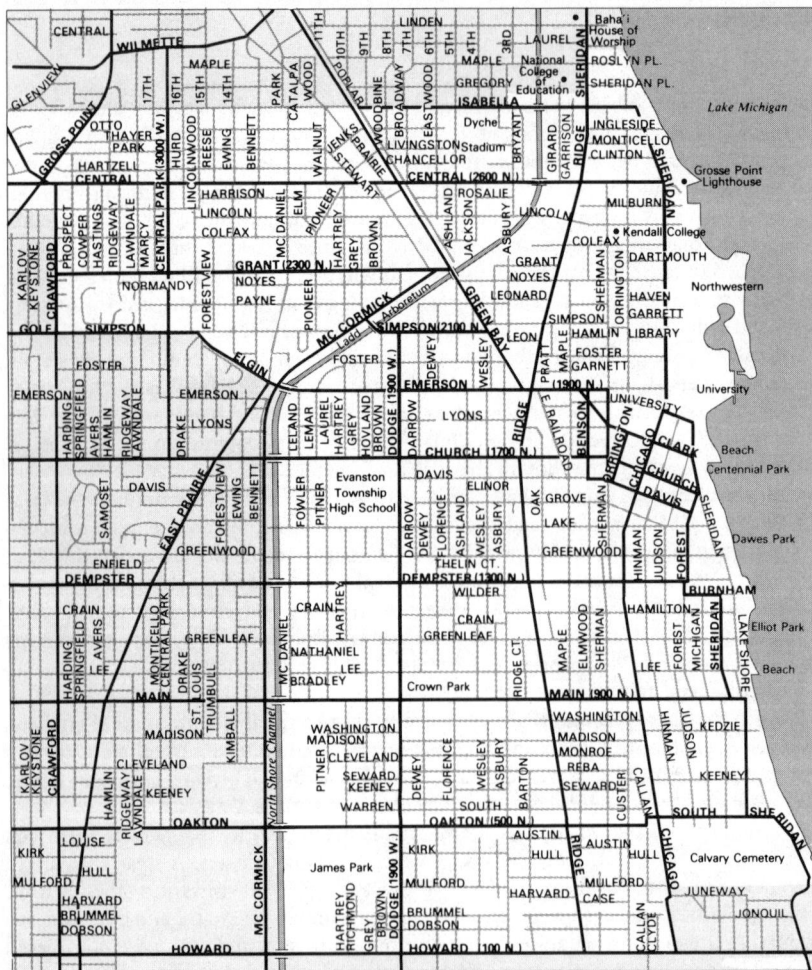

women is also available at **Khaki**. Handcrafted toys, jewelry, soft sculptures, rugs, and quilts are among the items by local and out-of-town artists available at **Mostly Handmade**.

Two Main Street stores rival anything Chicago has to offer. **Good's of Evanston** stocks a wealth of artists' supplies and a strong selection of custom frames. **Vogue Fabrics** is even more amazing. The immense textile supermarket offers one of the Midwest's largest arrays of materials: a whole room of designer fabrics, luxurious silks, and hard-to-find novelties like rayon Hawaiian prints; several others of upholstery and drapery yarn goods and accouterments; and yet another of patterns and findings. Of course, huge selections of cottons, wools, and synthetics are also available.

For handsomely displayed original fibers and yarns for weaving, crocheting, and knitting, go to the **Shepherd's Harvest**, which offers weaving and spinning classes as well.

Like many towns housing major universities, Evanston is graced with numerous wonderful bookstores, including **Great Expectations,** an old-style maze-like store with comfortable chairs adjacent to each section. The store, presided over by Truman Metzel, specializes in philosophy and economics. Great Expectations is only one of a number of shops clustered around the Foster Street el stop. Others include **Wm. Caxton, Ltd.**, and **Richard Barnes & Co.**, both of which sell used and antique books, and **Europa Bookstore**, which deals in new foreign books. If you're still not sated, try **Beck's Used Bookstore**, **Preservation Book**, and **Bookman's Alley**. For new books, try **Kroch's & Brentano's**.

One of Evanston's more unusual places is **Lekotek**, the country's first toy-lending library for handicapped children (by appointment).

RESTAURANTS

One of the coziest and finest restaurants in Evanston is **Café Provençal**, which turns out aromatic dishes with complex flavors. Owner Leslee Reis, who patrols the dining room chatting amiably with guests, is justifiably proud of the quality of what she serves. Try the grilled fillet of beef with roasted sweet onions and Merlot sauce flavored with truffled olive oil and fresh basil, the Provence fish soup, or the Wisconsin pheasant with rosemary-honey glaze. For dessert, don't miss the homemade ice cream, which often includes unusual flavors, such as Armagnac with prunes.

Striking décor and an eclectic menu make Ms. Reis's other Evanston venture, **Leslee's**, a popular spot as well

Another fine choice for dining is **Daruma**, a stylish Japanese restaurant with good food at reasonable prices. Best bets here include crisp tempura, noodle soups, tempura-fried stuffed chicken wings, and goma-ae (cold spinach in unusually sweet soy-sesame dressing), among others. Lines out the door at the **Pine Yard** attest to the top-quality ingredients and, for the most part, expertly cooked dishes at this no-nonsense Chinese restaurant. Pot stickers are well seasoned; peppery hot-and-sour soup is chock-full of all the right stuff, and the flavorful moo shu pork comes with properly thin pancakes.

Health-food-type restaurants abound in Evanston, and one of the best is **The Cornerstone Cafe**. Fish, especially rainbow trout served with nutty brown rice and delicious greens, probably makes the best meal at this macrobiotic/vegetarian storefront. Another good choice for healthful meals is the **Blind Faith Cafe**.

Evanston

Not surprisingly, numerous area restaurants cater with aplomb to Northwestern's 10,000 hungry mouths. **Dave's Italian Kitchen** is a popular pizza joint but serves pretty good and pretty inexpensive pastas as well. It's usually crowded, but the convivial staff and college-y surroundings always make for a pleasant time. Other good bets for pizza include **Giordano's** and **Carmen's**, both of which specialize in the tasty stuffed variety. For morning muffins or bagels, stop in at **J. K. Sweets**, which also serves ice cream and croissants. Fresh fish, clever specials, the salad bar, and pleasant help make **The Keg** the best of the obligatory rough-cut-cedar-stained-glass-and-lots-of-plants college places. Another campus hangout worth a visit even by non-Northwesterners is **Yesterday's**, which serves up excellent barbecued ribs and sandwiches.

Interesting Places

▶ **Baha'i House of Worship**
Linden Ave. and Sheridan Rd.,
Wilmette
256-4400

▶ **Robert Crown Ice Center**
1701 Main St.
328-9400

▶ **Emmanuel United Methodist Church**
Oak Ave. and Greenwood St.
864-9637

▶ **Evanston Civic Center**
2100 Ridge Ave.
328-2100

▶ **Evanston Ecology Center**
2024 McCormick Blvd.
864-5181

▶ **Evanston Historical Society**
225 Greenwood St.
475-3410

▶ **First Congregational Church**
Hinman Ave. and Grove St.
864-8332

▶ **First Presbyterian Church**
Chicago Ave. and Lake St.
864-1472

▶ **First United Methodist Church**
Hinman Ave. and Church St.
864-6181

▶ **Ladd Arboretum**
2024 McCormick Blvd.
864-5181

▶ **Lighthouse Landing Park**
2535 Sheridan Rd.
864-5198

▶ **Mitchell Indian Museum**
Kendall College
2408 Orrington Ave.
866-1395

▶ **Northwestern University**
Admissions Office
1801 Hinman Ave.
491-7271

▶ **Noyes Cultural Arts Center**
927 Noyes St.
491-0266

▶ **St. Mark's Episcopal Church**
Ridge Ave. and Grove St.
864-4806

▶ **St. Mary's Church**
Oak Ave. and Lake St.
864-0333

▶ **Willard House**
1730 Chicago Ave.
864-1397

Shopping

▶ **Richard S. Barnes & Co. Books**
821 Foster St.
869-2272

▶ **Beck's Used Book Store**
1583 Maple Ave.
869-6099

▶ **Bookman's Alley**
1712 Sherman Ave. (rear)
869-6999

▶ **Botti Studio of Architectural Arts**
919 Grove St.
869-5933

▶ **Calf & Dragon**
507 Davis St.
328-3128

▶ **Wm. Caxton, Ltd.**
917 Foster St.
475-1800

Chicago Main Compleat Newsstand
Chicago Ave. and Main St.
864-2727

Corner Store
1511 Chicago Ave.
475-0036

▶ **Europa Book Store**
915 Foster St.
866-6262

Evanston Seed & Bulb Co.
1004 Church St.
864-2050

▶ **Good's of Evanston**
714 Main St.
864-0001

▶ **Great Expectations**
911 Foster St.
864-3881

▶ **Grove Street Galleries**
921 Grove St.
866-7341

► **Hogeye Music**
1920 Central St.
475-0206

Kaehler Luggage Shop
1421 Sherman Ave.
328-0744

► **Khaki**
1245 Chicago Ave.
869-8090

► **Kroch's & Brentano's**
1711 Sherman Ave.
328-7220

► **Lekotek**
2100 Ridge Ave.
328-0001

► **Mexican Shop**
801 Dempster St.
475-8665

► **Mindscape Gallery**
1521 Sherman Ave.
864-2660

► **Mostly Handmade**
1622 Orrington Ave,
864-0845

► **Off the Hoof**
838 Custer Ave.
864-4830

Pot Shop
604 Dempster St.
864-7778

► **Preservation Book Shop**
1911 Central St.
864-4449

► **Peggie Robinson Design**
1514 Sherman Ave.
475-2121

► **Saxophone Shop, Ltd.**
2834 Central St.
491-0075

Scandinavian Design
1701 Sherman Ave.
869-6100

**Scandinavian Design
Clearance Center**
2510 Green Bay Rd.
491-1583

► **Shepherd's Harvest**
1930 Central St.
491-1353

► **Sound Post**
1239 Chicago Ave.
866-6866

► **Vogue Fabrics**
718 Main St.
864-9600

► **Mary Walter**
One Rotary Center
475-6644

✕ Restaurants

► **Blind Faith Cafe**
525 Dempster St.
328-6875

► **Café Provençal**
1625 Hinman Ave.
475-2233

► **Carmen's of Evanston**
1601 Sherman Ave.
328-6131

► **Cornerstone Cafe**
800 Dempster St.
328-6161

► **Daruma**
2901 Central St.
864-6633

► **Dave's Italian Kitchen**
906 Church St.
864-6000

► **Giordano's of Evanston**
500 Davis St.
475-5000

► **J. K. Sweets**
720½ Clark St.
864-3073

► **The Keg**
810 Grove St.
866-7780

► **Leslee's**
One Rotary Center
328-8304

► **Pine Yard Chinese
Restaurant**
924 Church St.
475-4940

► **Yesterday's**
1850 Sherman Ave.
864-8464

Oak Park and River Forest

"WRIGHT MAKES MIGHT" in Oak Park. The world's largest collection of Frank Lloyd Wright buildings — 25 — has long been the village's strongest draw. But there's more to Oak Park architecture than that. Prairie-school landmarks share the broad, tree-lined streets with Italianate, neoclassical, Victorian, and Queen Anne mansions, and some striking modern structures are interspersed.

Although the building stock is a great source of pride, locals are working hard to dispel the misconception that Oak Park is nothing more than a museum of the last hundred years' architectural development. There are antiques stores and crafts studios, and trendy shops in the Oak Park Mall, which was created in the mid-1970s to enliven the moribund central shopping district.

Like Hyde Park and Evanston, Oak Park is about ten miles from the Loop, and its history is linked to railroads. In 1848, the area (then called Harlem) was the destination of the very first train from Chicago (on the Galena & Chicago Western line), but the development didn't really take off until the Chicago & North Western built a station here in 1872. Although it never caught up with Hyde Park and Evanston, which had commuter service earlier, Oak Park prospered until the Depression. Then, lacking the attractions of a lakefront location and a major university, the village stagnated until the 1950s.

INTERESTING PLACES

The lack of growth may have been fortunate, since it undoubtedly saved many older buildings from redevelopment. Between Harlem and Ridgeland avenues and Madison and Division streets, almost every block is worth a look, even though all but two Wright buildings are in the **Oak Park Historic District**, which starts just north of Lake Street. The **Oak Park Visitors Center** is a good place to begin a tour. Here you'll find a ten-minute introductory slide show, an annotated street map, a variety of helpful pamphlets, and recorded self-guided tours.

Frank Sprague's *Guide to Frank Lloyd Wright and Prairie School Architecture in Oak Park* and the *Architectural Guide Map of Oak Park and River Forest* are both available at the center and are an excellent introduction to Wright and his local contemporaries — among them George Maher, Robert Spencer, E. E. Roberts, Tallmadge and Watson, and John S. Van Bergen — who rejected traditional styles to create an architectural vocabulary that was uniquely American and in tune with the prairie's flatness. Strong planes; angularity; stark, stylized ornament; and flat or low-pitched hip roofs, which combine to reduce spaces to their basic, geometric shapes, characterize their style.

Because he designed them for himself, **Wright's Home and Studio** are perhaps

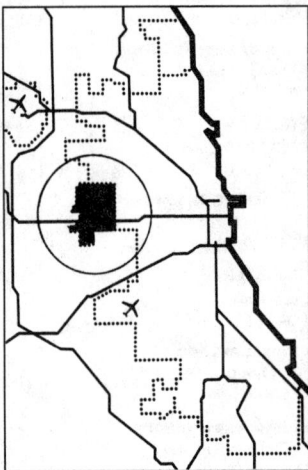

the most personal statement of his theories; however, they also grew organically over time to reflect the changing needs of his family. Built in 1889 when he was only 22, the house was extensively remodeled in 1895 to expand the kitchen-dining room, where the architect installed the first furniture he designed. A second-story, barrel-vaulted playroom with a Giannini mural of the *Arabian Nights* was also added. The octagonal, two-story studio was built in 1898 to accommodate Wright's flourishing practice and is more typically "Wrightian," with art-glass windows and plain geometric forms. Attached to the home and studio is the Ginkgo Tree Bookshop, which sells numerous books about Wright and Prairie-school architecture, as well as gifts and memorabilia.

Designed in 1905, the starkly geometric **Unity Temple** is a showplace of Wright's Prairie-school vocabulary. Despite the massive concrete exterior, the inside is intimate and inviting. Wood ornamentation leads the eye toward the pulpit and up to the sky-

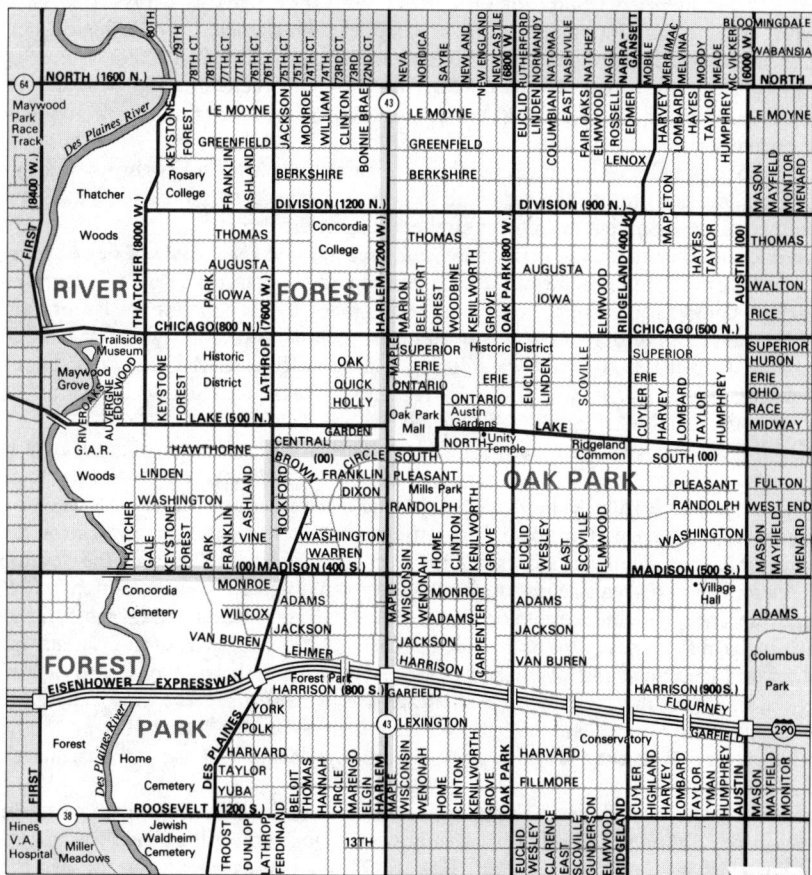

Note: River Forest street numbers are an extension of Chicago's. Forest Park uses the Chicago system but numbers N-S streets south from Central Ave. Oak Park uses Austin Blvd. as a base for E-W numbering. The elevated track between North and South Blvds. is the base line for addresses on N-S streets.

lights and clerestory windows.

Wright's contemporary, George Maher, known for his many houses in Chicago's Hutchinson Street District, designed the **Farson-Mills House** and its furniture. Built in 1897 and set on spacious grounds (now a public park), this formal mansion houses a senior citizens' center and the Historical Society of Oak Park and River Forest museum.

The village's literary links are noted by plaques in front of Ernest Hemingway's birthplace (339 North Oak Park Avenue), his boyhood home (600 North Kenilworth Avenue), and the house where Edgar Rice Burroughs knocked off several of his Tarzan novels.

Lake Street has several handsome churches (in addition to the Unity Temple), including **Calvary Memorial Church**, designed by W. G. Williamson and built in 1902 as the First Presbyterian Church of Oak Park. The **First United Church of Oak Park**, designed by Norman S. Patton, was modeled on chapels at Oxford and Cambridge and is graced with beautiful stained-glass windows. Oak Park's oldest house of worship, **Pilgrim Congregational Church**, was constructed in 1889. The shingle-style church survived the lightning that struck down many of the taller-steepled ones on the open prairie.

Overshadowed by Oak Park, River Forest remains today what it has always been: an upper-middle-class residential area with large homes on spacious lots and virtually no commercial development except on peripheral through streets.

While the early houses are Italianate, the irregularly shaped **River Forest Historic District** in the center of the village — separated from Oak Park's by just two blocks — contains six Wright houses, as well as many by his contemporaries, both in the Prairie-school idiom and in the medieval- and classical-revival styles that became fashionable in the 1920s. Before exploring, pick up a copy of *A Guidebook to the Architecture of River Forest*, edited by Jeanette S. Fields, available locally or at the ArchiCenter and the Art Institute of Chicago.

Driving around River Forest under tall elms that shade the streets and broad lawns is a tranquil pleasure. Be sure not to miss the magnificent **William Winslow House** at 515 Auvergne Place, a little, hidden street behind brick gateposts off Lake Street at the village's western edge. Winslow's firm produced the ornamental metalwork for the façade of Adler and Sullivan's Carson Pirie Scott & Company building and the elevator grilles for Wright's remodeling of the Rookery Building. This house, Wright's first important independent commission after he left Adler and Sullivan, betrays their influence in its massiveness, use of rounded arches, and applied naturalistic ornament. Edgewood Place, just east of Auvergne Place, sports a superb group of Prairie-school homes, including the Japanese-style **William Drummond House** (559), designed by Guenzel and Drummond in 1910; Wright's **Chauncey Williams House** (530); and his **Isabel Roberts House** (603), built for the daughter of one of the architect's early benefactors.

Follow Edgewood Place to Thatcher Avenue and continue north to the **Trailside Museum** (738) on the edge of the forest preserve. One of the village's earliest surviving homes, it was built by A. J. Hoffman in 1874. Four years later, he established the River Forest Young Ladies' Seminary in the house; in 1881, he converted it into a home for boys from broken homes. In 1917, the house and grounds became part of the forest preserve; the museum opened in 1932. Most of it is given over to a small zoo for indigenous forest-preserve animals, birds, and fish.

River Forest isn't all grand homes, however. Smaller houses dot most streets, and the 700 block of William Street is lined with 46 modest, Prairie-school-related dwellings — the largest collection of its kind around. **Rosary College**, established in 1918, looks just like a small-town, Gothic college campus should look.

Interesting Places

Ascension Church
East Ave. and Van Buren St.
Oak Park
848-2703

▶ **Calvary Memorial Church**
Lake St. between Kenilworth
and Forest avenues
Oak Park
386-3900

▶ **Farson-Mills House**
217 S. Home Ave.
Oak Park
848-6755

▶ **First United Church
of Oak Park**
Lake St. and Kenilworth Ave.
Oak Park
386-5215

▶ **Frank Lloyd Wright Home
and Studio**
951 Chicago Ave.
Oak Park
848-1976

Oak Park Conservatory
617 Garfield St.
Oak Park
386-4700

▶ **Oak Park Historic
District**
Bounded roughly by Lake St.,
Marion St., Division St., and
Ridgeland Ave.

▶ **Oak Park Visitors Center**
158 N. Forest Ave.
Oak Park
848-1978

▶ **Pilgrim Congregational
Church**
Scoville Ave. and Lake St.
Oak Park
848-5860

▶ **River Forest Historic
District**
Bounded roughly by Lake St.,
the Des Plaines River,
Chicago Ave., and
Harlem Ave.

▶ **Rosary College**
7900 Division St.
River Forest
366-2490

▶ **Trailside Museum of
Natural History**
738 Thatcher Ave.
River Forest
366-6530

▶ **Unity Temple**
Lake St. at Kenilworth Ave.
Oak Park
848-6225

▶ **William Winslow House**
515 Auvergne Pl.
River Forest

INDEX

INDEX

Index

Index

Index

Index

Index

Index

D

Da Nicola, 161, 166
Dae Ho, 180, 182
Daley, Mayor Richard J., 19
Daley, Richard J., Bicentennial Plaza Ice Skating Rink, 18
Daley, Richard J., Center, 65
Daley, Richard J., Bicentennial Plaza, 51, 52
Dalton, B., Bookseller, 69, 132
D'Amato's Bakery, 187
Dance Hotline, 46
D & L Office Furniture, 133
Danilo's, 79, 81
Dankhaus, 174, 177
Dan Ryan Expressway, 11
Dan Ryan Woods, 52
D'Arcy, Martin, Gallery of Art, 30
Darkroom Aids, 164
Darrow, Clarence, 67
Dart Gallery, 34
Darts, 51
Daruma Restaurant, 195, 197
Dave's Italian Kitchen, 196, 197
Davis Sq. Park, 92, 94
Dawes, Charles Gates, 31, 191
Dawson, Douglas, Gallery, 34
Dearborn Observatory, 29
Dearborn St. Station, 54, 65
Debevic's, Ed, 136
Deer Grove, 52
Deerfield, 12
Dégagé, 153
De Goyler, Robert S., 108
De Graef Fine Art, 34
De La Salle Institute, 90
Delaware Bldg., 65
Delicatessen Meyer, 176, 177
Delta Import Co., 186, 187
Denslow, William W., 65
DePaul Univ., 40, 49, 68, 147, 152; Loop Campus, 68, 147; School for New Learning, 68 ; School of Music, 40; sports, 49
Deson, Marianne, Gallery, 34
Deutsch Luggage, 133
Dewes, Francis J., House, 147, 148, 152
Diana Grocery & Restaurant, 79, 80
Diana's Bakery, 83
Diaz, Aurelio, 82

Dickey House, 119
Dillinger, John, 153
Dillion, David, 43
Dinkel's Bakery, 158, 164
Dinosaur Days, 56
Direct Auctioneers, 180, 182
Ditka, Mike, 48
Diversey Driving Range, 24
Doane Observatory, 26
Dobson, Henry Austin, 20
Dr. Michael's Products, 175, 177
Do-It-Yourself *Messiah*, 38
Dolese, John, 95
Dong Kee, 86, 87
Don Roth's River Plaza, 74
Dos Hermanos Cantina, 129
Douglas Park, 20; Field House, 24
Dove Candies & Ice Cream, 99, 102
Downers Grove, 12
Drake Hotel, 128
Drehobl Bros. Art Glass, 158, 164
Dreiser, Theodore, 76, 105
Drew Sales, 110, 111
Driftstone Wedding Cake-A-Rama, 99, 102
Drummond, William, House, 200
Drury Lane Oakbrook Terrace, 43
Dryad (sculpture), 129
DuBois, O. R., 124
Dubuffet, Jean, sculpture, 67
Duckworth, Ruth, 103
Du Page County Historic Museum, 31
DuSable Museum of African American History, 20, 30, 53
Dyche Stadium, 49
Dyfverman, John, 20

E

E.T.A. Creative Arts Foundation, 43
Earl's Pub, 152, 155
Early Music Series, 40
Eastern Bakery & Grocery, 99, 102
Eastern Oriental Rug Co., 120
East Side Archery, 113, 114
East West Gallery, 34

Eberhart, John E., 98
Eberhart, John E., House, 102
Economos, James E., 141
Edelman, Catherine, Gallery, 34
Edens Expressway, 11
Edgewater Beach Apts., 167, 172
Edgewater Beach Hotel, 167
Edgewater Golf Course, 167
Edgewater Presbyterian Church, 169, 172
Edwardo's, 106, 107
Edwardo's Pizzeria, 182
Egghead Discount Software, 164
Eidlitz, Cyrus L. W., 65
Eisenhower Expressway, 11
860-880 Lake Shore Dr. Apts., 123
Elaine's Bakery, 182
Elements, 133
Elf Shoppe, 149, 153
Elgin, 12
Elk Grove Village, 12
Elks Natl. Meml. Bldg., 152
Elle, 159, 164
Elmhurst, 12
Elm St. Cafe, 145
Elvia's, 93, 94
Emmanuel United Methodist Church, 192, 196
Ensemble Espanol, 46
Erdmann, Robert, 141
Erikson's Delicatessen, 170, 172
Erik the Red, 120, 121
Erinisle, 150, 153
Escargot, L', 154
Essanay Studios, 168, 172
Essex Inn, 68
Essex Restaurant, 37
Estevez, George, 37
Europa Bookstore, 160, 164, 195, 196
European Import Center, 175, 177
European Pastry Shop, 176, 177
European Sausage House, 176, 177
Europejska Lounge, 101, 102
Evans House, 118
Evans, Inc., 130
Evans, John, 191
Evanston, 12

Index

Index

Index

Index

Index

Index

Y

Z